DATE DUE

B.J. Harrison Library
Marshalltown Community College
Iowa Valley Community College District
Marshalltown, Iowa 50158

DEMCO

Recent Historians of Great Britain

Donated
To The Library by

Dr. Thomas Colbert

Recent Historians *of* Great Britain

ESSAYS ON THE POST-1945 GENERATION

Edited by WALTER L. ARNSTEIN

IOWA STATE UNIVERSITY PRESS / AMES

WALTER L. ARNSTEIN is L.A.S. Jubilee Professor of History at the University of Illinois at Urbana-Champaign.

PHOTO CREDITS: *Page ix,* photo by Susan Lukes; *page 37,* photo from *The English Commonwealth 1547–1640: Essays in Politics and Society,* ed. Peter Clark, Alan Smith, and Nicholas Tyacke (Leicester: Leicester Univ. Press, 1979), used by permission; *page 57,* photo © Billett Potter, Oxford.

© 1990 Iowa State University Press, Ames, Iowa 50010
All rights reserved

Manufactured in the United States of America
∞ This book is printed on acid-free paper.

No part of this book may be reproduced in any form or by any electronic or mechanical means, including information storage and retrieval systems, without written permission from the publisher, except for brief passages quoted in a review.

Authorization to photocopy items for internal or personal use, or the internal or personal use of specific clients, is granted by Iowa State University Press, provided that the base fee of $.10 per copy is paid directly to the Copyright Clearance Center, 27 Congress Street, Salem, MA 01970. For those organizations that have been granted a photocopy license by CCC, a separate system of payments has been arranged. The fee code for users of the Transactional Reporting Service is 0-8138-0592-9/90 $.10.

First edition, 1990

Library of Congress Cataloging-in-Publication Data

Recent historians of Great Britain : Essays on the post-1945 generation / edited by Walter L. Arnstein. — 1st ed.
    p. cm.
    Includes bibliographical references.
    ISBN 0-8138-0592-9 (alk. paper)
    1. Great Britain—Historiography. 2. Historiography—Great Britain—History—20th century.   I. Arnstein, Walter L.
DA1.R39 1990
941.08′072—dc20   90-4478

To Lacey Baldwin Smith

TEACHER, MENTOR, COLLEAGUE, FRIEND

Contents

Preface	ix
Introduction *Walter L. Arnstein*	3
G. R. Elton: Tudor Champion *Barrett L. Beer*	13
Joel Hurstfield: Historian for All Seasons *M. J. Tucker*	37
Christopher Hill and the People of Stuart England *Cynthia Herrup*	57
Lawrence Stone: Social Science and History *Joel Berlatsky*	75
J. H. Plumb and the Whig Tradition *Robert C. Braddock*	101
E. P. Thompson: Moralist as Marxist Historian *Thomas William Heyck*	121
Norman Gash: Peelite *Walter L. Arnstein*	147
F. S. L. Lyons: Historian of Modern Ireland *Alan O'Day*	173
Contributors	193
Index	197

Preface ༄

This collection of essays has a historiographical purpose that is explained in detail in the introduction. The collection also has a more personal purpose: to pay tribute to Lacey Baldwin Smith. Of the eight contributors to this volume, six received the Ph.D. degree in history from Northwestern University and wrote their doctoral dissertations under Smith's supervision; another was his student and assistant but ultimately completed his Ph.D. dissertation at the University of London; yet another has been his colleague for more than two decades. All of us have known Lacey Baldwin Smith for many years, and we take enormous satisfaction in this opportunity to honor him:

༄ *As a scholar and as one of the preeminent American historians of early modern England.* Whether the work be an article in a scholarly journal, a specialized monograph, a biography, or the general survey of three centuries of English history that has—in five successive editions—remained in print since 1966, Lacey Smith has been noted for painstaking research, thought-provoking exposition, and a style of writing recognizably, indeed uniquely, his own.

༄ *As a dedicated and highly respected member of the historical profession in the United States,* a position reflected in the offices of president of the Midwest Conference on British Studies, president of the North American Conference of British Studies, and member of the Council

ix

of the American Historical Association, as well as in such related posts as president of the Illinois Humanities Council.

As a teacher of rare force and effectiveness, first at the Massachusetts Institute of Technology and now for more than three decades at Northwestern University, where in 1986 he was named Peter B. Ritzma Professor in the Humanities. One of us can still recall the very first time that in 1955 Lacey Smith entered a Northwestern classroom — the twinkle in his eye, the sense of urgency in his voice, and the sheer vitality of his manner as he made it clear in lecture after lecture that the past is not dead but continues to speak to us even now. Those characteristics remain. As a captivated undergraduate remarked to another of us after hearing Lacey Smith retell the story of the Norman conquest, "You are there!" That same sense of immediacy, of passion barely held in check, has also transformed many a paper delivered to a professional convention into a memorable occasion rather than an invitation to slumber. To emphasize this facet of his pedagogy is not to suggest that for Lacey Smith the teaching of history has meant merely weaving romantic spells. In his undergraduate courses and in his graduate seminars, it has also meant demanding questions and a continual challenge to unexamined assumptions.

As a mentor and adviser who continues to take a genuine interest in all his students and in particular in those who, since 1961, have completed doctoral dissertations under his supervision. As a dissertation adviser, his tone was encouraging but his standards were high. He has not only remained involved in the subsequent careers of those graduate students but has often helped make those careers possible in the first instance. As he said to one of us while writing a letter in support of a fellowship application, "If words can get you money, mine will!"

Therefore, with an enduring sense of respect and affection, we dedicate this volume to Lacey Baldwin Smith.

Recent Historians of Great Britain

Introduction

WALTER L. ARNSTEIN

Most historians of modern Britain have preferred to practice their craft rather than to analyze it. They thus continue to adhere to the dominant philosophical tradition in Great Britain during the past three centuries—the empiricism of John Locke, David Hume, John Stuart Mill, and Bertrand Russell. For historians following that tradition, the prime basis of human knowledge remains the experience of the senses rather than either innate ideas or the a priori logical systems identified with continental philosophers like René Descartes, the seventeenth-century rationalist, and Georg Friedrich Hegel, the early nineteenth-century dialectical idealist.

Although the England and Scotland of the Georgian and Victorian eras could take pride in a number of prolific and successful historians—Edward Gibbon, David Hume, Thomas Babington Macaulay, and Thomas Carlyle among them—it was in nineteenth-century Germany that history first developed as a self-conscious, "scientific" academic discipline as distinct from a branch of literature. The most influential modern philosophy of history also originated in Germany, that of Karl Marx—the assumption that the history of a people, indeed of humanity at large, is determined ultimately by its economy, by changes in the forms of production, and by the social class struggles that such economic alterations set into motion. It was in France of the 1930s, 1940s, and 1950s rather than in Great Britain that the so-called *Annales* school of Fernand Braudel and his colleagues emerged.[1] These theorists were devoted to the assumption that historians ought to be less preoccupied with specific people and events—concerns of chronology and of narrative—than with the provision of a "total history" that constituted a kind of retrospective geographical and sociological assessment of the development of societies over the course of centuries.

As Harold Parker noted a decade ago, the prime characteristic of

British history writing remains "its strong empirical strain. For most British historians from Thomas Carlyle to the present, the study of history has been a reality-seeking enterprise." More recently Sir Geoffrey Elton, the subject of an essay in this book, observed with mingled pride and alarm that Britain was "now a beleaguered bastion of empiricist and non-ideological history."[2] Historians of Britain have been less apt than those of Germany and France and, for that matter, the United States to originate all-embracing schools of history — whether based on Marxist economics, Freudian psychology, feminist theory, "total history," or the utilization of the computer in the form of cliometrics.[3] That is not to say, however, that these historians (whether British, Irish, American, or Australian) have been altogether uninfluenced by the approaches noted above. Nor does it mean that they have been inactive. As David Cannadine has recently pointed out, "Undeniably, the period from the late 1940s to the early 1970s was indeed a Golden Age for professional British historians, a time when academe in general was an affluent society, and when Clio in particular had never had it so good."[4] During the very years that witnessed the eclipse of Britain as a great power, British historical scholarship paradoxically attained a scope and a scale for which no earlier generation can provide a precedent. As a consequence of a doubling in the number of British universities and a quadrupling in the number of university students,[5] more historical research and writing were done than ever before. The adoption by Britain after World War II of that nineteenth-century German invention, the doctoral dissertation, meant, moreover, that many more potentially publishable studies, based on research in primary sources, were undertaken. Such expansion in the realm of higher education was not limited to the United Kingdom; more research than ever in British history was being carried on in American universities as well as in those of Canada, Australia, and other lands of the erstwhile British Empire. During that "golden age," hitherto unexplored bodies of parliamentary and legal records were utilized, and old parish registers were examined to clarify the kingdom's social and demographic history.[6] There was widespread agreement that the two world wars not only had altered the balance of European and world power but also had done much to transform Britain's economy and its social and political structure. In the aftermath of those wars, the historians of the post-1945 generation were prepared to reexamine old assumptions, to experiment with new approaches, and to provide new syntheses.

Historians of modern Britain may have done less than their continental counterparts to pioneer all-inclusive (and perhaps meretricious) historical systems, but they have reflected from time to time about the assumptions that they and their predecessors have brought to the study of history. Thus back in 1967, J. R. Hale provided a helpful seventy-page introduction to his collection of characteristic excerpts, *The Evolution of British Historiography from Bacon to Namier.* More recently J. W. Burrow, in *A Liberal Descent: Victorian Historians and the English Past,*[7] has reassessed the writings of four great narrative historians: Macaulay, William Stubbs, Edward Freeman, and James Anthony Froude. Nor have more recent historians been excluded from such reconsideration. Cases in point include Michael Finlayson's *Historians, Puritanism, and the English Revolution,* Harvey Kaye's *The British Marxist Historians,* and pre-eminently, John Kenyon's *The History Men: The Historical Profession in England since the Renaissance,* a highly personal but wide-ranging survey that focuses primarily on twentieth-century scholars. Approaching modern writing about British history in a highly informative but somewhat different fashion is Richard Schlatter's *Recent Views on British History,* a collection of chronologically arranged bibliographical essays by different authors.[8]

Although the concerns of this book overlap those of several of the works cited above, it is distinct both in purpose and in organization.[9] Its goal is to clarify the work of the post-1945 generation of historians of Britain by focusing on eight major scholars. Each essay is written by a different author, but all essays share three common purposes: (1) to provide helpful information about the personal and academic background of the historian; (2) to call attention to all his major publications and to alert the reader to those aspects of the recorded past (both chronological and topical) with which he has been most immediately concerned; and (3) to indicate where in the spectrum of modern history writing the subject of the essay fits. The primary purpose of each essay is to introduce the body of work and to indicate how much support it has received and how much controversy it has aroused within the profession. Evaluation cannot be excluded, however, from essays of this type, and each contributor has been left free in this respect. The essays possess a common purpose and analogous organization. They do not, however, seek to impose a common historiographical "party line."

In one respect only, the choice of historians discussed in this volume has been arbitrary. All contributors had to feel persuaded of the importance of their subjects and had then to complete essays that abided by the agreed criteria. Although other historians might readily have been added to the list, there is widespread consensus that all eight are among the most influential scholars concerned with the last five centuries of the British past. The eight (six of whom are living and active) do, moreover, constitute a generation, a generation that came to prominence during the decade after 1945. The oldest of them was born in 1911, the youngest in 1924. Christopher Hill published his first book in 1940; the first books of the others appeared between 1947 and 1953. They have much else in common as well. All were influenced significantly by World War II; six served in the armed forces, another as civil servant and official war historian. Only F. S. L. (Leland) Lyons, a citizen of the neutral Irish Republic, was less immediately affected by the war. For the rest, it meant an interruption in their education or their academic careers while it broadened their experience by plunging them into a nonacademic sector of society. All have proved to be prolific writers of books and articles — Christopher Hill and Geoffrey Elton overwhelmingly so — and the others not far behind. All have focused their historical research primarily on the domestic history of Britain during the past five centuries.

At a time when the art of biography was at a discount among academic historians, almost every one of the eight has written a major biography. Geoffrey Elton, it is true, has argued that "even at its best biography is a poor way of writing history,"[10] and none of his own studies of Thomas Cromwell is a biography in a technical sense. Yet even Elton has recently (1985) become the biographer of the late-Victorian historian, Frederic Maitland. Joel Hurstfield wrote a brief life of Queen Elizabeth I; Christopher Hill has produced biographical studies of Oliver Cromwell and John Milton; Lawrence Stone provided a biography of a relatively obscure Elizabethan, Sir Horatio Palavicino. The list goes on: J. H. Plumb is the biographer of Robert Walpole; E. P. Thompson, of William Morris; Norman Gash is the author of the classic modern biography of Sir Robert Peel as well as of the first twentieth-century life of Lord Liverpool; Leland Lyons wrote the first scholarly biography of John Dillon and the only complete, fully documented modern life of Charles Stewart Parnell. All of these historians have written about flesh-and-blood individuals — as opposed to abstractions — as prime agents in shaping the past.

For none of the eight, moreover, has history served as a cloister in which to share research only with fellow academic initiates. Each of the historians to be discussed has provided at least one major synthesis, designed to summarize half a century or more and incorporating the researches of fellow historians. In 1955 Geoffrey Elton published *England under the Tudors,* "a text that shaped the teaching of Tudor history for the next thirty years."¹¹ Later he brought out a more specialized survey, *Reform and Reformation: England 1509–1558* (1977). Joel Hurstfield contributed a significant work of synthesis, *Elizabeth I and the Unity of England* (1960) to the popular *Teach Yourself History* series edited by A. L. Rowse. Christopher Hill is the author of the oft-reprinted volume, *The Century of Revolution, 1603–1714* (1961) in the *Norton History of England*. The work of Lawrence Stone most readily described as a general overview is *The Causes of the English Revolution, 1529–1642* (1972), but his books on the English aristocracy and the English family are also noted for their chronological sweep. *England in the Eighteenth Century* (1950), J. H. Plumb's contribution to the *Pelican History of England*, has remained in print ever since first publication. Although E. P. Thompson's *The Making of the English Working Class: 1790–1830* (1963) may not have been intended as a general survey of the period in question, it has proved to be a highly comprehensive form of social history that has stimulated thought and research by students and scholars in Europe and North America. Norman Gash's *Aristocracy and People: Britain 1815–1865* (1979) was intended as just such a survey, volume eight of a *New History of England* coedited by A. G. Dickens and Gash himself.¹² Finally, F. S. L. Lyons's *Ireland Since the Famine* (1971) provides the most comprehensive and highly regarded survey of its subject.

To suggest that the eight historians studied in this volume have much in common is not to pretend that, as members of the same historical generation, they have been concerned with the same facets of the past or that they approach history in the same way. The hitherto neglected legal documents in which Geoffrey Elton has immersed himself may have implications for our understanding of Tudor society. Nevertheless, his approach to the past remains consciously "political"¹³ in a fashion with which scholars who describe themselves as "social historians" take issue. As Barrett Beer points out in his essay, Elton denounced as "false gods" many of the alternative approaches to the past that were becoming popular in the 1960s. His book, *Political History: Principles and Practice* (1970), remains dedicated to the proposition that the structure of sound narrative history remains "overwhelmingly political, overwhelmingly concerned with those fortunes and manipulations of power in society which form the main recorded activities of men."¹⁴ The approach of Norman Gash, and to a lesser degree that of J. H. Plumb, also remains predominantly "political." Christopher Hill, the senior British Marxist historian of his generation, obviously belongs to a quite different category.

Yet (as Cynthia Herrup suggests in her essay), Hill, although never disowning his basic Marxism, has built upon it in an increasingly sophisticated manner. Certainly no other Marxist historian of our day has become so fascinated with the study of ideas, especially religious ideas.

E. P. Thompson's interests as a historian—especially his concern with the protorevolutionary and at best semiliterate masses—overlap those of Hill, except that Thompson's chronological arena has been the eighteenth century rather than the seventeenth. He has served as this generation's most influential British exponent of "history from the bottom up." It is Thompson's professed purpose "to rescue the poor stockinger, the Luddite cropper, the 'obsolete' weaver" and their ilk "from the enormous condescension of posterity."[15] As William Heyck makes clear in his essay on Thompson, not all professedly Marxist historians think alike, and many of Thompson's articles in historical journals have castigated other Marxist historians for their methodological errors. Indeed, Thompson appears to take as much pride in his English particularism as in his Marxism.[16] Though not a Marxist,[17] Lawrence Stone may also justly be described as a social historian, but Stone's focus has been not on the anonymous masses but on the better-recorded upper ranks of society in early modern England: the sources of their wealth, their land-holding practices, and their family relations. In successive works Stone has shown himself willing to apply a variety of social-science techniques—economic, sociological, anthropological, and studies of *mentalité*. In recent years he has been equally ready to call attention to the limitations of quantification and of the "new social history." As Joel Berlatsky notes in his essay, in 1979 Stone called for a revival of "narrative history." Joel Hurstfield's studies of "fiscal feudalism" and the Tudor Court of Wards may justify categorizing him as an economic historian, but his predominant interests were general rather than narrowly topical.

The inclusion of F. S. L. Lyons in this collection of essays serves as a reminder of the single most obvious constant in any study of the history of England (or Britain) during the past five centuries—Ireland. No historian of our time has dealt with the interaction of the modern Irish with their immediate geographical and cultural neighbors in a more comprehensive or judicious spirit than Lyons.

To argue for the inclusion of these eight historians in this volume is not to suggest that others of comparable merit might not have been added to the list. Even if we had limited ourselves to the same generation and to historians who have focused all their attention on Britain itself (unlike, say, Hugh Trevor-Roper and A. J. P. Taylor), we might appropriately have added essays on A. G. Dickens, the respected student of the English Reformation, or on Gordon Donaldson, holder of the chair of Scottish history at the University of Edinburgh until 1979 and a major inspiration for a renewed academic interest in the history of medieval and early modern Scotland.[18] Had we included historians who are American by birth, we might have devoted an essay to Lacey Baldwin Smith, whose *This Realm of England, 1399–1688* (1966), has introduced more American university students to the history of early modern England than has any other book.[19] Smith has been responsible for numerous other works, including biographies of Henry VIII and Elizabeth I.[20] We might also have added Jack Hexter, the incisive critic of historical sacred cows of the sixteenth and seventeenth centuries.[21] Another possibility would have been an essay on Dame Veronica Wedgwood, the perceptive chronicler of the England that entered the Civil War of the 1640s.[22] John Kenyon has written illuminating studies on late seventeenth- and early eighteenth-century politics and ideas, and Ian Christie, a disciple of the late Sir Lewis Namier, has made the Britain of the era of the American and French revolutions peculiarly his own.[23] George Rudé has made numerous contributions to the social history of eighteenth-century England.[24]

Of all modern historians of nineteenth- and twentieth-century Britain, Asa Briggs (now Lord Briggs) has proved to be the most prolific. In addition to producing the influential survey, *The Age of Improvement, 1783–1867* (1959), he has written detailed studies ranging from the Victorian wine industry to a five-volume history of the British Broadcasting Corporation. More recently he has also produced a comprehensive *Social History of England: From the Romans to Mrs. Thatcher* (1983). The late George Kitson Clark may have published less, but he guided more doctoral students into the highways and byways of Victorian history than any other university adviser of his generation, and his *Making of Victorian England* (1961) remains a highly influential introduction to nineteenth-century attitudes and assumptions. Among American historians of the same era, Gertrude Himmelfarb has done much to elucidate Victorian ideas; her subjects have ranged from Jeremy Bentham to John Stuart Mill, Charles Darwin, and Lord Acton. In *The Idea of Poverty* (1985), she canvassed and assessed the beliefs of two generations of economists, publicists, and novelists. Eric Hobsbawm has been the most prolific Marxist historian concerned with the social and economic history of nineteenth- and twentieth-century Britain.[25] And Henry Pelling has made the origins of the twentieth-century British Labour party peculiarly his own, while also surveying British trade unionism, communism, the impact of World War II, and the extraordinary life of Winston Churchill.[26]

The purpose of this introduction, however, is to set the scene not for a possible sequel but for essays designed to introduce and to illuminate the life and works of eight of the most eminent historians of modern Britain—Geoffrey Elton, Joel Hurstfield, Christopher Hill, Lawrence Stone, J. H. Plumb, E. P. Thompson, Norman Gash, and F. S. L. Lyons. No introductory essay can, or should, serve as a substitute for reading the historian's own books and articles, but it may serve graduate students and readers of history generally as a reminder of what those works are, when they were published, and what their import has been. The result should be a fuller understanding of some of the masters of Britain's modern "golden age" of historical writing.

NOTES

I am grateful to Professor T. William Heyck of Northwestern University and to professors Caroline Hibbard and Paul W. Schroeder, my colleagues at the University of Illinois, for reading an earlier draft of this introduction and for making a number of helpful suggestions. John Beeler provided invaluable assistance in the preparation of the index.

1. *Annales: Economies, Sociétés* was begun in 1929. Seven volumes of translated essays from the journal, edited by Robert Forster and Orest A. Ranum, were published between 1975 and 1982 in Baltimore by the Johns Hopkins University Press. The titles of the first three volumes are *Biology of Man in History, Family and Society,* and *Rural Society in France.*

2. See Elton's essay, "Great Britain," in *International Handbook for Historical Studies,* ed. Georg G. Iggers and Harold T. Parker (Westport, Conn., 1979), 204. As the essays that follow will suggest, even historians like Christopher Hill and E. P. Thompson constitute only partial exceptions to this generalization.

3. For cliometrics see R. W. Fogel and G. R. Elton, *Which Road to the Past? Two Views of History* (New Haven, 1983); for a psychological approach see Peter Gay, *Freud for Historians* (New York, 1985); for feminism see Joan W. Scott, "Gender: A Useful Category of Historical Analysis," *American Historical Review* (Dec. 1986):1053–75. There are a few exceptions to the generalization that modern British historians have failed to produce historical systems. The most obvious was Arnold Toynbee, who proposed in a twelve-volume *Study of History* (London, 1934–1961) that the twenty-one distinct civilizations he identified in recorded history (and treated as organic entities) constitute the historian's appropriate foci of study. In *The Idea of History* (Oxford, 1946), R. G. Collingwood put forward the neo-idealist notion that "all history is the history of thought" and "therefore all history is the re-enactment of past thoughts in the historian's mind" (215). The tradition known as the Whig Interpretation of history, though definitely English, was less a self-conscious system than a set of assumptions that, as Herbert Butterfield demonstrated in *The Whig Interpretation*

of History (London, 1931), was shared by numerous nineteenth-century British historians looking back on their country's past. Their tendency was to look on most human history as fundamentally progressive and "to produce a story which is the ratification if not the glorification of the present" (Preface).

4. David Cannadine, "The State of British History," *Times Literary Supplement,* Oct. 10, 1987, 1139.

5. The number of full-time British university students grew from 51,000 in 1945–1946 to 82,800 in 1953–1954 and to 226,600 in 1982–1983. By the last year there were an additional 248,800 full-time students in polytechnics and colleges of higher education, many of which included departments of history. See Her Majesty's Stationery Office, *Annual Abstract of Statistics* (1953), 90; *Social Trends* (1971), 121; *Social Trends* (1985), 53.

6. One obvious example is E. A. Wrigley and R. S. Schofield, *The Population History of England, 1541–1871: A Reconstruction* (Cambridge, 1982). In his pioneering work, *The Making of the English Working Class: 1790–1830* (New York, 1963), E. P. Thompson is far less concerned with statistics than with utilizing obscure pamphlets, periodicals, and government documents.

7. J. W. Burrow, *A Liberal Descent: Victorian Historians and the English Past* (Cambridge, 1981). Rosemary Jann has supplemented Burrow's book with *The Art and Science of Victorian History* (Columbus, Ohio, 1985).

8. Michael G. Finlayson, *Historians, Puritanism, and the English Revolution* (Toronto, 1983); Harvey J. Kaye, *The British Marxist Historians: An Introductory Analysis* (Cambridge, 1984); John P. Kenyon, *The History Men: The Historical Profession in England since the Renaissance* (London, 1983; Pittsburgh, 1984); Richard Schlatter, ed., *Recent Views on British History* (New Brunswick, N.J., 1984).

9. The closest analogy is Herman Ausubel et al., eds., *Some Modern Historians of Britain: Essays in Honor of R. L. Schuyler* (New York, 1951). That volume includes brief essays on twenty-one different nineteenth- and twentieth-century British historians. Among the latter are Elie Halévy, Sir William Holdsworth, R. H. Tawney, Sir Lewis Namier, and Sir Winston Churchill.

10. G. R. Elton, *The Practice of History* (London, 1967), 169.

11. See Barrett Beer's essay on Elton in this volume.

12. Elton's *Reform and Reformation* constitutes volume 2 of the same series.

13. See Elton's debate with the American cliometrician R. W. Fogel in Fogel and Elton, *Which Road to the Past?*

14. G. R. Elton, *Political History: Principles and Practice* (London, 1970), 177.

15. E. P. Thompson, *English Working Class,* 12.

16. See Thompson's preface to the *English Working Class* and his essay, "The Peculiarities of the English," in his *The Poverty of Theory and Other Essays* (London, 1978), 35–91.

17. As Stone has noted, "The Marxist interpretation of the role of the aristocracy in the English revolution, with which I had set out, had been shattered by close contact with the empirical evidence." Self-defined liberal historians like Stone managed to cooperate with Marxist historians, however, on the editorial board of *Past and Present,* the journal begun in 1952 as a British counterpart to *Annales.* See Lawrence Stone, "A Life of Learning," *ACLS Newsletter* (Winter/Spring, 1985):13, 15.

18. Donaldson is the general editor as well as the author of volume 3 of the four-volume Edinburgh *History of Scotland* (Edinburgh, 1965). His other works include *The Scottish Reformation* (Cambridge, 1960) and *Scottish Church History* (Edinburgh, 1985).

19. The book constitutes volume 2 of a four-volume *History of England,* ed., Lacey Baldwin Smith (Lexington, Mass., 1966). A fifth edition of the entire series appeared early in 1988.

20. Lacey Baldwin Smith, *Henry VIII: The Mask of Royalty* (London, 1971); and *Elizabeth Tudor: Biography of a Queen* (Boston, 1975). Smith's other works include *Tudor Prelates and Politics* (Princeton, 1953); *A Tudor Tragedy: The Life and Times of Catherine Howard* (London, 1961); *The Horizon Book of the Elizabethan World* (New York, 1967); and *Treason in Tudor England: Politics and Paranoia* (Princeton, 1986).

21. See J. H. Hexter, *Reappraisals in History* (Evanston, Ill., 1961); and *Reflections on Historians* (Cambridge, Mass., 1978).

22. C. V. Wedgwood's works include *The King's Peace, 1637–1641* (London, 1955); *The King's War, 1641–1647* (London, 1958); and *The Trial of Charles I* (London, 1964).

23. Christie is responsible for numerous monographs and essays as well as a general survey, *Wars and Revolutions: Britain, 1760–1815* (Cambridge, Mass., 1982).

24. For example, *Hanoverian London, 1714–1808* (London, 1971); and *Wilkes and Liberty* (Oxford, 1962).

25. See, for example, *Essays in Labour History* (London, 1961); and *Industry and Empire: An Economic History of Britain since 1750* (London, 1968).

26. See, for example, *The Origins of the Labour Party, 1880–1900* (Oxford, 1954); *A History of British Trade Unionism,* 4th ed. (London, 1987); and *Winston Churchill* (London, 1974).

G. R. Elton ⧞ *Tudor Champion*

BARRETT L. BEER

The appointment of G. R. Elton as Regius Professor of Modern History at Cambridge University in 1983 marked the climax of one of the most extraordinary academic careers since 1945. Born in Germany in 1921, Elton began his education in Prague and emigrated to Britain with his family in 1939. In spite of his roots in Central Europe, Elton's education was partly British, as he received his undergraduate and graduate degrees from the University of London. If Elton's origins and education set him apart from the traditional path to eminence at Cambridge, his highly specialized research, his neglect of the nonprofessional reading public, and his hostility toward new historical methodologies have given him a unique position among the historians of his own generation. Whereas Sir Lewis Namier moved from eighteenth-century politics to the larger stage of European diplomacy and R. H. Tawney wrestled with the difficult problems of poverty among the sixteenth-century peasantry and the complex relationship between religion and the rise of capitalism, Elton spent thirty years studying Thomas Cromwell, an early Tudor politician whose public career lasted only a decade. Yet Elton received the regius professorship denied Namier and Tawney, a prize that was also denied Sir John Neale, A. L. Rowse, and A. J. P. Taylor.

Elton's roots place him outside the mainstream of British academic life, but he is descended from a long and distinguished European intellectual tradition. As he remarked in his inaugural address, his ancestor, Samuel Meyer Ehrenberg, founded "a modest scholarly dynasty" in 1808 when he took over an ailing school at Wolfenbüttel, a few miles from Hanover, Germany.¹ But it was Elton's father, Victor Ehrenberg, who provided a link with the world of scholarship and university teaching.

Victor Ehrenberg (1891–1976), born in Altona, Germany, the son of a banker, Otto Maximilian Ehrenberg, studied at Stuttgart, Göttingen, Berlin, and Tübingen. He received the Dr. phil. degree in 1920 and began teaching at the University of Frankfurt in 1922. Seven years later Ehrenberg was appointed professor of ancient history at the German University of Prague, a post that he held until 1939. After emigrating to Britain under a grant from the Society for the Protection of Science and Learning (SPSL), he taught at secondary schools in Carlisle and York and had university appointments at Dublin and Newcastle before becoming lecturer and then reader in ancient history at Bedford College, University of London.² Following his retirement in 1957, Ehrenberg visited the United States on several occasions. In 1958 he was visiting professor at Brandeis University, and in 1962 he was Martin lecturer at Oberlin College. Ehrenberg was a prolific writer whose works spanned a period of forty-five years. The range of his learning reached from specialized articles on the rise of the polis and encyclopedia entries to general works that included *The Greek State* and *From Solon to Socrates: Greek History and Civilization during the Sixth and Fifth Centuries B.C.*

Writing in *The Times* after Ehrenberg's death, a former colleague described the scholar's background as a compound of emancipated Judaism and the German cultural heritage. He praised Ehrenberg's ability to connect Greek constitutional and political history with the history of ideas.³ Insight into Ehrenberg's view of history and the work of the historian may be found in a preface written toward the end of his life where he commented on the difficulty of writing in a field that was a jungle of ancient traditions and modern conjectures:

> We may be less critical than our immediate predecessors in our search for absolute historical truth, not least because we no longer believe in the possibility of discovering that truth. We are a generation in between, no longer sure of critical positivism, nor on the other hand, of the rationalist intuition now so much in vogue. I myself cannot claim that my love for the ancient Greeks has found a safe route through the jungle, much as I have tried.⁴

Ehrenberg, who was praised as a European liberal, was one of an important group of scholars who sought refuge in Britain from persecution in Hitler's Germany. His career is significant in itself, and it also suggests similarities and contrasts to the career pursued by his son.

After his birth on August 17, 1921, at Tübingen, Geoffrey Rudolph Ehrenberg lived with his family in Frankfurt and later in Prague where his formal, classical education began. The family left Prague early in 1939 traveling on Czech passports through Germany to Britain where Geoffrey and his younger brother, Lewis, enrolled at Rydal School. Located at Colwyn Bay in Wales, Rydal was a Methodist-related public school. Many years later Lewis recalled their arrival: "My brother and I . . . had come to Rydal as refugees from Prague through the generosity of the School Governors, and we had only a week in England before we were exposed to the strange and mysterious entity of an English Public School. . . . We knew virtually no English, and after trying to understand the Head, were convinced we knew none."[5]

Both young men progressed rapidly, and by 1941 Geoffrey began teaching duties as an assistant master. As the war had created serious staff shortages at Rydal, the young master taught a wide range of subjects including fifth form history, German, fourth form mathematics, and commercial arithmetic. While teaching occupied Geoffrey's daytime hours, he studied at night for an external degree of the University of London. His special subject, the late Roman Republic, reflected the influence of his father, and in 1943 he received a first class honors degree, an extraordinary feat for any external student and especially one who had lived in Britain for only four years. The next year he joined the British army, at which time he changed his name to Elton under an army council instruction. Until 1946 Geoffrey Ehrenberg, now Elton, served in the East Surrey Regiment and the Intelligence Corps where his duties included service in Allied-occupied Austria. He left the army with the rank of sergeant to continue his education at the University of London.

In 1946 Elton began research for a Ph.D. in English history under the direction of Professor J. E. Neale. The author of a highly regarded biography of Elizabeth I and a number of important pioneering articles on Elizabethan parliaments, Neale was a leading authority on the Tudor period. He suggested that Elton should examine the state papers at the Public Record Office from the reign of Henry VIII, a period that had received little attention since A. F. Pollard published what was regarded as the authoritative and definitive biography of the king in 1902. Elton was drawn to the extensive collection of documents connected with the administration of Thomas Cromwell in the 1530s and, working almost entirely on his own, produced a dissertation that was to form the basis of his life's work. For that research, "Thomas Cromwell, Aspects of His Administrative Work," he was awarded a Ph.D. in 1949.[6] When Elton completed his doctorate, teaching positions in British universities were regularly filled by persons without advanced research degrees. To many British scholars of the day, the doctorate of philosophy with its German origins and its American modifications was inappropriate for a bright young recipient of a first class honors degree, especially from Oxford or Cambridge. However, times and attitudes were changing, with the result that Elton's graduate study gave him discipline and technical skills possessed by few of his contemporaries and future rivals.

Elton's research and publications opened the door to a career of university teaching, and his advancement was steady but conventional. His first academic appointment took Elton to Scotland, where he was assistant in history at Glasgow University (1948–1949). After a year he was able to return to England where he was offered an assistant lectureship at Cambridge University replacing Kenneth Pickthorn, a Tudor constitutional historian, who had entered Parliament. The move to Cambridge proved to be permanent; Elton served as assistant lecturer from 1949–1953 and lecturer from 1953–1963. He was elected a fellow of Clare College in 1954. In 1963 he was promoted to reader in Tudor studies, a position that he held until 1967 when he received a personal chair as professor of English constitutional history.

G. R. Elton succeeded Owen Chadwick as Regius Professor of Modern History at Cambridge in 1983 and served until retirement in 1988. The political nature of the regius professorships often provokes comment in the press because the monarch makes the appointments on the recommendation of the prime minister. Successful candidates traditionally offer a combination of scholarly and political credentials.[7] Following Elton's appointment, the *Guardian* labeled Elton as "the current spokesman of Tory history" and "a favourite in [Margaret] Thatcher's England" and deplored his unashamed call "for an elitist and nationalistic history." At the other end of the political spectrum, John Kenyon hailed Elton's appointment and asserted that he and Sir Lewis Namier were the two greatest British historians of the twentieth century.[8]

Many other honors accompanied Elton's professional advancement. He was elected fellow of the British Academy in 1967 and president of the Royal Historical Society in 1972. He has received honorary degrees from Glasgow (1979), Newcastle (1981), Bristol

(1981), and London (1984). On three occasions Elton held visiting professorships in the United States, at Pittsburgh in 1963, Colorado in 1967, and Minnesota in 1976. He was Ford lecturer at Oxford in 1972, and these lectures were published as *Policy and Police: The Enforcement of the Reformation in the Age of Thomas Cromwell.* In 1986 he received a knighthood.[9]

The major focus of Elton's research and writing has been Thomas Cromwell, a minister of Henry VIII, who held office from 1531 until his execution in 1540 and played a critical role in the early Reformation. Cromwell was the subject of Elton's dissertation and the central figure in three major scholarly books, *The Tudor Revolution in Government: Administrative Changes in the Reign of Henry VIII, Policy and Police,* and *Reform and Renewal: Thomas Cromwell and the Common Weal.* Beginning in 1949, Elton published over thirty scholarly articles that deal with Cromwell either directly or indirectly; many of these were reprinted in the three volumes of his collected works. Beyond this, Cromwell appears prominently in Elton's two textbooks, *England under the Tudors* and *Reform and Reformation,* as well as in a collection of documents, *The Tudor Constitution,* and other works. Rarely, if ever, has a major British historian pursued such specialized study over so many years.[10]

When Elton began his doctoral research, the standard authority on Cromwell was the two-volume work of Roger B. Merriman, *Life and Letters of Thomas Cromwell,* published when the author was only twenty-six years of age. Merriman was an American, born in Boston, educated at Harvard and Oxford, who was a prominent member of the Harvard faculty from 1908 until his death in 1945. Unlike Elton, Merriman moved on to other subjects after completing his work on Cromwell. Best known for a four-volume study, *The Rise of the Spanish Empire* (1918–1934), Merriman also wrote a biography of the great Turk, *Suleiman the Magnificent,* which appeared in 1944. Merriman differed from Elton in that he did not find Cromwell an attractive historical figure, although he clearly demonstrated Cromwell's importance and furnished insights that were subsequently taken over by Elton.[11]

Merriman's life of Cromwell was a critical, political biography based on printed sources and British and European manuscripts. Included with the biography were 351 of Cromwell's letters. Merriman concluded from his research that Cromwell "familiarized himself with every detail of domestic administration to an extent that no king or minister had ever done in England before." "From the close of the year 1532 until his fall," Merriman wrote, "the entire domestic administration of England was in Cromwell's hands." Merriman posed what was to become fifty years later a highly contentious question: Who was the "real cause of the secular and religious revolution of the years 1530 to 1640," Thomas Cromwell or Henry VIII? Merriman's answer was that probabilities pointed to Cromwell "as the true originator of the startling changes which occurred after his accession to power."[12] Although Merriman recognized the revolutionary character of the 1530s and blazed trails that were followed later by Elton, the latter never acknowledged any indebtedness and indeed dismissed Merriman's work in a footnote as one that did "little but recount the political history of the time with Cromwell put in the middle of it."[13]

The Tudor Revolution in Government, Elton's first book, set the tone for most of his later work. He argued that English government had a special claim to be studied and firmly rejected the idea of Tudor despotism:

> To speak of despotism and a reign of terror in sixteenth-century England was easier for a generation which had not met these things at first hand; however it remains true that it was a time when men were ready to be governed, and when order and peace seemed more important than principles and rights. What distinguished the Tudors from their European contemporaries, who were facing similar problems, was just that they provided peace and order without despotism — certainly without the weapons of a despot.[14]

Here was the voice of a man who had experienced the beginning of the German Holocaust firsthand, not that of the cloistered academic. Elton not only rejected the concept of Tudor despotism but also used Cromwell's career to reinterpret the end of the Middle Ages and the beginning of the modern period. Elton argued that 1485 was not the beginning of modern English history; on the contrary, the early Tudor period was medieval, with the era of Cardinal Wolsey signalling the climax of medieval household administration. In contrast, Cromwell was "a modern type of English statesman," who brought to government the talents of the lay businessman and the professional bureaucrat. Cromwell revolutionized administration so completely, according to Elton, that in 1603 "Elizabeth handed to her successor a country administered on modern lines."[15]

Elton supported his bold assertions by a meticulous analysis of Cromwell's financial and administrative policies. Cromwell's firm hand controlled the collection of firstfruits and tenths and the management of the dissolution of the monasteries through the Court of Augmentations. In 1540, during his last weeks in office, Cromwell drafted legislation for the reorganization of the Court of Wards along bureaucratic lines. Elton revealed how Cromwell, unlike his predecessors, controlled the lesser seals, the signet and the privy seal, and enlarged the office of principal secretary to achieve his reforming goals. The development of the King's Council during the 1530s also received careful attention. Wolsey, according to Elton, had interrupted the growth of a small, powerful council, but Cromwell governed through the council and contributed to the emergence of the Privy Council, a body that was to have a long and important history under the later Tudors and early Stuarts. Although there was no Privy Council in 1532, the appearance of such a council in 1540 was a consequence of Cromwell's work between 1534 and 1536. Elton conceded that Cromwell did not start from scratch in developing the Privy Council and that his reforms were not entirely original. While the reformed council was "essential for that more energetic, efficient, and bureaucratic government which Cromwell desired, the establishment of a board of equally powerful members, subject to and dependent only on the king, could not but militate against the supremacy of one minister." Consequently, it was the new Privy Council that in the end enabled Cromwell's enemies to unite against him. After Cromwell was gone, "the newly emancipated councillors finished the elaboration of the board of government which would in itself prevent the rise of another Cromwell."[16]

The Tudor revolution, as defined by Elton, was a complex series of administrative changes caused by Henry VIII's determination to break with Rome and establish a national church under his own authority. The revolution was reformist and on the whole beneficial to England. After 1540 there was a period of decline during the reigns of Edward VI and Mary, but Elizabeth successfully restored good government "without major administrative reforms and merely by putting fresh energy and drive into the existing institutions."[17] The Tudor revolution, according to Elton, was essentially the work of a single man, Thomas Cromwell. He did not deny that Cromwell was an autocrat who exercised great power but insisted that the country needed strong leadership and that this leadership successfully changed England into a modern state.

The Tudor Revolution in Government established Elton's reputation as the leading authority on the reign of Henry VIII and the most vigorous and dynamic interpreter of the Tudor period. During the years that immediately followed its publication, Elton enlarged the concept of the Tudor revolution in a series of journal articles and in two highly influential textbooks. In one article he expanded Cromwell's leadership role and argued that he was the man behind the Henrician Reformation; in another he contended that Cromwell was not a Machiavellian but a constitutionalist who believed in parliamentary government and in the rule of law.[18] In 1955, only two years after the appearance of *The Tudor Revolution,* Elton published *England under the Tudors,* a text that shaped the teaching of Tudor history for the next thirty years. This powerful and persuasive book placed Thomas Cromwell at the very center of the Tudor era and made the Tudor revolution the principal historical event of the sixteenth century. The enlarged concept of the Tudor revolution reached far beyond administrative change and included the development of national sovereignty, the creation of the Church of England, the growth of parliamentary government, and the emergence of conservative and paternalistic social policies. It is no exaggeration to state that *England under the Tudors* and its companion volume of documents, *The Tudor Constitution,* published in 1960, influenced the historical understanding of an entire generation.

After *The Tudor Revolution* Elton concentrated less on administrative history but continued to study Thomas Cromwell and the decade of the 1530s. In his second monograph, *Policy and Police,* Elton examined the problem of law enforcement in what he called "the age of Thomas Cromwell." The Reformation under Henry VIII, Elton argued, meant the end of domestic peace. "Many resented and, to the best of their ability, resisted the innovations; others who welcomed them were fewer but noisier and by their frequent excess of zeal provoked reactions in village and town which, taken together, could amount to the sort of violence that might endanger the security of the King's government."[19] Elton found examples of unlawful behavior and disorder throughout the country, but *Policy and Police* concentrated on the region south of the river Trent and excluded the major rebellion of the period, the Pilgrimage of Grace.

In considering the government's response to popular unrest, Elton attempted to answer the question whether the regime of Cromwell practiced a "reign of terror." The reformed Treason Act of 1534, championed by Cromwell, was severe but necessary, and revealed that the common law and due process had triumphed over the legal procedures of the fourteenth century. An analysis of treason trials demonstrated that constitutional procedures were followed, with the result that acquittal frequently occurred. Out of 883 cases of treason between 1532 and 1540, 308 persons were executed and 32 acquitted. In addition, there were 96 pardons and 223 cases that were either dropped or probably dropped. Two hundred and eighty-seven of those charged with treason were "people involved in open and manifest rebellion, having raised war against the King." After a meticulous examination of law enforcement and of prosecutions for treason, Elton concluded that the rule of law prevailed and Cromwell's leadership assured that "there should be neither holocaust nor reign of terror."[20] Although Cromwell was himself numbered among the victims of the Tudor revolution, Elton insisted that he alone was both victim and victor because he successfully guided England toward a constructive goal.

Elton described his third book on Cromwell, *Reform and Renewal: Thomas Cromwell and the Common Weal* (1973), as "my last engagement with Thomas Cromwell, at least at book-length." Whereas *Policy and Police* examined negative aspects of government — the need for law enforcement in a country where people would not obey the law — *Reform and Renewal,* the shortest of Elton's major works, considered the more positive reforms initiated under Cromwell. The study of reformist thought and policy led the author toward intellectual history where he again encountered solid American scholarship, especially the work of W. Gordon Zeeveld, Arthur B. Ferguson, and Stanford E. Lehmberg. Yet Elton sought to break new ground, arguing that none of those historians had "attempted a systematic study of the way in which articulate protest and intellectual remedy-mongering may have percolated into statutes and proclamations."[21]

In *Reform and Renewal,* Elton examined Cromwell's work in Parliament where his reforming proposals were debated and passed into law. He viewed the enactment of parliamentary legislation as the major test of Cromwell's achievement, because an act of Parliament was "a powerful instrument: once made, it commanded obedience of a virtually religious character, and more practically it had the whole weight of the common law's organs of enforcement behind it." Elton revealed Cromwell's long hours of labor in preparing bills for Parliament and also shed new light on the distinction between bills officially promoted and those originating with a private interest. Cromwell's major achievements included the Sheep and Enclosure Act, a new Poor Law, and the Statutes of Uses and Wills which "revolutionized" the land law.[22] But Cromwell encountered strong parliamentary opposition and fell from power at the height of his career. He therefore achieved less than he desired; yet his reforms set new standards for the commonwealth, and after his death reforming efforts continued.

The Thomas Cromwell who emerged in *Reform and Renewal* was different in many respects from the man in Elton's earlier work. "His cast of mind was less determinedly secular and less ruthlessly radical than I had once supposed." This new Cromwell also possessed greater intellectual resources. Elton noted with approval the assessment of Gabriel Harvey, an Elizabethan scholar, who admired Cromwell's Roman disposition, his powers of speech, and his "natural heroical audacity," talents that he shared with three others, John Dudley, Duke of Northumberland, Thomas Stukeley, and Francis Drake. Moreover, Cromwell is seen in the book as a statesman possessed of substantial religious commitment. His interest in the Bible "was not so exclusively political and pragmatical." He was essentially an evangelical—a man of the gospel—whose religious thought combined humanist and Protestant concepts into a sound middle-of-the-road zeal for reform of the English church.[23]

Elton's research on Cromwell and his concept of the Tudor revolution received critical acclaim in Britain and in the United States. By 1960 his name was a household word among Tudor scholars, graduate students, and British undergraduates. In England his textbooks filled a need for up-to-date scholarship, with the result that his influence in the grammar schools soon equalled his influence in the universities. As Elton's innovative interpretations became the new orthodoxy, criticism appeared. In 1959 the revised edition of the *Bibliography of British History: Tudor Period, 1485–1603* had contained cautionary annotations of Elton's work by Conyers Read,[24] but it was not until 1963 that two British scholars, Penry Williams and G. L. Harriss, mounted a major assault on Elton in *Past and Present*. Harriss, a medievalist, argued that Elton neglected the medieval precedents for Cromwell's policies, while Williams challenged Elton's more extreme claims for Cromwell's unique contributions to sixteenth-century government.[25] Both rejected the idea of a Tudor revolution in government. J. J. Scarisbrick, a former student of Elton's, published a biography of Henry VIII in 1968 in which he argued that the King, not Cromwell, was the principal architect of the royal supremacy. In the same year Oxford University Press reprinted Roger Merriman's biography of Cromwell.[26]

Although Elton responded to his critics with a vigorous defense of his work combined with tactical retreats from exposed positions, the concept of a Tudor revolution in government began to lose favor during the 1970s. In *The Crisis of Parliaments: English History 1509–*

1660, Conrad Russell rejected the idea that Cromwell's administrative policies heralded the beginning of modern government, while another text, *Peace, Print and Protestantism, 1450–1558,* by C. S. L. Davies included more than five pages of criticism of Elton's views.[27] In 1986 six scholars, including former Elton students, collaborated in *Revolution Reassessed: Revisions in the History of Tudor Government and Administration,* a collection of essays that attacked Elton's research on the court, the Privy Council, and government finance, and proclaimed that little of the original Cromwellian revolution survived. This critical work, according to Penry Williams, was nothing less than "a garland of hemlock" delivered to the master by his "academic children." Elton did not retreat before his adversaries, however, and continued to insist that the financial reforms of the 1530s and 1540s had been far more important than the supposedly more sophisticated program of reform of the previous century.[28]

After the publication of Elton's last book on Cromwell, *Reform and Renewal,* his research led to yet further challenges to older interpretations of Tudor history. The topic to which he gave most attention was Parliament. In four highly technical articles, he examined the materials of parliamentary history, arguing that a sound understanding of the sources must precede an understanding of the institution itself.[29] In two important lectures he outlined the conclusions drawn from his study of the sources of parliamentary history. The first, a presidential address to the Royal Historical Society in 1974, discussed the contribution of Parliament to political stability. Elton posed the question whether Parliament and other institutions of central government "provided known and accessible instruments which enabled positive interests, demands, and ambitions on the part of the politically powerful to achieve their ends." It was his conclusion that the Tudor Parliament fulfilled "its function as a stabilizing mechanism." "It mediated in the touchy area of taxation; by producing the required general and particular laws it kept necessary change in decent order; it assisted the rich in the arranging of their affairs; and it helped the ambitious to scale the heights of public power." The older view, based on liberal preconceptions, that Parliament should oppose or undo lawful and legitimate government represented, according to Elton, a misunderstanding of sixteenth-century political theory.[30]

A second lecture given as a memorial to Sir John Neale in 1978 was in fact a severe critique of Neale's work and that of his American colleague, Wallace Notestein. Using methods similar to those employed to attack the Tudor revolution in government, Elton argued that surviving records do not sustain Neale's view that the Elizabethan House of Commons grew in self-esteem and importance, because "the 'true' modern parliament" began earlier with the constitutional developments of the reign of Henry VIII. In Elton's view, Neale's narrative history neglected the House of Lords and exaggerated the importance of a few outspoken opposition leaders. "The evidence of the parliamentary record thus suggests that bills and acts—the making of every sort of law—should be treated as the first business of the Elizabethan Parliament." Elton also contended that Parliament was not called for political reasons; "nor was it thought of as a political assembly: it was a court, and the best contemporary opinion of its functions brings in politics only very obliquely."[31]

What was required, according to Elton, was nothing less than a complete reexamination of Elizabethan parliamentary history. His reassessment of the early Elizabethan period appeared in *The Parliament of England, 1559-1581* in which he emphasized the importance of procedure and legislation rather than Parliament's role in the great affairs of state. Elton came to the surprising conclusion that it was doubtful whether Parliament "ever really mattered all that much in the politics of the nation, except perhaps as a stage sometimes used by the real contenders over government and policy." He dismissed older notions about the rise of the House of Commons and an active Puritan opposition as varieties of myth and nonsense.[32]

Elton's later writings—like his earlier research on Cromwell and the Tudor revolution—were revisionist and combative. His topics had been thoroughly studied by major scholars of the previous generation: Elizabethan parliaments, the political career of Sir Thomas More, and the commonwealth reformers of the reign of Edward VI. Historians whose work he criticized and corrected included Neale, Notestein, Tawney, and R. W. Chambers, the biographer of More. By scrutinizing well-known sources and emphasizing neglected or unknown ones, Elton found that his predecessors had made serious errors or failed to comprehend the meaning of important documents. Elton argued that a proper understanding of even the most ambiguous sources would yield only one correct interpretation. His research therefore demolished old interpretations and destroyed theories that were no longer tenable. Interest in Elton's revisionism was heightened when he included his own early research as work requiring reassessment.[33]

Elton attracted the attention of scholars and advanced himself through his published research, but he also took a keen interest in the teaching of history in schools and universities. He became prominent at a time when secondary school enrollments, especially in the university-preparatory sixth form, were increasing. Expansion of the secondary schools led to the growth of existing universities and the establishment of new ones.[34] At both levels there was a heavy demand for teachers and textbooks. Elton's first text, *England under the Tudors* was an immediate success; it was frequently reprinted and appeared in a second edition in 1974. In the schools, sixth-form pupils preparing for the advanced (A) level General Certificate of Education examination in Tudor and Stuart England read *England under the Tudors* as a required text. A-level pupils were expected to analyze the interpretations of several authorities, but some were tempted merely to memorize Elton's persuasive arguments and to reproduce them on examination papers that were graded by university lecturers who were admirers of his work. As the effectiveness of teachers was measured by the success of their pupils in passing examinations, the readable new text rapidly became the authoritative interpretation of the Tudor period.

A similar situation existed in the universities which began admitting students from families whose children had never before received the benefits of higher education. Here students of the Tudor period could read the weighty and dated volumes of the *Oxford History of England* by J. D. Mackie and J. B. Black or S. T. Bindoff's short and highly compressed *Tudor England* in the *Pelican History of England* series. One could argue that the Oxford tomes were too long and Bindoff was too short, but *England under the Tudors* was just right. To supplement the text, Cambridge University Press issued a paperback edition of *The Tudor Revolution in Government* (1959). The following year Elton, who initially had considered revising J. R. Tanner's *Tudor Constitutional Documents*, published an entirely new book, *The Tudor Constitution: Documents and Commentary,* which provided the documents to support his interpretation of the Tudor period.[35] History undergraduates who were seeking a sound and respected scholar to guide them in writing essays and in preparing for university examinations found a ready friend and mentor in G. R. Elton.

Later, when criticism and outright rejection of Elton's Tudor revolution appeared, and when Elton also modified his original positions, problems for the student increased. A paperback edition of *Reform and Renewal* (1973) offered Elton's newer views, and the second edition of *England under the Tudors,* while not rewritten, included an additional chapter of corrections and revisions. The revisions notwithstanding, Elton asserted:

> I have to confess that the description and interpretation here put forward do not seem to me to have been invalidated by those twenty years [since the first edition]; however I might nowadays wish to modify this judgment or reconsider that assessment, I continue in general to stand by the view expressed here from the first. The massive research and publication of the past generation, though of course they demand some alterations in the book, have not, to my mind, undermined its main theses and have indeed confirmed some of its originally rash speculations.[36]

In view of this defense of *England under the Tudors,* it is surprising that Elton was actually preparing a new, and quite different text, *Reform and Reformation: England 1509–1558,* which was completed in 1976 and published the next year.

Reform and Reformation differs from *England under the Tudors* in scope, tone, and substance. Whereas the earlier book covers the whole Tudor century, *Reform and Reformation* begins with the accession of Henry VIII and ends with the death of Mary. It is an eclectic work that takes note of other research, including that of American scholars, and draws heavily on unpublished dissertations directed by Elton at Cambridge. In this remarkable text, the critical comments usually directed against other historians are now aimed at Elton himself. It would be difficult to find another book of the past twenty years that contains as much self-criticism as *Reform and Reformation.* Every chapter reveals the fruits of recent research, much of which was inspired by Elton. The Dudleys, a family formerly scorned by Tudor historians, appear in a new light. Indeed *Reform and Reformation* opens with Edmund Dudley's call for reform and includes a portrait of John Dudley, Duke of Northumberland, dressed in the costume of a practical politician and reformer. The character and achievements of Elton's new Henry VIII reveal the influence of Lacey Baldwin Smith and J. J. Scarisbrick. Like *England under the Tudors,* the new text emphasizes the 1530s at the expense of other periods, but the character of the decade has greatly changed. As Arthur J. Slavin has observed, "the revolution in government" is now no more than a prelude to reform. "Cromwell, now a man of ideas, is also more eclectic and less single-minded, though he has a vast steadiness of purpose."[37] In short, in *Reform and Reformation* Elton transformed the Tudor revolution into an age of reform.

Elton's impact on the teaching of history includes a strong commitment to the training of graduate students. As the ranks of graduate students swelled in the 1960s, Elton's seminar at Cambridge replaced the University of London as the major center of Tudor research. Many British and American students completed doctoral dissertations under his direction, while others acknowledged his guidance in research completed elsewhere. Elton's students received careful supervision and rigorous training that helped them compete successfully in an academic environment, which by the 1970s was becoming overcrowded with research scholars and underpopulated by undergraduates wishing to study history. Among the most successful of Elton's former students were D. M. Loades, John J. Scarisbrick, Stanford E. Lehmberg, John Guy, and Christopher Haigh, each of whom has made important contributions to Tudor studies. Elton developed strong transatlantic connections, and in 1982 a group identifying themselves as "his American friends" published a collection of essays entitled *Tudor Rule and Revolution* on the occasion of his sixtieth birthday. Although nothing like a formal Elton school of historical studies ever developed, close personal ties linked the master and his former students in Britain and the United States. His influence was greatest among those who researched sixteenth-century topics under his direction, but he also inspired revisionist scholars who undertook to rewrite the history of the early Stuart period and to free it from Whiggish preconceptions. Independent researchers in a variety of areas benefited from his advice.[38] A prolific correspondent, Elton found time to help almost any serious historian who requested his assistance.

Although Elton's textbooks and seminar influenced an entire generation of students of the sixteenth century, his views on the writing of history were aimed at a larger audience. Historians in all fields need to use documents correctly, and Elton believed that traditional academic history required protection against an assortment of "false gods."[39] These included Whigs, who studied the past to understand the present, and Marxists, whose understanding of sources was clouded by adherence to false theories. The new social and economic history, psychohistory, and computer-assisted social science also threatened the integrity of history, as Elton understood it.[40] The various false gods flourished particularly in American universities. Elton noted that while the United States had very little history, it was often badly written by professional historians.[41] In the United States, "one still encounters the old double standard; men who express themselves very prettily in conversation or, occasionally on the platform, pull out some special dictionary of polysyllabic jargon when they write, in the conviction that the fraternity will not otherwise recognize them as scholars."[42] He faulted American graduate schools for allowing students to study historical problems "through the contrasting opinions of selected writers rather than from the evidence" and for following a curriculum that places too little emphasis on the dissertation.[43] It is not easy to gauge Elton's true attitude toward the false gods of history: *The Practice of History* is a manifesto written in anger, while "Two Kinds of History" is a thoughtful dialogue with Robert Fogel.[44] In these and other writings, flashes of wit and humor are juxtaposed with a relentless attack on the enemy.[45]

However one reacts to Elton's diagnosis of the ills of history in general and the inadequacies of American historians in particular, no one can fault him for failing to spell out exactly what history ought to be. Good history, according to Elton, must be based on sound documentary scholarship and presented in an intelligible narrative. The structure of good narrative history will be "overwhelmingly political, overwhelmingly concerned with those fortunes and manipulations of power in society which form the main recorded activities of men."[46] The political history Elton recommends emphasizes legal, constitutional, and administrative aspects but avoids biography. In Britain, said Elton, "the historians' task consists among other things, if I may put it, in a crude re-kindling of a certain respect for a country whose past justifies that respect."[47] In his inaugural lecture as regius professor at Cambridge, Elton again called for a renewed interest in English history and praised the achievements of his country.[48]

Elton's commitment to good history reaches far beyond the classroom, lecture hall, and seminar and transcends professional rivalries and national boundaries. He proclaimed boldly in *The Practice of History* that "modern civilization is peculiar rather than ordinary in that it rests upon the two intellectual pillars of natural science and analytical history." He further elaborated his views:

> Theology and philosophy can both claim to have commanded the minds of men for longer stretches of time and over larger areas than these characteristic thought systems of the twentieth century, thought systems which, significantly enough, came jointly to dominance in the seventeenth. Their triumph, now universal, has itself been the outcome of an historical situation, for the political and technological advantages which gave Europe the victory in the struggle of civilizations brought to the top a complex of societies whose thinking had been influenced by the longest traditions of a real concern with the past.[49]

To protect this civilization, says Elton, historians must reject the restraint of established authorities and commit themselves to the cause of reason, freedom, and truth. They must also surrender "the very human desire to discover great schemes, large answers, words that may save or damn mankind." They will be "limited, particular—and free." The social function of the historian is to serve as "mankind's intellectual conscience" and to oppose absolutist system-builders, political dictators, and social equalizers.[50]

Although historians may prefer to devote themselves to the world of ideas and the study of historical records as they teach and conduct research, few, if any, can escape the influence of the environment in which they live. As Lawrence Stone has remarked, "They are driven by hidden or not so hidden passions and political prejudices."[51] G. R. Elton, like other successful scholars, had to assess received opinion and established authorities at the beginning of his career and identify what was erroneous or deficient. At the same time he had to compete with contemporaries for a position of authority. After achieving these two objectives, Elton could evaluate the work of newcomers and defend himself against aspiring rivals. His chosen field of study, Tudor England, was a minefield of professional and ideological controversies long before he began his research. J. A. Froude, the greatest Tudor historian of the Victorian period, was attacked mercilessly for faulty scholarship and subjected to character assassination. E. A. Freeman, a regius professor at Oxford, referred to Froude as a beast and scribbled in a book margin, "May I live to disembowel James Anthony Froude"; "Froude is the vilest beast that ever wrote a book."[52] The darker side of the British historical profession, described by John Kenyon in *The History Men,* could not fail to affect Elton's work.

When Elton began his studies, the established authorities in British history included A. F. Pollard, R. H. Tawney, G. M. Trevelyan, and L. B. Namier. In addition, there was the American, Roger B. Merriman, whose book on Thomas Cromwell was the first obstacle to Elton's advancement. He first devalued Merriman's work and then ignored him altogether. Turning to targets in Britain, Elton approached Pollard more cautiously. Although he lived until 1948, Pollard was viewed as a "sound Victorian liberal" who gave Henry VIII "not only the respect of the historian but also the worship of the devotee." This was perhaps not an injudicious assessment in 1962, but later Pollard's reputation plummeted with the result that the revised, 1974 edition of *England under the Tudors* omitted his biography of

Henry VIII from a bibliography of over two hundred entries and mentioned it only as "an ancient classic" that was entirely superseded by modern work.[53] Harsher judgments were reserved for Trevelyan and Tawney. Although not lacking defenders, Trevelyan became an easy target for critics; in 1981 Elton dismissed him as a "long discarded" author "who knew nothing at firsthand about the sixteenth century."[54] Among the scholars who had made their mark before World War II, Tawney was singled out for the greatest abuse. In 1968 Elton wrote, "I don't think there has been a historian at work in this country who has had a worse, more disastrous effect upon what I may call the national self-consciousness than that very good man Richard Tawney. With great regret I am coming to think increasingly that there is not a single work which Tawney wrote which can be trusted."[55] Elton's disdain for older authorities was not complete. He was an admirer of Namier, and although he claimed to be the disciple of no one, he held a high opinion of two medievalists: T. F. Tout and F. W. Maitland. The latter, a Victorian legal historian, was the subject of Elton's first biography, published in 1985.[56]

Elton was especially severe with contemporary historians, especially scholars working in his own field and arriving at conclusions different from his own. He often based his criticism on misuse of sources but did not always demonstrate how the sources were misinterpreted. Inadequate research was another charge leveled against his victims. Accordingly, Elton faulted Joel Hurstfield's essays on liberty and authority in Tudor England with the comment, "None of these is based on intensive new research, and all rest on a rather thin foundation of evidential material."[57] Lacey Baldwin Smith's masterful *Henry VIII: The Mask of Royalty* was "a highly personal but interesting essay [which] would be more convincing if the evidence behind it were more trustworthy,"[58] while Lawrence Stone's *The Causes of the English Revolution* was "shot through with tradition-hallowed but doubtful statements."[59] Ideological differences, which stood behind the attack on Tawney, led Elton to write of W. G. Hoskins's "waffle about a 'working class' in Tudor England."[60] When Penry Williams criticized Elton's views on the Tudor revolution in *The Tudor Regime,* he countered with the charge that the author was poorly informed about legal and administrative history and concluded that "it should be clearly said that the book is by no means all gallant failure."[61] In the first Sir Herbert Butterfield lecture given in 1983, Elton said many kind things about his former colleague but also gave two reasons why he failed to become a major historian. "One of these is highly technical: deficiencies in Butterfield's understanding of historical evidence and its treatment, just the area in which he is reckoned to have been learned and illuminating. The other is the conflict within him between the historian and the Christian."[62]

After his death in 1975, Sir John Neale replaced R. H. Tawney as the historian most frequently and most harshly attacked by Elton. He initially wrote of his mentor at the University of London with respect and recommended his works on Elizabethan parliaments enthusiastically. As late as 1975 Elton held that Neale's biography of Elizabeth, although too indulgent toward the queen, was the best available life. He wrote that *The Elizabethan House of Commons* was an "important analysis of elections, membership, and procedure," and gave even higher marks to *Elizabeth I and Her Parliaments,* which was a "brilliant narrative of parliamentary affairs, indispensable to an understanding of the political, constitutional, and ecclesiastical history of the reign," although it concentrated "too exclusively on occasions of political dispute and conflict."[63] In his presidential address to the Royal Historical Society in 1974, however, Elton called for a new approach to parliamentary history and cautiously raised questions about Neale's methods of research. Four years later in the J. E. Neale Memorial Lecture, he spoke appreciatively of Neale's work and concluded, "Thanks to him—and it is heartfelt thanks—we know where we must start in order to go further." On the other hand, he argued that Neale had been influenced by the misconceptions of the American scholar, Wallace Notestein, whose interpretation of parliamentary history was "crumbling before the onslaughts" of modern research.[64]

Elton intensified his attack on Neale in 1984 when he proclaimed that the time had arrived for "denying him outright." "For much of his interpretation," Neale had relied on the Whiggish views of Notestein, whose "venerable works pretty thoroughly misinterpret what happened and leave important parts of the story untold." The writings of Notestein and Neale, properly understood, were "a mixture of political conviction and of tendentious misreadings of selected evidence." Fearing that the demolition of Neale might have gone too far, Elton felt compelled to caution his readers: "Neale got some things right. His narrative of parliamentary events is quite often correct in detail, though often also falsely slanted in interpretation."[65]

Elton's assaults on prominent historians stand as a reminder that Victorian traditions of ideological conflict and personal animosity among British academics have lasted well into the twentieth century, but a balanced assessment of his career must give greater weight to his impressive scholarly output and his significant contributions to the historical profession.[66] Moreover, since Elton remains actively at work even in retirement, any evaluation of his overall achievement must be something of an interim report. Years must pass before it can be determined whether he will suffer the fate of Tawney or Neale at the hands of a new generation of critical scholars or whether his reputation will survive as Maitland's has done. It may also be premature to judge whether G. R. Elton will be remembered primarily as the formulator of the (now largely discredited) concept of "the Tudor revolution in government," or as a skillful and zealous historiographical controversialist, or as an extraordinarily diligent researcher in the archives, or as a defender of intellectual freedom. His contemporaries have come to recognize him as a bold and combative academic historian who aspires to dominate his field and to vanquish those who fail to share his vision of the past. In the process he has also become one of that tiny handful of individuals in the world of British history who can justly be deemed a household name.

NOTES

I am pleased to acknowledge the assistance of Frances Armytage, W. H. G. Armytage, Anthony Fletcher, John Mackrell, Roger Manning, Harold Schwartz, and Lawrence Stone. None of these, however, is in any way responsible for what is contained in this essay.

1. G. R. Elton, *The History of England* (Cambridge, 1984), 1.
2. The SPSL was founded shortly after Hitler came to power. It was privately funded, with a substantial contribution coming from British university teachers. See Marion Berghahn, *German-Jewish Refugees in England* (New York, 1984), 78.
3. *The Times,* 6 Feb. 1976.
4. Victor Ehrenberg, *From Solon to Socrates* (London, 1968), xiii–xiv.
5. Lewis Ehrenberg, *Rydal School 1936–1963* (Colwyn Bay, n.d.), 22–27, 125.
6. Information in this and the preceding paragraph is in part based on an interview with Professor Elton at Clare College, Cambridge, on May 27, 1985. Notes from the interview are in the possession of the author.
7. For comments on regius professorships see H. R. Trevor-Roper, *History: Professional and Lay* (Oxford, 1957); and A. J. P. Taylor, *A Personal History* (New York, 1983), 214–17.
8. Richard Gott, "Reaction and Reform among History Men—and Women," *Guardian Weekly,* 4 Feb. 1984, 5; John P. Kenyon, *The History Men: The Historical Profession in England since the Renaissance* (London, 1983), 273.
9. The following collections of essays have been published in honor of Professor Elton: *Tudor Rule and Revolution: Essays for G. R. Elton from His American Friends,* ed. D. J. Guth and J. W. McKenna (Cambridge, 1982); *Politics and Society in Reformation Europe: Essays for Sir Geoffrey Elton on his Sixty-fifth Birthday,* ed. E. I. Kouri and Tom Scott (New York, 1987); *Law and Government under the Tudors: Essays Presented to Sir Geoffrey Elton, Regius Professor of Modern History in the University of Cambridge on the Occasion of His Retirement,* ed. Claire Cross, David Loades, and J. J. Scarisbrick (Cambridge, 1988); and *Rulers, Religion and Rhetoric in Early Modern England: A Festschrift for Geoffrey Elton from His Australasian Friends.* In

Parergon, new ser., no. 6 (Sydney, Australia, 1988). Bibliographies of Elton's published works appear in *Tudor Rule and Revolution* and *Law and Government under the Tudors.*

10. Thomas Cromwell emerged as a major European statesman in Elton's *Reformation Europe, 1517–1559* (London, 1963), 168, 185, 297.

11. The recipient of many honors, Merriman was Gurney Professor of History and Political Science and master of Eliot House at Harvard. In 1935 Cambridge University awarded him an honorary doctorate.

12. Roger B. Merriman, *Life and Letters of Thomas Cromwell* (1902; reprint, Oxford, 1968), 1:89, 103, 112.

13. G. R. Elton, *The Tudor Revolution in Government* (Cambridge, 1953), 6 n.2. In *England under the Tudors* (London, 1956), 478, Elton wrote, "There is no life of Cromwell worth mentioning."

14. Elton, *Tudor Revolution,* 1–2.

15. Ibid., 3, 71.

16. Ibid., 320, 350, 351–52.

17. Ibid., 417.

18. G. R. Elton, "King or Minister? The Man behind the Henrician Reformation," (1954; reprinted in his *Studies in Tudor and Stuart Politics and Government* [Cambridge, 1974]), 1:173–88; "The Political Creed of Thomas Cromwell," (1956; reprinted in *Studies*) 2:215–35.

19. G. R. Elton, *Policy and Police: The Enforcement of the Reformation in the Age of Thomas Cromwell* (Cambridge, 1972), 45.

20. Ibid., vii, 387, 389, 399–400.

21. G. R. Elton, *Reform and Renewal: Thomas Cromwell and the Common Weal* (Cambridge, 1973), vii, 7.

22. Ibid., 68, 160.

23. Ibid., vii–viii, 11, 34–37.

24. Conyers Read, ed., *Bibliography of British History: Tudor Period, 1485–1603,* 2d rev. ed. (Oxford, 1959), 30, 44, 87.

25. Penry Williams and G. L. Harriss, "A Revolution in Tudor History?" *Past and Present* 25(July 1963):3–58.

26. J. J. Scarisbrick, *Henry VIII* (London, 1968), 304. For further criticism of the Tudor revolution as formulated by Elton, see Lawrence Stone, "How Nasty was Thomas Cromwell?" *New York Review of Books,* 22 Mar. 1973; "Terrible Times," *New Republic,* 5 May 1982; and John Guy, "The Tudor Age (1485–1603)," in *The Oxford Illustrated History of Britain,* ed. Kenneth O. Morgan (Oxford, 1984), 246–48.

27. Conrad Russell, *The Crisis of Parliaments: English History 1509–1660* (London, 1971), 110–11; C. S. L. Davies, *Peace, Print and Protestantism, 1450–1558* (St. Albans, Herts., 1977), 226–32.

28. Christopher Coleman and David Starkey, eds., *Revolution Reassessed: Revisions in the History of Tudor Government and Administration* (Oxford, 1986), 199; Penry Williams, "Pathways of Reform," *Times Literary Supplement,* 5 Dec. 1986; G. R. Elton, "A New Age of Reform?" *Historical Journal* 30, no. 3(1987):709–16.

29. G. R. Elton, "The Early Journals of the House of Lords"; "The Sessional Printing of Statutes, 1484–1547"; "The Rolls of Parliament, 1449–1547"; "Enacting Clauses and Legislative Initiative, 1559–1581"; reprinted in *Studies in Tudor and Stuart Politics and Government* (Cambridge, 1983), 3:58–155.

30. G. R. Elton, "Tudor Government: The Points of Contact," in his *Studies* 3:5, 21.

31. G. R. Elton, "Parliament in the Sixteenth Century: Functions and Fortunes," in his *Studies* 3:157, 163, 159.

32. G. R. Elton, *The Parliament of England, 1559–1581* (Cambridge, 1986), ix, 350, 378.

33. For Elton's work on More and the commonwealth reformers, see "Sir Thomas More and the Opposition to Henry VIII," in his *Studies* 1:155–72; "Thomas More," *Studies* 3:344–72; and "Reform and the 'Commonwealth-Men' of Edward VI's Reign," *Studies* 3:234–53. For an example of self-criticism see "Thomas Cromwell Redivivus," *Studies* 3:373.

34. See W. H. G. Armytage, *Four Hundred Years of English Education*, 2d ed. (Cambridge, 1970), 246–52.

35. Elton's views on Tanner are found in the preface to *The Tudor Constitution: Documents and Commentary* (Cambridge, 1960), v–vi.

36. G. R. Elton, *England under the Tudors*, 2d ed. (London, 1974), v.

37. Arthur J. Slavin, "G. R. Elton and His Era: Thirty Years On," *Albion* 15(1983): 217.

38. For early examples of Elton's influence on Stuart revisionist historiography see Conrad Russell, ed., *The Origins of English Civil War* (London, 1973), 16; and J. P. Kenyon, *Stuart England* (Harmondsworth, Mddx., 1978), 41.

39. G. R. Elton, *Future of the Past* (Cambridge, 1968), 32.

40. G. R. Elton, *Political History: Principles and Practice* (London, 1970), 160.

41. Elton, *Future of the Past*, 9.

42. G. R. Elton, *Practice of History* (London, 1967), 109.

43. Ibid., 103, 171.

44. R. W. Fogel and G. R. Elton, *Which Road to the Past? Two Views of History* (New Haven, 1983), 71–121.

45. An example of Elton's wit may be found in "The Historian's Social Function," *Studies* 3:413, where he wrote, "People will continue to read history, even serious history, and people will continue to write history, even good history. Still, there are enemies, some lurking in thickets, some boldly skirmishing across the plain, and while their peashooters cannot kill they can and do hurt." On another occasion he lashed out at British scientists and said that history is "the only subject which makes you grow up and takes you past adolescence." *Chronicle of Higher Education*, 19 Feb. 1986, 31.

46. Elton, *Political History*, 5, 163, 177.

47. Elton, *Future of the Past*, 22.

48. Elton, *History of England*, 23–27.

49. Elton, *Practice of History*, 1.

50. Elton, *Studies* 3:424–28.

51. Lawrence Stone, "Not a Nice Lot," *New York Times Book Review*, 18 Mar. 1984. H. R. Trevor-Roper expressed a similar view in *History and Imagination* (Oxford, 1980), 2: "Even the most 'objective' of historians, we soon discover, are imprisoned, though they may not know it, in a philosophy which is conditioned by subjective experience."

52. Kenyon, *History Men*, 118.

53. G. R. Elton, *Henry VIII: An Essay in Revision* (London, 1962), 4; *England under the Tudors*, 2d ed., 494. Curiously, the 1969 reprint of the first edition of *England under the Tudors* states that Pollard had written the best life of Henry VIII, 478.

54. Elton, *Studies* 3:438. A more favorable assessment of Trevelyan may be found in Walter L. Arnstein, "George Macaulay Trevelyan and the Art of History: A Cen-

tenary Reappraisal," *The Midwest Quarterly,* 18, no. 1(Autumn, 1976): 78-97.

55. Elton, *Future of the Past,* 15-16. There is also vigorous criticism of Tawney in *Reformation Europe: 1517-1559* (London, 1963), 314-18.

56. G. R. Elton, *F. W. Maitland* (New Haven, 1985). David Cannadine, "The First of the Modern Historians," *Sunday Times,* 4 Aug. 1985, suggested that this book contains important autobiographical insights.

57. Elton, *Studies* 3:433.

58. G. R. Elton, *Reform and Reformation: England 1509-1558* (London, 1977), 406.

59. Elton, *Studies* 3:477.

60. G. R. Elton, *Renaissance Quarterly* 36, no. 3(1983): 427.

61. G. R. Elton, "The Tudors So Far," *Times Literary Supplement,* 15 Feb. 1980, 183.

62. G. R. Elton, "Herbert Butterfield and the Study of History," *Historical Journal* 27, no. 3(1984): 729-43.

63. Elton, *England under the Tudors,* 2d ed., 495, 497.

64. Elton, *Studies* 3:182.

65. Elton, "Parliament," in *The Reign of Elizabeth I,* ed. Christopher Haigh (London, 1984), 80, 81, 84. A full assessment of Neale appears in the *Dictionary of National Biography, 1971-1980,* ed. Lord Blake and C. S. Nicholls (Oxford, 1986), 623-24.

66. Cf. C. S. L. Davies, "Twentieth Century Thomas Cromwell," *Times Higher Education Supplement,* 3 May 1974, 13. See also Peter Scott, "Textbook Revolution of a Natural Englishman," *Times Higher Education Supplement,* 13 June 1980, 7. Scott viewed Elton not as an exile, "but someone who has come home" and emphasized his conservatism and attraction to nationalism.

Joel Hurstfield
Historian for All Seasons

M. J. TUCKER

Although he has been neglected since his death in 1980, Joel Hurstfield was a major figure in the post-1945 generation of British historians.[1] For seventeen years, from 1962 to 1979, he was Astor Professor of English History at the University of London, a prestigious chair occupied for many years by his mentor, Sir John Neale, the leading specialist in Elizabethan studies during the 1930s and 1940s.[2] Appropriately enough, G. R. Elton allotted Hurstfield six references in his critical bibliography, *Modern Historians on British History* (1970).[3] To study Hurstfield is to learn what kind of history was in vogue during the time he rose to prominence (1946–1959) and during his heyday in the 1960s and early 1970s.

Joel Hurstfield was born on November 4, 1911, of a line of "émigré forebears who had sought refuge in England from persecution."[4] He received his basic education at Owen's school in the London borough of Islington. Even as a child he was drawn to the great political figures of the day, spending his free time at political meetings or in rapt attention in the gallery of the House of Commons, savoring the great debates of his time. Later, as an undergraduate at University College, London, he attended Hugh Gaitskell's lectures in economics, and with him established a college socialist society. He also began to think about how persons came to achieve fame and to use power. Two of the key questions he would later pose as a historian were: "What is the relationship between a man and the people among whom he lives; and . . . what is the relationship between the crown and society?"[5] Hurstfield's experiences sitting in the parliamentary gallery and study-

37

ing contemporary politicians would stand him in good stead when he wrote about Elizabeth I and William and Robert Cecil.

At the University of London in 1934, Hurstfield earned a coveted first class honors degree in history and won the Pollard and Gladstone prizes. These achievements opened the doors to an academic career, first as a graduate research student for two years under J. R. Neale. The work with Neale made a deep impression on Hurstfield, and many years later he noted how productive historians like Neale and his contemporary, A. H. Dodd, had been able to transmute dusty archives so that people and institutions long dead lived once more "in the recreative imagination of the historian."[6]

In 1937 Hurstfield was appointed to his first academic post, assistant lecturer at University College, Southampton; a year later he advanced to lecturer. Since Hurstfield constituted one-third of the entire history department, he spent twenty hours a week in the classroom teaching a variety of courses. Sometimes his preparation for a nine o'clock lecture stopped at two A.M., and he would arise at seven to finish the job. The college could claim only 250 students, and Hurstfield was warned that if the enrollment did not increase, he would lose his job. There was even the possibility that the college (later the University of Southampton) would be placed under the jurisdiction of the municipal authority and be turned into a nonacademic technical college. Hurstfield found that the townspeople looked on the college faculty as "arrogant, underemployed intellectuals, living comfortable lives with long holidays . . . [who] could only rouse [themselves] sufficiently to deliver unsavoury political speeches attacking the diplomacy of Neville Chamberlain."[7] While at Southampton the young lecturer officially changed his last name from Hirschfeld to Hurstfield.

Possessing a marvelous speaking voice, a quick intelligence, and a love of debate, Hurstfield toured the United States as a member of the 1934 interuniversity debating team. While at Southampton his love of politics led him to stand as a Labour party candidate for Parliament, but the outbreak of World War II frustrated a role at Westminster. He became a civil servant instead, first as assistant commissioner of the National Savings Committee, 1940–1942, and then as official historian for the Office of the War Cabinet, 1942–1946.[8] The years spent in the civil service proved invaluable for Hurstfield. He learned how large the gap was between what official directives and memoranda proclaimed and what administrators and their staffs actually did. Later he discerned an analogous gulf between the directives issued by Tudor authorities, such as Elizabeth I and the Cecils, and the actions of their underlings. His experiences as a civil servant informed and enriched his teaching as well as his research. Nor could he ever forget that he had played a role in one of the great events of the twentieth century—Britain's successful stand against Hitler's onslaught.[9] To have survived that epic conflict imbued him and many of his contemporaries with a renewed spirit of confidence.

With the war over, Hurstfield reentered academic life, determined to make it his sole career. His first postwar appointment was as lecturer at Queen Mary College, University of London, 1946–1951.[10] Looking back on those years, he recalled the exhilaration of teaching the returning veterans, who knew about life at an elemental level. To Hurstfield these were "the best years of his life. . . . The days were long and money was short. The work was hard but the life was good."[11] From Queen Mary College he moved in 1951 to his alma mater, University College, London, where he became reader (a position comparable to that of an American associate professor) in 1953 and professor in 1959. In 1962 he succeeded M. A. Thomson as Astor Professor of History. From 1964 to 1966 he also served as dean of the faculty of Arts for the college, and from 1966 to 1970 he was chair of the history department. In 1979 he retired from active teaching to the Huntington Library in California and died there a year later—on November 19, 1980, at the age of sixty-nine. His survivors included a wife, Elizabeth Valmai Walters of Hirwaun, Glamorgan, and a son and daughter.[12]

Hurstfield's first book, *The Control of Raw Materials* (1953), was a volume in the series *The History of the Second World War,* edited by W. K. Hancock, which was highly regarded by professional historians. Hurstfield's book provided a solid 530 pages of economic history. As was his habit with later books, he furnished a preview of the volume in article form. In "The Control of British Raw Material Supplies, 1919–1939" in the *Economic History Review,* he castigated—with the aphoristic skill that was to become a trademark—the British control of the supply system. He noted that if it had not been "established in a moment of absence of mind, it was certainly set up with a complete absence of plan."[13]

Reviewers were high in their praise of Hurstfield's narrative ability. Ronald Brech, in *International Affairs,* deemed the chapters on Anglo-French and Anglo-American collaboration "worthy of study by any student of international relations." He regretted only that official histories did not allow reference to personalities or to the process by which personal decisions led to the solution of technical problems.

In *Political Studies,* R. S. Milne also deplored "the reticence which clothes official histories," but J. P. T. Bury in the *English Historical Review* admired "the masterly way" in which Hurstfield had overcome such handicaps in order to produce "a lucid and readable account of the British Government's policy."[14]

Hurstfield's second major publication was *The Queen's Wards: Wardship and Marriage Under Elizabeth I* (1958). This book was his masterpiece. Hurstfield had worked on it intermittently for twenty years since first becoming a research student. In the preface, he thanked Sir John Neale not only for suggesting the topic but also for editing it in typescript.[15] He also noted how World War II had forced him to set the study aside for several years; yet it had also provided him with the experience of living under rigid wartime government controls. The foci of *The Queen's Wards* were the revival of feudal wardship and marriage, its effects upon government, and the Elizabethan struggle for power. In the course of the book he developed a further theme—the contrast between two successive masters of the Court of Wards, William Cecil, Lord Burghley, and his son Robert. Hurstfield carefully delineated both "the political conservatism of the father and the vigourous, imaginative approach of the son."[16]

Hurstfield's American contemporary, Garrett Mattingly, had been similarly affected by wartime experience when he wrote *The Armada* (1959). His years in the navy motivated Mattingly not only to focus on the relevant archives but also to concentrate on the international dimensions of the crisis to endow sixteenth-century drama with an air of immediacy.[17] Both scholars had been interrupted by the war and yet found that the experience had enhanced their historical vision. They looked at the historical world they wrote about thereafter with the eyes of life. Far from deflecting them, the enforced delay enriched their work and contributed in each case to the production of a historical masterpiece.

During the six years that led to the appearance of *The Queen's Wards,* Hurstfield had published six articles on the significance of wardship and the role of the Cecils. In "The Revival of Feudalism in Early Tudor England,"[18] he showed that the early Tudor monarchs had subverted feudal intentions in order to make feudalism pay. Selling the marriage rights of Crown wards became a major source of Tudor revenue. In a companion article, "The Profits of Fiscal Feudalism, 1541–1602," Hurstfield coined the phrase, "fiscal feudalism," that was to be universally adopted by specialists in Tudor history. Hurstfield's basic thesis was that the Crown reasserted its feudal rights for revenue purposes, thus distorting the original military purpose of feudalism. This article also dealt with the technical economic aspects of fiscal feudalism and calculated the revenues that the Crown had derived from the practice between 1541 and 1602.[19] Hurstfield based his calculations on a method set forth in his earlier article, "Lord Burghley as Master of the Court of Wards, 1561–98."[20] By a patient reconstruction of the manner in which wardships were sold, he was able to conclude that the Crown did not get all the profits from wardship; purchasers also had to give gifts to officials and go-betweens. Hurstfield estimated that if Elizabeth had secured all the profits she would have obtained a surplus of two million pounds, but that in fact she received only one-fourth, with the remainder appropriated by her highly placed subjects.[21]

The different approach to the mastership of wards by the Cecils, father and son, intrigued Hurstfield. He noted that Robert Cecil, responding to the Crown's severe financial difficulties, managed to extract 48 percent more from the Court of Wards. "There was nothing here of the temperate conservatism of the father but the resolution of a young man in a hurry, turning his back on his father's ways." Hurstfield went on to observe that Robert demonstrated a wider vision of government finance than his father; thus as lord treasurer he recommended replacing fiscal feudalism by the Great Contract, which would have resulted in the Crown giving up the right to wardship in exchange for an annual sum supplied by Parliament.[22] Hurstfield applauded Robert Cecil's statesmanship, but the Great Contract was seen by King James as a betrayal of his prerogatives, while the Commons disdained it for other reasons, making Cecil's "efforts to hammer out a new revenue system . . . a gallant failure."[23]

This was a major theme of *The Queen's Wards:* the contrast between the two faithful Crown servants, each energetic and forceful, with the son having the imagination to devise a bargain that would have allowed the Stuart monarchs to have an independent income, thus frustrating by that very independence the development of parliamentary liberties. Three other articles on the Cecils and the Court of Wards adapted for popular consumption in *History Today* what Hurstfield was to say in his scholarly book: "Wardship and Marriage under Elizabeth I"; "William Cecil, Lord Burghley: Minister to Elizabeth I"; and "Robert Cecil, Earl of Salisbury: Minister to Elizabeth I and James I."[24] In "Corruption and Reform under Edward VI and Mary: The Example of Wardship,"[25] Hurstfield extended his interest to bribery, a subject that was to become the central theme of his subsequent book, *Freedom, Corruption and Government in Elizabethan England* (1973).

In his recreation of the world of wardship, Hurstfield demonstrated the gift of being able to think himself back into the minds of those about whom he wrote. It is true that he denied our ultimate ability to see the world through Tudor eyes,[26] but Hurstfield did come to know the Tudors in a manner that few other historians have done. Thus he found an answer to a puzzle that had long baffled Tudor specialists: Why did so many Englishmen, scattered as far away as Yorkshire, Cheshire, and Northamptonshire, all hold land of the manor of Greenwich in Kent? His investigation revealed that by holding land of Greenwich, the possessor could claim "socage tenure" rather than the status of "tenant-in-chief" of the Crown. The astute landholder could thereby avoid onerous duties and escape the fiscal encroachments of the Crown.[27] Hurstfield explained the process in detail in "The Greenwich Tenures of the Reign of Edward VI."[28]

With these articles and the book, Hurstfield succeeded in making the complex legal institution of wardship understandable, illuminating, and even entertaining. One of the distinguishing marks of his scholarship was that he always sought as wide an audience as possible. Hurstfield had faith in his ability to explain and in that of his readers to understand and profit thereby.

In *History Today,* A. H. Dodd heralded *The Queen's Wards* as "an important chapter in the history of Elizabethan administration and society and of the transition from the feudal state to the new monarchy." He described the book as the best available introduction to English feudalism, and noted in passing that Hurstfield portrayed Robert Cecil in more favorable a light than Neale had done.[29] In the *English Historical Review,* A. L. Rowse agreed that "Mr. Hurstfield has something important that is new to tell us" and characterized the work as an "excellent book." He went on to add a dash or two of vinegar to the honey by suggesting that Hurstfield had not got the relationship of Elizabeth I and Burghley quite right and that, although an excellent delineator of institutions, "Hurstfield is not quite so perceptive about persons."[30] All the same, Rowse invited Hurstfield to write a volume for the highly popular *Teach Yourself History* series that he was then editing.

The notable American interpreter of the Tudors, Conyers Read, reviewed *The Queen's Wards* for *History.* Read noted the coincidence of the book's appearance with H. E. Bell's *Introduction to the History and Records of the Court of Wards and Liveries* (1953), and found the two books "equally admirable." Read suggested that Hurstfield had overreacted to the evils of the sale of marriage rights, and was not entirely persuaded by the manner in which he—on technical grounds—had exonerated Burghley from the charge of corrupt practice.³¹ Such criticisms, however, did not debar Read from asking Hurstfield to provide a thirty-two–page contribution on constitutional history for the second edition of Read's magisterial *Bibliography of British History, Tudor Period, 1485–1603* (1959).³² Hurstfield had been examined by three severe masters of Tudor history and had triumphed. His immediate reward was a personal professorship.

Hurstfield's next project enabled him to demonstrate his aptitude as a teacher. His contribution to the *Teach Yourself History* series, *Elizabeth I and the Unity of England* (1960), was brief (226 pages) and popular.³³ Like his onetime colleague at Queen Mary College, Professor S. T. Bindoff, who used *Tudor England,* his contribution to the paperback *Pelican History of England,* to make new, important judgments,³⁴ so Hurstfield used *Elizabeth I and the Unity of England* to propose a major reconsideration of Neale's ideas. Rather than accepting Neale's view of Elizabeth as a resurgent, triumphant queen who wavered only near the end of her life, Hurstfield dated that decline to 1584.

Reviewing the book for *History,* R. B. Werham described it as "a brilliant little book." He found Hurstfield's revisionist approach altogether persuasive. In the *English Historical Review,* Lawrence Stone praised the work for its elegant, economical style and for Hurstfield's candid reflection that the Elizabethan age was perhaps "not a heroic age after all" but "rather one of complacent conservatism." For Stone the book provided an "intellectual challenge" that elevated it "above the level of a competent political textbook."³⁵

Hurstfield's success as a writer, his skill as a speaker, and his promotion in 1962 to Astor Professor of English History led to numerous opportunities to present history to a wider audience during the 1960s and 1970s. He became a popular radio speaker on the BBC Third Programme on all manner of subjects historical. Two of his books originated as radio lecture series: *The Elizabethan Nation* and *The Reformation Crisis.*³⁶ The former included eight lectures for first and second year students; they constituted part of a degree course in history and English and were originally broadcast early in 1965. Hurstfield supplemented these lectures with a separate series on Elizabethan culture and ideas that focused on art as a way of investigating the *mentalité* of the Elizabethan era.³⁷

The Elizabethan Nation is a brief and readable introduction to Elizabethan times. It possesses all the best Hurstfield qualities: revealing details, arresting quotations, and sound generalizations. On the printed page it has the marvelous quality of drawing readers in, just as eloquent speakers bind their listeners. Consider this statement: "Henry VIII was a revolutionary who was suspicious of all revolt. He believed—as many others have since vainly believed—that he who starts a revolution can tell it where to stop."[38]

The Reformation Crisis, edited by Hurstfield, originated in a series of lectures broadcast by the BBC in 1962. Hurstfield set the scene in an introductory lecture and was followed by nine experts, including such luminaries as G. R. Elton, A. G. Dickens, and C. V. Wedgwood. Hurstfield's subject was "The Search for Compromise in England and France." Reviewing the book for the *Catholic Historical Review,* John R. Meyer noted its value "for those instructing the initiate and, of course, for the initiate himself." Patrick McGrath in *History* called it a "lively and refreshing little book."[39]

Hurstfield's other radio talks included distillations of themes drawn from his own writings, for example, "Liberty and Authority under Elizabeth I," reviews of major new historical works of others, for example, *The Crisis of the Aristocracy* by Lawrence Stone, and discussions of famous historians, such as Conyers Read and V. H. Galbraith. He also provided detailed reviews of two immensely popular television series of the late 1960s, *Henry VIII and His Six Wives* and *Elizabeth R.*[40] Hurstfield began by setting the scene; he then went on to contrast the manner in which the television series presented Henry, Elizabeth, and their world with the way in which, in the judgment of a professional historian, the work ought to have been done. He admired the characterization of Henry's Duke of Norfolk, but Hurstfield concluded that the writers and producers had failed miserably with Thomas Cromwell. He also complained that the series revealed nothing of the court's connection with Parliament or the wider society of the realm, nor—he noted pointedly—had the producers ever bothered to mention a single date. His conclusion was succinct: "Fact is more exciting—and disturbing—than fiction—most of all in the 16th century. The Parliaments, the social life, the religious crises of Elizabeth's reign are incomparably more exciting than her love affairs, real or imaginary."[41]

Hurstfield's last book, *Freedom, Corruption and Government in Elizabethan England* (1973) plumbs the depths of liberty and corruption, themes that had begun to intrigue him during the early 1950s and perhaps even during his years as a research student in the 1930s. Hurstfield's professed purpose was "to search into the minds and experiences of sixteenth-century Englishmen, to see what they felt about freedom, corruption and the nature of government." The book is composed of ten chapters and a Retrospect, all of which had been independently published between 1953 and 1971 in first-rate journals or collections, such as the *English Historical Review, History,* the *Cambridge Modern History,* the *Transactions of the Royal Historical Society,* and *Victoria County History.*[42]

Alan Haynes, reviewing the book for *History Today,* praised Hurstfield's thoughtfulness and his willingness, in contrast to A. L. Rowse, to make generalizations. He noted that Hurstfield, unlike G. R. Elton, described Thomas Cromwell's actions as Henry VIII's first minister as "despotic." Haynes demurred, however, at Hurstfield's defense of the Cecils from charges of corruption in the accumulation of their vast fortune because he suspected that the Cecils obtained that fortune "by dubious means."[43]

At the time of his death, Hurstfield, who was working on a major biography on Robert Cecil, had completed chapters tentatively titled: "Robert Cecil and the Government of the Tudor State," "A Courtier from the Cradle," and "The Apprenticeship: Foreign Affairs."[44] Tudor historians are the poorer that Hurstfield failed to complete his projected life of Cecil as well as for the fact that these and other unpublished essays have not appeared in print.

In addition to the works already mentioned, Hurstfield edited several other books: *Shakespeare's World* (1964), coedited with James Sutherland; *Tudor Times, English History in Pictures* (1964); and *Elizabethan People: State and Society* (1973), coedited with Alan Smith.[45] In his memoir of Hurstfield, A. G. Dickens described him perceptively as "a persuasive editor [who] improves work submitted to his judgment while yet leaving the author's self-regard unimpaired. One ends by half believing one has done the job unaided! The same tact, based upon a deep respect for other personalities and viewpoints, has enabled him to collaborate most effectively with his able juniors."[46]

Hurstfield was an assiduous book reviewer, and an almost complete list of his reviews in academic journals may be found in "The Historical Writings of Joel Hurstfield, 1944 to 1978," in *The English Commonwealth, 1547–1640,* the festschrift published in 1979 in Hurstfield's honor.[47] No one has yet provided an index, however, to his reviews in newspapers such as the *Times,* the *Daily Telegraph,* and the *Guardian.*

As a reviewer, Hurstfield was never fearful of calling attention to the errors authors had made in quoting or interpreting texts. Nor was he afraid to challenge the revisionist theses of eminent contemporaries. Hurstfield's appraisal of Lawrence Stone's *The Crisis of the Aristocracy, 1558–1641* is a case in point. Hurstfield praised Stone's work as a highly readable and truly "major contribution" to scholarship that according to Hurstfield's own kitchen scales "weighs three pounds eleven ounces, without wrappers." He was fully prepared to agree with Stone's portrayal of a Stuart nobility that was "under stress and in decay." On the other hand, he dissented from Stone's overall approach, and was doubtful about the manner in which Stone had used literary evidence and had credited the seventeenth-century Puritans with being the first to define marriage as a spiritual union. Hurstfield also questioned Stone's suggestion that the growth of freedom of choice in the marriages of the nobility was directly related to the destruction of the Court of Wards.[48] On the whole, Hurstfield was a generous encourager of works that he thought advanced Tudor studies. One example is his review of F. G. Emmison's *Elizabethan Life*.[49]

> With Dr. Emmison's volume on Essex we come nearest to the texture and temper of daily life, its sights and sounds and smells, its gaiety and faith and despair, the hard life and the close companionship of death. Its author enjoys a considerable reputation among historians for his long and valued [study of] Essex records; and for this volume, the third of a continuing series, he deserves a second reputation for his mastery of a diverse and complex range of sources. I know of few comparable works which display so well in an abundance of fascinating detail the quality of life of the ordinary people of an Elizabethan county.[50]

Hurstfield approached his work with care and deliberation. He knew from his own experience that years of struggle and effort went into the books he reviewed, and he always dealt humanely and as generously as possible with the authors. In a radio conversation with V. H. Galbraith, he recalled his own experience in preparing his first publication in a scholarly journal. The twenty-page article that appeared in the *Economic History Review* in 1944 had taken him an entire year to complete, work for which, of course, he received no compensation. He decried the more recent tendency of pushing younger scholars to write popular books quickly.[51]

Hurstfield, who had learned his trade by much hard work, shared his insights gladly. As a student in his Tudor-Stuart research methods class in the autumn and winter terms of 1958–1959 at the Institute of Historical Research, London, I was introduced to the records at the Public Record Office — reports of commissions of the peace and inquisitions post mortem. In a painstaking and patient manner, Hurstfield explicated the meaning of such records and how his students might best make use of them. He cautioned us to reread carefully any direct quotations copied from a document and then to make a marginal dated notation that the quotation had been checked. His advice on presenting a thesis has been passed on many times to my own students: abjure perfectionism; begin writing as quickly as possible and draft a chapter—though not necessarily the one that will come first in the finished work. Hurstfield noted that there is an architectonic quality to every good thesis—a theme.[52] He possessed the gift of never losing sight of his theme. Perhaps that was the result of his youthful training as a debater. His listeners and readers were always aware that he was arguing a case, developing a theme. As a teacher, Hurstfield had the ability to direct a student to where he intended to go—even when the student had not yet clarified his own intentions!

Hurstfield's students would arrive at the seminar filled with joyful anticipation; one never knew with what kind of anecdote or observation he would begin. He gave a discourse one day on how revolutionary a document the New Testament was.[53] It should be noted that from 1956 until 1975, Hurstfield conducted that seminar in collaboration with the ageing Sir John Neale. In her essay, "Joel Hurstfield and the Tudor Seminar," Norah Fuidge vividly recalls Hurstfield as a teacher. She observed that, although it might have been plausible to sum up Neale's subject as "Parliament and Puritanism" and Hurstfield's as "Consent, Consistency, and Corruption," such labeling would not have done justice to the multifarious interests of either man. In Hurstfield's seminars, she remembered, discussions ranged widely in an atmosphere of courtesy and friendliness. Hurstfield would go on to devote long hours to private conferences with seminar members.[54] Like his colleague, S. T. Bindoff, Hurstfield believed that time granted to budding historians was time well spent. If the great man will not teach, who will? And Hurstfield gladly taught.

A special postscript was added to Hurstfield's obituary in the *Times* calling attention to his contributions to the administration of University College, London, as dean of the Faculty of Arts, as chair of the history department, as fellow of the University of London, and as a faithful member of innumerable committees. In the wider world he was lauded for the manner in which he fearlessly expressed his opinions as well as for the pleasure he afforded as a public lecturer and afterdinner speaker, where "his wit and spontaneity were unrivalled."[55] In his memoir, A. G. Dickens remembers Hurstfield's versatility: his contributions as the author of *Don's Diary* in the *Times Higher Education Supplement,* as a broadcaster, and as a University of London public orator during the years 1967-1971. In the latter role "he somehow managed to be even better on zoologists than on historians: the less he knew of the subject, the more easily and civilly did he impale the eminent victim. He never forgot that the honorary graduand must appear not just a little larger than life, but also distinctly more amusing."[56] The demand for his lectures led Hurstfield to serve as Shakespeare birthday lecturer in Washington, D.C., in 1969, as James Ford special lecturer in history at Oxford in 1972, as John Coffin memorial lecturer at the University of London in 1974, as A. H. Dodd memorial lecturer at University College, Bangor, Wales, in 1978, and as Creighton lecturer at the University of London in 1978. The University of Southampton and the University of London conferred on him honorary degrees as Doctor of Literature.

Hurstfield returned to the United States many times after his first visiting professorship in 1967. He was a fellow of the Folger Library in 1973, Andrew Mellon research fellow at the Huntington Library for 1977–1978, and senior research associate there in 1979.[57] Wherever he went, he reminded Americans of their heritage and its importance, and he made that heritage come alive when he spoke.

Where does Hurstfield fit in the world of historical scholarship? Unlike Sir Lewis Namier and the "Namierization" of history, Hurstfield's name has not been transmuted into either a noun or a verb. Unlike Peter Laslett, he did not found a community of disciples like the Cambridge Group to collect data so that future generations would have a more reliable accumulation of demographic information. Hurstfield's own work spawned neither new methodologies nor created new schools. He recognized that historians would make increased use of social sciences—anthropology, demography, econometrics, psephology, and sociology.[58] He did not, however, include in his list of auxiliary sciences for the historian either psychology or psychobiography. He did not think it necessary to share with his readers his political views or insights into his private life. Indeed, customarily he dismissed queries about himself with the remark that "all autobiography is self-indulgence."[59] The public historical record is therefore bare when it comes to many details of his life, and his *Who's Who* sketch omits the names of his parents and the year of his marriage.

Hurstfield's strengths lay in solid economic history (after the fashion of R. H. Tawney), as well as political, constitutional-legal, biographical, and literary history. He was first-rate at whatever he turned his hand to. His primary contributions to Tudor-Stuart historiography were his explanation of fiscal feudalism and probing the issues of power, corruption, and authority. Though he was in many ways Sir John Neale's successor, he was still his own man, and his work on the Cecils amply showed where the two masters of Tudor history differed. His work also complemented that of Conyers Read, the great interpreter of Burghley's diplomatic career. He filled a major research gap by clarifying Burghley's role as master of the Court of Wards. Work still needs to be done on the Elizabethan Exchequer, which both Cecils headed as Lords Treasurer, and Hurstfield was aware of the need for more research on the lesser members of the Tudor parliaments. He recognized that his own studies might have to be redone, but he objected to applying the prosopographical techniques of Namier and of Neale in a mechanical manner. He insisted that what men *said* and what they *did* was as important as who they *were*. An unimaginative Namierite could apply an unreflecting determinism to the past as readily as could an unimaginative Marxist. But a study of the lesser figures casts new light on the greater, and Hurstfield foresaw that "we shall one day begin all over again to write the biographies of Leicester, Walsingham, and even Burghley himself."[60]

Hurstfield's own investigations led him to differ with A. L. Rowse on the degree of liberty to be found in Tudor England. "Freedom was limited in the Tudor period. And to speak of it as an age of liberty the way A. L. Rowse does is simply anachronistic."[61] Hurstfield conceded that Elizabethan England lacked a modern police force, a state of affairs that limited the extent of governmental power. Elizabethan liberty, he insisted, was therefore less a matter of popular principle than of government weakness. "There is always a discrepancy between the will of the Government and the power of the Government," he concluded, "and the power lagged behind the will."[62] As Nicholas Tyacke has plausibly suggested, this "abiding concern with the theme of liberty" may well have originated in Hurstfield's memory of his own ancestors who had found refuge in England.[63]

Like Rowse, Hurstfield was conversant with the literature of the sixteenth and early seventeenth centuries. As A. G. Dickens observes in his memoir:

> Though primarily a historian of government, Hurstfield has held the balance more evenly than most, and it was not merely by following Tawney's example that he came to investigate the Tudor social and cultural scene. From an early stage he stood convinced of the need for historians to draw closer toward literary scholars. He has accordingly written several articles linking Shakespeare studies and Elizabethan historiography, together with at least one book which extends across both fields: *The Elizabethan Nation*

(1964). That in addition he could as easily have become a major figure in local and regional history is shown by his chapter on county government 1530–1660 in the *Victoria County History* of Wiltshire, in which he reveals a fresh vista of provincial politics and of their relation to national affairs. Yet again, he has edited individually or jointly several important collections of studies covering diverse aspects of the period.[64]

Nor was Hurstfield afraid to differ with his contemporaries, however eminent. "You know, of course," he recalled, "of my arguments with G. R. Elton, who, I think, gets this upside down. He sees a great efficient, vigorous minister like Cromwell trying to extend the liberties of Parliament. I think he's trying to restrict them in the interests of efficiency." A. F. Pollard, the early twentieth-century biographer of Henry VIII and Wolsey, as well as the founder of the Institute of Historical Research in London, remained, in Hurstfield's view, a more insightful interpreter of the Tudors than Elton. As Hurstfield pointed out, "Pollard argued, as I would argue, that it's no good saying [that a particular action] follows the law without asking who makes the law."[65]

It may be fair to conclude that in his specialized studies of the economic and legal activities of the Cecils, Hurstfield used a microscope and in his more generalized studies, and as a BBC lecturer, he used a telescope. His additions to our knowledge of fiscal feudalism and Tudor legal fictions have already been noted, as has the manner in which he expanded our notions of Tudor liberty, power, and corruption and dampened unduly sunny appraisals of the scope of individual freedom during the Elizabethan era. Two of Hurstfield's works, *The Queen's Wards* and *Freedom, Corruption and Government in Elizabethan England*, are likely to remain standard publications, to be read by all students of the period. In his bibliographical appraisal, "Recent Writings in Tudor History," Wallace MacCaffrey praises both books. He calls the former work authoritative and he also singles out for praise Hurstfield's "illuminating" essay, "Queen and State: The Emergence of an Elizabethan Myth," in J. S. Bromley and E. H. Kossman, eds., *Britain and the Netherlands*, vol. 5 (1975). In a related survey, David Underdown lauds Hurstfield for "judiciously avoiding the anachronistic application of later norms" in his assessment of the corruption of the early Stuart period.[66]

Hurstfield once observed that historians could benefit from training in business and work in the Civil Service, as he had done. Experience in creating government records in our century was helpful when interpreting analogous documents from an earlier era. It was also helpful to have a model. "I, as you know," he once explained, "was a pupil of Neale. I became a historian because I could see from him the excitement of being a historian, of working on Tudor material." Hurstfield rebelled against the philosophy of historians like V. H. Galbraith, the medievalist, for whom historiography meant historical specialists writing esoteric books for fellow specialists. Hurstfield agreed with Neale that historians should write so as to be understood by all who were literate. Neale had taught him, he noted, that it was possible to address the specialist and the lay reader in the same tone; "and if you can't," he added, "then it's a failure of your literary talents—not a failure of the subject or of the purpose."[67] Hurstfield differed from Neale, however, in his attitude toward the public responsibilities of his professorship. Neale once confided to Hurstfield that he had turned down the opportunity to give several lectures to launch a distinguished endowment because "it would have deflected him from research to which he was committed over the next few years."[68] Hurstfield, in contrast, appears to have accepted most of the opportunities that came his way to lecture, review, administer, write the occasional article, and to edit books. Each historian was prodigious in his own fashion, but Hurstfield covered a wider variety of subjects and appeared more conscious of the responsibilities that appertained to his position and his university. Perhaps in accepting so many engagements, he was prevented from completing more scholarly books based, as was *The Queen's Wards,* on research in the Public Record Office. But life is larger than scholarly books. Hurstfield may have thought there would be time in retirement to do the big book on Robert Cecil; that time was not granted to him.[69]

Hurstfield did not believe that the past should be approached by means of a preconceived party line but simply by utilizing the best evidence available. We know that he did not believe in historical inevitability. As he observed in another of his taped public conversations, "Nothing is inevitable in history until five minutes before it happens."[70] He was ever conscious of the role of chance in the lives of all historical players. But for World War II and the postponement of the general election scheduled for 1940, he might, after all, have devoted his life to Parliament rather than to scholarship.

Although Professors Dickens and Tyacke have suggested that Hurstfield was able to play such a variety of roles because he wasted no time on either alcohol or tobacco and because he was blessed by a supportive family,[71] yet important aspects of Hurstfield's background and life remain tantalizingly elusive. We know little, for example, about his impressions of the United States or about his reactions to the great events that occurred in his lifetime. And we would like to know more about his association with Winston Churchill, who thanked Hurstfield for a prepublication review of Churchill's *The New World,* volume 2 of his *History of the English-speaking People.*[72] We do know, however, that Joel Hurstfield was a man of many talents—a superb scholar, a knowledgeable reviewer, a stimulating and genial teacher, a wise and witty lecturer[73]—and that he employed all these talents to add life and vigor to the world of history of the post-1945 era.

NOTES

I am grateful to Walter Arnstein for the opportunity to participate in this project, for his encouragement, and for his helpful suggestions. I am similarly grateful for useful criticism to Barrett Beer of Kent State University and F. J. Platt of Northern Arizona University. I am also indebted to the late J. F. Larkin for sharing his insights about Hurstfield; to John M. Currin for his essay on Sir Robert Cecil and for his advice; and to Professor Hurstfield's son, Dr. Julian Hurstfield of the history department, University of Kent at Canterbury, for information about his father.

1. John P. Kenyon refers to Hurstfield only twice in *The History Men: The Historical Profession in England since the Renaissance* (London: Weidenfeld and Nicolson, 1983), 206, 318.

2. *Times* (London), 1 Dec. 1980; 6 Dec. 1980; 9 Dec. 1980.

3. G. R. Elton, *Modern Historians on British History, 1485–1945: A Critical Bibliography, 1945–1969* (London: Methuen, 1970), 125, 157, 161, 188, 206, 1014. Numbers refer to bibliographical items.

4. Nicholas Tyacke, "Joel Hurstfield, 1911–1980," Univ. College, London, *Bulletin* (Feb. 1981), 12. I am grateful to Maldwyn A. Jones, head of the history department, University College, London, for supplying me with a copy. This account of Hurstfield's career is based on Tyacke's article; *Who Was Who, 1971–1980,* 394; and *Times* as cited in note 2.

5. "Personal and Political Biography: A Note on Mary Tudor," *University of Newcastle Historical Journal* 2(February 1973):17.

6. Joel Hurstfield, *Man as Prisoner of His Past: The Elizabethan Experience,* A. H. Dodd memorial lecture, delivered 12 May 1978 (Cardiff: Univ. of Wales Press, 1980), 1.

7. Joel Hurstfield, "What Went Wrong with the Universities?", *Times Higher Education Supplement,* 13 June 1975, 6.

8. *Who Was Who, 1971–1980,* 394; Tyacke, "Hurstfield," 12. The timing of the change of surname can be approximated by a comparison of the Univ. College, London, *Calendar, 1933–1934,* 508–9, with the *Southampton Univ. Calendar* for 1938–1939.

9. Joel Hurstfield, "Conyers Read and Historical Biography," *Listener,* 28 April 1966, 747.

10. *Who Was Who,* 394.

11. Hurstfield, "What Went Wrong?", 6.

12. *Who Was Who,* 349; *Times,* 6 Dec. 1980; *Contemporary Authors,* 102:285;

Tyacke, "Hurstfield," 12. "The explanation of the fact that he was twice appointed to Professorships is as follows. In this country there are both *personal* chairs and *named* or *endowed* chairs, both being awarded for distinction in scholarship. Joel Hurstfield was promoted to a personal chair in 1959 and then in 1962 he succeeded to the vacant Astor Chair in English History." Letter from Maldwyn Jones, 18 June 1987.

13. Joel Hurstfield, *The Control of Raw Materials*, in *The History of the Second World War*, ed., W. K. Hancock (London: HMSO and Longmans, Green, 1953); *Economic History Review* 14(1944):31.

14. Reviews of *The Control of Raw Materials:* by Ronald Brech, *International Affairs* 34(1954):91; by R. S. Milne, *Political Studies* 2(1954):91, by J. P. T. Bury, *English Historical Review* 69(1954):508–9.

15. Joel Hurstfield, *The Queen's Wards: Wardship and Marriage under Elizabeth I*, 2d ed., ed. Frank Cass (London, 1973), xi–xii. Later Hurstfield would do the same for his student, A. G. R. Smith. See Alan G. R. Smith, *Servant of the Cecils: The Life of Sir Michael Hickes, 1543–1612* (Totowa, N.J.: Rowman & Littlefield, 1977), 12. I owe this reference to Marjorie K. McIntosh of the department of history, Univ. of Colorado at Boulder.

16. Hurstfield, *Queen's Wards,* xi.

17. Garrett Mattingly, *The Armada* (Boston: Houghton Mifflin, 1959), vi–vii.

18. *History* 37(1952):31–45.

19. Joel Hurstfield, "The Profits of Fiscal Feudalism, 1541–1602," *Economic History Review,* 2d ser., 8(1955):53–61.

20. *Trans. R. Hist. Soc.,* 4th ser., 31(1949):102 n3.

21. Hurstfield, "Fiscal Feudalism," 58.

22. Ibid., 60, 61. For a first-rate evaluation of Robert Cecil's public career that adds to Hurstfield's work by dealing more fully with Cecil's career under King James VI and I, see Thomas M. Coakley, "Robert Cecil in Power: Elizabethan Politics in Two Reigns," in *Early-Stuart Studies: Essays in Honor of David Harris Willson,* ed. Howard S. Reinmuth, Jr. (Minneapolis: Univ. of Minnesota Press, 1970), 64–94.

23. Ibid., 61.

24. *History Today* 4(1954):605–12; 6(1956):791–99; and 7(1957):279–89.

25. *English Historical Review* 68(1953):22–36.

26. I owe this statement to my colleague Clifton Yearley's recollection of his conversation with Hurstfield.

27. Hurstfield, *Queen's Wards,* 19–20.

28. Joel Hurstfield, "The Greenwich Tenures of the Reign of Edward VI," *Law Quarterly Review* 65(1949):72–81.

29. *History Today* 9(1959):143–44.

30. *English Historical Review* 74(1959):503–4.

31. *History* 44(1959):165–66.

32. Listed in "The Historical Writings of Joel Hurstfield, 1944 to 1978" in *The English Commonwealth, 1547–1640: Essays in Politics and Society,* ed. Peter Clark, Alan G. R. Smith, and Nicholas Tyacke (N.Y.: Barnes & Noble, 1979), 206.

33. Joel Hurstfield, *Elizabeth I and the Unity of England,* in *Teach Yourself History* series (London: English Univ. Press and Penguin; N.Y.: Macmillan, 1960).

34. G. R. Elton in *England under the Tudors,* rev. ed. (London: Methuen & Co., 1959) called Bindoff's book a "brilliant short study," v.

35. *History* 47(1962):193–94; *English Historical Review* 77(1962):366.

36. Joel Hurstfield, *The Elizabethan Nation* (London: BBC publications, 1964); *The Reformation Crisis* (N.Y.: Harper Torchbooks, 1965).

37. Hurstfield, *Elizabethan Nation,* 7-8.
38. Ibid., 10.
39. Hurstfield, *Reformation Crisis,* v-vii; *Catholic Historical Review* 55(1969):87; *History* 51(1966):215.
40. Hurstfield, *Listener,* 29 Dec. 1960, 1177-79; 24 June 1965, 934-35; 28 Apr. 1966, 747-48; 4 Apr. 1968, 439-40; 11 Mar. 1971, 289-92.
41. *Listener,* 11 Mar. 1971, 292.
42. Joel Hurstfield, *Freedom, Corruption and Government in Elizabethan England* (London: Jonathan Cape, 1973), author's note, 9-10.
43. *History Today* 23(1973):674-75.
44. I owe the information about the unpublished essays to Dr. Julian Hurstfield. The scholar hard at work on a full modern account of the career of Robert Cecil is Pauline Croft of Royal Holloway College and Bedford New College, director of the Tudor-Stuart seminar at the University of London Institute of Historical Research. Her published articles about Cecil include "Fresh Light on Bate's Case," *Historical Journal* 30, no. 3(1987):523-39, as well as contributions to *Parliamentary History* 2(1983); 4(1984); and 6(1987). She has also edited "A Collection of Several Speeches and Treatises of the Late Treasurer Cecil" for the Royal Historical Society, *Camden Miscellany* 29(1987). The tentative title of her forthcoming book is *Robert Cecil in Power, 1593-1612.* I am grateful to Dr. Croft for her willingness to read and to make helpful suggestions about an earlier draft of this essay.
45. Joel Hurstfield and James Sutherland, eds., *Shakespeare's World* (New York: St. Martin's Press, 1964); Hurstfield, ed., *Tudor Times, English History in Pictures* (London: Historical Assoc., 1964); Hurstfield and Alan Smith, eds., *Elizabethan People, State and Society* (New York: St. Martin's Press, 1973). See also Clark et al., eds., *English Commonwealth,* 206-8.
46. Clark et al., eds., *English Commonwealth,* 15.
47. Ibid., 209-14.
48. *Listener,* 24 June 1965, 934-35.
49. F. G. Emmison, *Elizabethan Life* (Chelmsford: Essex Record Office, 1977).
50. *Times,* 20 Jan. 1977. I owe a copy of this review to the kindness of Dr. F. G. Emmison. In the judgment of many scholars, Emmison transformed the Essex Record Office into the foremost county archival repository during his tenure as chief archivist.
51. "The Gospel According to Galbraith—Professor V. H. Galbraith Talks to Professor Joel Hurstfield about the Work of the Historian," *Listener,* 14 Apr. 1968, 444.
52. Personal notes of author in blue notebook for Bindoff-Hurstfield course for 1958-1959.
53. I owe this reference to Dr. John J. Morrison, editor of the *Wing* short title catalogue at Yale University Library.
54. Clark et al., eds., *English Commonwealth,* 19-21. In a letter to me (2 June 1987), Thomas M. Coakley of the department of history of Miami University confirms my impression of Hurstfield as a positive and helpful teacher.
55. *Times,* 9 Dec. 1980.
56. Clark et al., eds., *English Commonwealth,* 16.
57. *Who Was Who,* 394.
58. Joel Hurstfield, "The Historian's Commitment," *Times Educational Supplement,* 26 Apr. 1968, 1384.
59. Cited by Tyacke, "Hurstfield," 12.

60. Joel Hurstfield, "Conyers Read and Historical Biography," *Listener,* 28 Apr. 1966, 748.

61. Joel Hurstfield and Penry Williams, *Elizabeth I: State and Religion,* London: Audio Learning, HEA002, 1975, Track B. Audiotape. I am grateful to my former chair, Professor Charles Stinger, and the department of history, SUNY at Buffalo, for purchasing this tape for my use.

62. Joel Hurstfield, "Liberty under the First Elizabeth," *Journal of the Royal Commonwealth Society* 8(1965):221.

63. Tyacke, "Hurstfield," 12.

64. Clark et al., eds., *English Commonwealth,* 14-15.

65. Hurstfield and Williams, *Elizabeth I,* Audiotape. For further exploration of his differences with Elton, see Joel Hurstfield, "Was There a Tudor Despotism After All?", *Trans. Roy. Hist. Soc.* 17, 5th ser. (1967):83-108.

66. Richard Schlatter, ed., *Recent Views in British History* (New Brunswick, N.J.: Rutgers Univ. Press, 1984), 78, 95. In another chapter, "New Ways and Old in Early Stuart History," David Underdown propounds similar views, 111, 132.

67. "Gospel According to Galbraith," 440.

68. Joel Hurstfield, "John Ernest Neale, 1890-1975," *Proceedings of the British Academy* 63(1977):403.

69. In a letter to the author (18 May 1988), Dr. Pauline Croft suggests that Hurstfield's failure to complete a full-scale biography of Robert Cecil may also be attributable to the fact that Hurstfield "understood the young man in a hurry, anxious in so many ways to update his father's administrative legacy," but found it far more difficult to come to grips with Robert Cecil as an older man. Hurstfield "had less empathy with, and knowledge of, Jacobean society than Elizabethan" and he may have found Cecil in his later years "an enigma and almost impossible as a biographical subject."

70. Hurstfield and Williams, *Elizabeth I,* audiotape, Track B.

71. Clark et al., eds., *English Commonwealth,* 16; Tyacke, "Hurstfield," 12.

72. Winston Churchill, *The New World,* vol. 2 of his *History of the English-speaking People* (New York, 1956), viii.

73. While in London in 1958-1959, I attended one of Hurstfield's undergraduate lectures. I remember vividly Hurstfield's magnificent voice and a packed lecture hall of University College students pleading with him for an entertainment before the main historical course. Hurstfield obliged and told a wonderful little story about a bird—much like his captive audience—that was hemmed in by a cage until, on a nice day, it eventually found the door to the cage and flew to freedom. The story held the rapt attention of his students and at its conclusion evoked tremendous applause.

Christopher Hill ᚖᚙᚖ
and the People of Stuart England

CYNTHIA HERRUP

One of the most prolific, most influential, and most controversial English historians alive, Christopher Hill has devoted more than fifty years to the study of England in the seventeenth century. He has published some twenty books, pamphlets, and collections of edited documents as well as scores of articles, introductions, book reviews, and occasional pieces.[1] Ranging from essays to monographs to lectures to textbooks, Hill's studies encompass such traditionally discrete subjects as religion, economics, literature, and science. Reviews of his work (this one being no exception) commonly begin with some attempt to convey the protean scale of his productivity and erudition. As even one of his sharpest critics conceded: "I doubt that a single scholar who has passed judgment on any considerable work of Dr. Hill's has ever read as extensively as he in the subject of their common concern.... Most historians know some of the published sources and scholarly works on a period or topic; Dr. Hill knows *all* of them for the century of English history between 1560 and 1660 and a good bit of what lies on either side of those time limits."[2]

But Hill's influence is not simply a result of the range and number of his interests. Hill has always striven to tie the particular to the general, and each of his specific subjects reinforces his synthesis of seventeenth-century English history. A Marxist since the 1930s, Hill's synthetic vision has given his work a coherence rarely matched in modern historiography. Over the years he has managed to accommodate an ever more sophisticated application of Marx within an essentially constant interpretation of the seventeenth century. Hill has consistently argued, first, that the English Civil War was primarily a social conflict; second, that it was a bourgeois revolution; and third, that its outcome cleared the path for the development of English capitalism.[3]

Moreover, Hill has always considered history too serious a task to be left only to historians. Naturally he has attracted Marxist readers with no specialist interest in the seventeenth century, but he has regularly addressed more general audiences as well.[4] The clarity of his arguments, the elegance of his language, and the conviction of his prose have made Hill's work widely accessible. Countless readers have been drawn to the seventeenth century by Hill's textbooks, and many know Milton, Marvell, and Richardson primarily through Hill.[5] Nevertheless, the qualities that have made Hill so influential outside his speciality have also qualified his influence within it.

John Edward Christopher Hill was born in York in 1912.[6] A member of a prosperous Methodist family, he attended St. Peter's School, York, where he won the Headmaster's prizes for history and Latin prose as well as a county major scholarship. Hill read history at Balliol College, Oxford, and received in 1934 the top First in the History Schools and a fellowship at All Souls College. While a fellow of All Souls, he went on to spend a year in the Soviet Union and then two as a lecturer in the history department, University College, Cardiff. By 1938, when Hill returned to Balliol as a fellow and tutor in modern history, he was also a member of the Communist party of Great Britain. In 1946, Hill, along with Eric Hobsbawm, Rodney Hilton, Victor Kiernan and others, helped to found the Communist party's Historians' Group; for the next decade, he was one of its most active members. The journal *Past and Present,* with Hill among its original editors, grew out of discussions within the Historians' Group.[7]

During his years in the Communist party, Hill tried to educate his readers about Marxism and the Soviet Union.[8] He published essays on Marxist theory, on Soviet scholarship concerning the seventeenth century, and on contemporary life under communism.[9] Nevertheless, he did not neglect English history; before 1956 he produced his first general statement on the Civil War as England's bourgeois revolution, a collection of documents (with Edmund Dell) supporting that interpretation, and several influential essays.[10] Much of this work was doctrinal, but it should not be discounted. Even when Hill was deliberately provocative, he was never careless. Stripped of rhetoric, his early essays on England provide a solid introduction to his later work;

they reveal sympathies that he has never abandoned and themes to which he has repeatedly returned.

Hill's most important historical essay from these years is "The English Revolution," one of three articles published in honor of the tricentennial of 1640. He hoped to expose the congratulatory nature of an English historiography that insisted that the good sense of the English people had spared them a violent revolution.[11] Rejecting the notion that England differed fundamentally from Europe, Hill equated what had happened in England in the seventeenth century with what had happened in France in 1789. Each, he later wrote, was "the story of how one social class was driven from power by another, and how the form of state power appropriate to the needs of the first was replaced by one appropriate to those of the second."[12]

In "The English Revolution," Hill argued that the struggles of the seventeenth century were social, rather than constitutional, conflicts that occurred because the most progressive elements of society (merchants, gentry, and yeomen) had outgrown the strictures of the feudal state (monarchy, aristocracy, and church). Since progressive development depended upon economic freedoms that the reactionary monarchy of Charles I denied, the bourgeoisie had to dismantle the outmoded social structure if they were to prosper. The Parliamentarians opposed, not merely the King or his councillors, but the entire social system. "The Parliamentarians thought they were fighting God's battles," Hill wrote, adding, "They were certainly fighting those of posterity, throwing off an intolerable incubus to further advance."[13]

But the incubus was actually a Hydra; many Parliamentarians were far from revolutionary. Hill contended that although they had allied against the King with "small people, whose intellectual vision was not restricted by anxieties for their own property," conservative Parliamentarians quickly grew uneasy about the implications of that partnership.[14] They had fought for their own freedom but saw popular freedom as mere license. By 1649 the real revolution was over. The radicals were silenced; the conservative Parliamentarians became property owners for whom peace was more important than social justice. The constitutional experiments of the 1650s demonstrated that the bourgeoisie were happy to have a king if they could control him. And Restoration England revealed the strength of that control; it was a society geared to trade and commerce, out of sympathy with feudal customs and revolutionary ideologies. Charles II was called "King by the Grace of God," but most people recognized that he "was really King by the grace of the merchants and squires."[15]

However he might now soften the passion of his prose, Hill still would agree with the general thesis of "The English Revolution." He has called the 1940 essay the writing of "a very angry young man, believing he was going to be killed in a world war."[16] But beneath the anger, the essay also contained an agenda for work to which Hill, reprieved from death, was remarkably faithful. Many of the hallmarks of his approach—the interweaving of religion, economics, social life, and politics; the insistence that these struggles (the one that failed and the one that succeeded) set the path for England's future; the firm belief in the heroism of the common people—were clear in the essay. Its broad outlines are recognizable in Hill's two textbooks, *Century of Revolution 1603–1714* (1961) and *Reformation to Industrial Revolution* (1967). Many insights that Hill later would elaborate into full-length studies also were recognizable. In "The English Revolution," Hill suggested the relationships between religion and economics that form the core of *Economic Problems of the Church* (1956) and of *Society and Puritanism in Pre-Revolutionary England* (1964). He also articulated the deep respect for seventeenth-century radicals that lies behind *The World Turned Upside Down* (1972) and *The Religion of Gerrard Winstanley* (1978). And he broached the interpretation of the Restoration that he would elaborate four decades later in *The Intellectual Consequences of the English Revolution* (1980) and in *The Experience of Defeat* (1984).

"The English Revolution" was not the only important history that Hill wrote during the years that preceded his break with the Communist party in 1956. Almost all of the pieces published in 1958 as *Puritanism and Revolution* were written before 1956. They revealed a more temperate Hill, but one absolutely engaged with his material. In the most important of these pieces, "The Norman Yoke," Hill brilliantly traced the influence that theories of lost rights have had in English history.[17] Showing how people came to see inequality as a historical rather than simply as a theological condition, Hill argued that to many people in the seventeenth century, the Norman Conquest, not the Fall of Man, explained England's hierarchical social system. Historical myths, like biblical ones, lent themselves to various interpretations. The belief that Norman victories destroyed a freer Anglo-Saxon world meant that England's woes were historically specific and historically remediable, but the definition of those woes differed significantly. Since the seventeenth century, what Hill called the Whig definition of that legacy has generally prevailed, but never without its more radical shadow. To constitutionalists such as Sir Edward Coke, the Anglo-Saxon past ensured the property rights of freeborn Englishmen, but to radicals such as the Levellers and then the Diggers, that past also held hopes of communal ownership and democracy. Hill concluded that the inspiration of the radical vision of the past, however mythical, however idealistic, helped to sustain the working class until it became self-confident enough to posit the forward-looking ideal of socialism.

In 1956, Hill resigned from the Communist party, disheartened, like many others, by disagreements about internal Party democracy, by the Soviet invasion of Hungary, and by Khrushchev's revelations about Stalin. In that same year, he also published his first monograph, *Economic Problems of the Church: From Archbishop Whitgift to the Long Parliament.* Hill's serious academic style was so different from the polemical tone of "The English Revolution" that one American reviewer confidently declared that "Mr. Hill is a Marxist who has come out of his trance."[18] But Hill has shown such skeptics that Marxism and lucidity are not mutually exclusive. Since his departure from the Communist party, Hill has written more books and written them less rhetorically, but he is still very much a Marxist. He credits his colleagues in the Communist Party Historians' Group with inspiring him to find more sophisticated ways to discuss historical development; they were the first to challenge the cruder categorizations of "The English Revolution." As Hill developed the arguments suggested by his earliest work, the reverence to Marxian orthodoxy disappeared, but the conclusions remained.[19]

Only Hill can say how deeply his break with the Party affected him, but between 1956 and 1965 his scholarship on the Revolution clearly took on a new direction. As Hill devoted himself more fully to Balliol and to Oxford, his work turned repeatedly to questions of beginnings. Focusing on the years before 1640, Hill explored how members of a traditional society gained the courage to participate in revolution; the interaction of ideas and material conditions was his unifying theme. This was not a new interest, but Hill was able to develop it more fully through his analyses of Puritanism.[20] In addition to the essays in *Puritanism and Revolution,* Hill's major contributions to this discussion were *Economic Problems of the Church* (1956), *Society and Puritanism in Pre-Revolutionary England* (1964), and *Intellectual Origins of the English Revolution* (1965).

At the outset of *Economic Problems of the Church,* Hill argued that historians had to recognize, as their subjects in the seventeenth century had, that one cannot divide religion from economics, social life, or politics. Hill maintained that scholars who studied seventeenth-century religion as if it were simply theology or simply "a mere economic reflex" misconstrued both its contemporary meaning and its contemporary power.[21] Social environment, religious belief, and ecclesiastical organization influenced and were influenced by one another. Puritanism was far more than a product of a capitalistic mentality, but Puritanism would have been unthinkable without the existence of that mentality. The English Revolution was far more than a product of Puritanism, but the Revolution would have been unthinkable without the existence of that faith. The historian's task, as Hill saw it, was to explain both the society that gave rise to a particular religiosity and the effect that this religiosity had upon society. Hill concluded:

> All I would suggest is that revolutions are made, not only by the great symbolic figures whom posterity recollects, but also by nameless masses of men and women. The higher flights of theory may have passed them by. They expected, however, that political ideas or platforms of church government should be rooted in experience. So the more we know about the facts of everyday life for the average man and woman, the better placed we are to understand the appeal of programmes worked out by the leaders, the heroes and the saints.[22]

To Hill, Puritanism was the natural refuge of the middling groups in early modern England. In an article written to honor R. H. Tawney, Hill argued that justification by faith made Protestantism, and later Puritanism, irrevocably individualistic. The idea that motives, not actions, determined virtue eroded the credibility of Catholic economic doctrines. No inevitable marriage existed between Puritanism and capitalism, but in an increasingly capitalistic society, Puritanism offered a way to legitimize new economic values. It also allowed the sort of confidence that helped individuals to challenge the authority of precedent with an authority of conscience.[23]

Each of Hill's three books on prerevolutionary Puritanism elaborated upon this vision. *Society and Puritanism in Pre-Revolutionary England* explored the social values that made Puritanism attractive to seventeenth-century men and women. Hill contended that the Puritan stress on labor and self-discipline, on preaching and conscience, on the household and the parish suited the economic values of industrious men and women who were anxious to improve their lot. "It [Puritanism] seemed to point the way to heaven," he concluded, "because it helped them to live on earth."[24] *Economic Problems of the Church* looked at Puritanism from a different perspective; it focused on the values that set people against the established Church. Arguing that the Reformation left the Church vulnerable economically while undermining its legitimacy as a landlord, Hill showed how by the seventeenth century the conjunction of theological and economic differences made the situation irremediable. The poverty of the Church barred ecclesiastical reform, but neither Puritans nor bishops trusted the other to rectify the situation. With so many livings in secular hands, reforms proposed by the Church threatened Puritan religious ideals and property rights; with so little room for constructive theological controversy, reforms proposed by Puritan laity threatened the ecclesiastical hierarchy.

The last of these three books, *Intellectual Origins of the English Revolution,* was also the most ambitious. Begun as the 1962 Ford lectures, the essays suggested positive relationships between not only Puritanism and capitalism, but also Puritanism and democracy, Puritanism and modern science, and Puritanism and the techniques of modern scholarship. Hoping to find England's Rousseau, instead in the writings of Raleigh, Coke, Bacon, and others, Hill found a core of ideas that brought him back repeatedly to the influence of religion. Hill wanted to spark an interest in the link between Puritanism and other intellectual changes in the seventeenth century, and he was successful; for twenty years, the book has inspired heated discussions about those relationships.[25]

In 1965, Hill became master of Balliol where he remained until his retirement in 1978. At Balliol, as elsewhere, these were years of turmoil. Student unrest seemed to threaten a revolution, albeit a revolution of limited ambitions. For a radical in power, as Hill was, this time must have been both exhilarating and frustrating. Like the poet about whom he would write so eloquently in these years, Hill was caught between two cultures. Always skeptical of authority without purpose, he was sympathetic to the students, but always aware of the value of the past, he recognized the dangers of abandoning established practices simply because they were established.[26]

Faced with new challenges in his own life, Hill turned to a new set of historical problems. His interest shifted from how individuals gained the courage to revolt to how individuals conducted themselves during a revolt. During his years as master, Hill's intellectual efforts focused on defending the intellectual integrity of radicalism in the seventeenth century. In *The World Turned Upside Down* (1972) and the *Religion of Gerrard Winstanley* (1978), Hill argued the coherence of the radical vision. In *God's Englishman: Oliver Cromwell and the English Revolution* (1970) and *Milton and the English Revolution*

(1977), he focused on two other men who found their radicalism tempered by the responsibilities of power. In addition to his regular rounds of reviews and articles, Hill published a second set of lectures in these years, *Antichrist in Seventeenth-Century England* (1971), and a second collection of essays, *Change and Continuity in Seventeenth-Century England* (1974). These works, too, illustrate Hill's concern with the impact of revolution, and with how, given the opportunity, societies and individuals reconstructed the world around them.

Having earlier argued that England in the seventeenth century contained two distinct cultures, the traditional and the progressive, in *The World Turned Upside Down* Hill tried to excavate the radical world normally obscured by censorship. He had devoted an earlier essay to what the propertied classes thought the meaner sort desired, but *The World Turned Upside Down* was a full-scale ethnography of that shadow culture, "a guidebook for the Island of Great Bedlam."[27] Hill found much to admire there, including an unwavering faith in the potentiality of humanity and a hatred of inequality. These ideals resonated not only forward to nineteenth- and twentieth-century radicalism but also backward at least as far as the Lollards. "The New Model Army," Hill wrote, "was the match which fired the gunpowder. But once the conflagration started, there was plenty of combustible material lying around."[28] *The World Turned Upside Down* investigated that material, its origins, development, and implications.

Milton and the English Revolution was the closest thing to biography that Hill had written, but it continued his exploration of radical ideas. Hoping to rescue Milton from the Milton scholars, Hill insisted that the great poet could only be understood historically. Hill argued that although Milton's elitism kept him more intellectual than activist, his writings supported a firm anticlericalism as well as a wide range of heresies (among them anti-Trinitarianism, materialism, mortalism, and antinomianism). Milton, Hill believed, was drawn to radicalism as a moth to a flame, "in permanent dialogue with the plebeian radical thinkers of the English Revolution."[29] He may have never identified publicly with the radicals, but he lived through many of the same experiences, drew on many of the same inspirations, and came to many of the same conclusions. Even Milton's greatest poems were meditations on the Revolution. In *Paradise Lost, Paradise Regained,* and *Samson Agonistes,* Milton tried to understand God's betrayal, to reconstitute the relationship between humanity and God, and to urge the just to remain hopeful. The defeat of the Revolution was one of the great traumas of Milton's life, but his life's greatest conflict, according to Hill, was that between respectability and the lure of radicalism.[30]

Hill's study of Milton was only the most extensive of his examinations of the social context of radical ideas. *Antichrist in Seventeenth-Century England,* a conceptual study reminiscent of "The Norman Yoke," showed how important the concept of the Beast was in intellectual life in the seventeenth century and how its meaning could be accommodated to different political uses.[31] *Change and Continuity* contained three studies of seventeenth-century hostility towards professions.[32] And *The Religion of Gerrard Winstanley* expanded the controversial secular interpretation of the leader of the Diggers that Hill had first posed in his introduction to Winstanley's collected works.[33] If Hill's work while a fellow of Balliol brought the social tensions of the seventeenth century back to the center of historiography, his work while the master of Balliol brought back the task of defining just who and what was revolutionary.

In 1978, Hill retired as the master of Balliol, and between 1978 and 1981, he held visiting professorships at the Open University in Britain, the Australian National University, and Rutgers University. Addressing the problem of reconciliation, his latest books analyze how people who believed passionately in the Revolution coped with the cause's failure.[34] *Some Intellectual Consequences of the English Revolution* (1980) (the Merle Curti lectures at the University of Wisconsin in 1976) surveyed the social legacy of 1640–1660. "A Bourgeois Revolution?" reaffirmed Hill's sense of why that legacy was so important.[35] *The Experience of Defeat: Milton and Some Contemporaries* (1984) used the lives of radicals who survived the Revolution to study different responses to the Restoration. And in two essays on Daniel Defoe, Hill illustrated how radical ideas can survive even under censorship.[36] Hill cautioned, "We should not exclude the possibility that a class-dominated society may contain an egalitarian society struggling to get out; nor assume that the hegemony of one set of values excludes the possibility that other values exist, at a lower social level, or in the interstices, geographical or social, of an apparently homogeneous society.[37] Hill's latest work has stressed how much the revolutionaries won even in defeat; it has emphasized the presence in England of both a radical and a bourgeois inheritance.

For more than forty years, Hill has refined his view of the seventeenth century with arguments that have proven remarkably resilient.

His ideas have changed but, to paraphrase one of his own titles, the changes are less obvious than the continuities.[38] His work rests on a consistent set of convictions. First, he insists that the events of 1640 to 1660 permanently altered British life. Hill inverts the interpretation of his predecessors; where they saw a Civil War interrupting England's peaceful progress toward constitutional monarchy, an interregnum from civilization as well as from kingship, Hill sees a Revolution that cleared the path for the reception of capitalism, experimental science, and democracy. To Hill, English history is not anomalous; as in other countries, the seeds of later triumphs were sown in revolution.

But those triumphs owed as much to the radical Revolution that failed as they did to the bourgeois Revolution that succeeded. Radicals as different as John Milton and Gerrard Winstanley envisioned a church without a hierarchy, a social structure without an aristocracy, and a government without a king. They hoped to replace private property with communal ownership, state religion with spiritual enlightenment, and formal law with natural justice. Because such changes threatened conservative Parliamentarians as much as they did Royalists, the authorities quashed the free market in ideas that had flourished since the end of censorship. By 1660 the older forms of government returned under new restrictions. Although their ideas became a legacy for future generations, the radicals were discredited. To Hill the failed Revolution is the great tragedy of the seventeenth century. It has inspired some of his most insightful work and some of his most poignant prose.

Second, Hill has demanded of himself and others historical explanations that express the intricacy of people's lives. Hill eschews the conventional categorizations of academic discourse; his books are not religious or economic or social or intellectual or cultural histories, but all of these and more. Whatever the specific subject, the intention is the same: to recreate as fully as possible the circumstances in which people lived. He sees religion in the seventeenth century as a vernacular for expressing ideas about economics, social life, and politics, but he also recognizes religion as religion. He refuses to see economic interests as a universal explanatory force, but he is equally skeptical about the independent power of ideas. Hill repeatedly reminds his readers of the complexities of human motivation. His best work illustrates the continual interaction between religious beliefs, economic interests, intellectual preferences, and political views. One of his most important contributions is his insistence on this complexity, in scholarship as well as in history.

Third, Hill sees a fundamental heroism played out in the daily lives of laboring people. Replacing a simplistic notion of class consciousness with a more flexible notion of self-awareness, Hill has argued that people in early modern England did not accept social inequality as natural. Hostilities were common, and fear was the foundation of the social structure. He contends that the "many-headed monster" played a crucial role in governance; directly and indirectly, it set the path of English history. Only by studying "what might have been" as well as "what was" can scholars understand that history. Without making unrealistic claims for their literary capacities, Hill accords an Arise Evans or a Roger Crab the same sympathy as their better-known counterparts.[39] Hill explains: "The fact that the revolution might have gone further should never allow us to forget the heroism and faith and disciplined energy with which ordinary decent people responded when in the interests of smashing the old order the Parliament's leaders freely and frankly appealed to them to support its cause."[40]

Hill's arguments are often compelling to general readers, but his vision is more problematic for specialists.[41] Few of his interpretations have gone unchallenged; little of his method has gone uncriticized. Reviewers have complained of Hill's "tidy-mindedness," pointing out that his desire to synthesize encourages black and white categorizations. Although Hill meticulously melds categories of motivation, he often allows too little room for individual irrationality or internal contradictions. Everything and everyone fits some part in a bigger picture. Yet even the fit of the clearly rational pieces can be questioned. Hill draws attention to parallels between changes in religious, economic, social, and intellectual life, but assumes their integration. He connects ideas and actions, but too often substitutes juxtaposition and repetition for evidence of causation. He suggests the continuity of ideas through generations, but provides few specific instances of the maintenance of such a legacy.[42] Some colleagues would attribute such difficulties to Hill's Marxism, but Marxist analysis restricts Hill no more and no less than other preconceptions restrict the work of other scholars. His shortcomings stem from his belief in a single, comprehensive explanation, not from the particular explanation he has chosen.

Hill's methodology further restricts his ability to persuade other seventeenth-century scholars. Commanding an unrivaled knowledge of printed sources, he has left the archival research to others. His longstanding interest in literature and his concern to "document the mental transformations which accompanied and facilitated the rise of capitalism" explain the logic of his choice, but do not compensate for the elitism inherent in his materials.[43] Hill has made the world of radical intellectuals his own, but the connection between that world and the lives of most English men and women remains uncertain. In reviewing *Society and Puritanism in Pre-Revolutionary England,* one of Hill's former students complained, "He seeks to relate ideas to society without an adequate study of society."[44] That social knowledge necessitates a type of archival work in which Hill has shown little interest.

And there have been more specific criticisms: *Economic Problems of the Church* is too schematic;[45] *Society and Puritanism in Pre-Revolutionary England* ignores the crucial group of Puritans who were gentry;[46] *Milton and the English Revolution* oversimplifies the process by which experience is translated into art;[47] *The World Turned Upside Down* identifies individuals whose ideas appeal to the twentieth century and then weaves a coherent culture from what was only a common lifespan.[48] But although specific interpretations have been contested or disproven, much of value remains. Thirty years after its publication, *Economic Problems of the Church* still contains the best modern discussion of ecclesiastical sources of revenue, and its thesis, while overstated, is generally sound. Twenty years after its publication, *Society and Puritanism* is still a superb introduction to the non-theological world of Puritanism. Even if its interpretation is too ambitious, *Milton and the English Revolution* has made it impossible to portray Milton convincingly as simply a scholarly product of European humanism. And even if the gallery of radicals is deceptively impressive, *The World Turned Upside Down* has ensured that life in revolutionary England cannot be dismissed simply as anarchic. Historians will continue to argue over Hill's radicals, their importance, their coherence, and their value. But the territory can never be the same as it was before Hill's explorations. Despite skepticism about his conclusions, to study the seventeenth century without reading Christopher Hill would surely be unthinkable.[49]

Over all these years and all these pages, what is Christopher Hill's contribution to understanding the history of England? He has made the Revolution the centerpiece of the seventeenth century and he has added the middling sort and the radical intellectuals to the cast of the historically articulate. But if his conclusions have not prevailed, why is he a great historian? To be sure, reading Hill is an enormous pleasure. He writes not only well but also with a conviction that harks back to a time when history was primarily a literary endeavor. Having mastered a vast contemporary literature, he shares it generously with his readers. He offers numerous examples and quotes sources rarely cited by other authors. And, despite his erudition, Hill's arguments are always clear; he is unafraid of big questions and bold theses.

Most importantly, Hill challenges not only historical interpretations but also the way most professionals now do history. A generalist in an age of specialists, he demands that his readers consider the unities between areas of life rather than rest comfortably as experts in economics or religion or ideas. By insisting that readers continually confront the relationship between the material and the mental, he emphasizes their intimate connection. And more than any other major historian of the seventeenth century, Hill values literature as an integral expression of English life. No one else makes literary evidence so central to their interpretations; no one else so regularly reminds a generation fascinated with the inarticulate of those who read and wrote. Despite the modest nature of many of his texts, Hill is a historian of ideas and he has preserved intellectual history in a generation that has rejected more conventional intellectual historians.[50]

Hill's work is provocative rather than definitive, but Hill would probably be pleased with that accomplishment. He has argued that the business of historians is to present arguments for discussion. The goal is to stimulate, as well as to inform. An honestly presented but flawed argument that provokes, Hill would contend, is better than an impeccable but minor addition to received wisdom.[51] No one is more generous than Hill at acknowledging errors or at drawing attention to trenchant criticisms of his own work. And few have so willingly trained historians whose style, views, and methods differed from their own.[52] The proper measure of his achievement is not his contribution to historical orthodoxy but his contribution to historical dialectic. As Gerald Aylmer, a former student of Hill's, has observed, learning from Hill's books does not necessitate agreement with Hill's arguments. "That a reader or pupil, can disagree and still be glad to acknowledge a continuing influence," Aylmer has written, "is perhaps one hall-mark of a great teacher."[53] That definition of greatness undeniably fits Christopher Hill.

NOTES

1. Since this essay was completed, Hill's most important publication has been *A Turbulent, Seditious and Factious People: John Bunyan and his Church* (Oxford: Clarendon Press, 1988; published in the United States in 1989 by Alfred A. Knopf under the title *A Tinker and a Poor Man*). Here Hill repositions Bunyan and his work in the specific world of England in the seventeenth century. The book presents a masterfully complex portrait of Bunyan, "warts and all," bringing readers considerably closer

to understanding the power of a man who was arguably England's greatest writer of prose. Hill has also continued producing regularly essays on a variety of topics. Some of his earlier pieces are now available in *The Collected Essays of Christopher Hill.* 3 vols. (Amherst: Univ. of Massachusetts Press, 1985–1986).

A select bibliography of Hill's writings between 1938 and 1977 may be found in Donald Pennington and Keith Thomas, eds., *Puritans and Revolutionaries: Essays in Seventeenth-Century History Presented to Christopher Hill* (Oxford, 1978). The paperback edition, published in 1982, includes an addendum for the years 1978–1981. Because Hill's works have different publishers on each side of the Atlantic and are reprinted frequently in both places, full bibliographical information has not been included in this essay. The notes that follow indicate the date of publication in England; specific citations include information on the edition being cited. For more extended comments on Hill's impact on seventeenth-century historiography, see Geoff Eley and William Hunt, eds. *Reviving the English Revolution: Reflections and Elaborations on the Work of Christopher Hill* (London: Verso, 1988).

2. J. H. Hexter, "The Burden of Proof," *Times Literary Supplement,* 24 Oct. 1975, 1250, 1252, reprinted in J. H. Hexter, *On Historians: Reappraisals of Some of the Makers of Modern History* (Cambridge, Mass., 1979), 227–51.

3. This is not to suggest that there has been no change within Hill's work, but simply that the changes have been modifications rather than major shifts. Compare, for example, the argument of "The English Revolution" in *The English Revolution, 1640: Three Essays,* ed. Christopher Hill (London, 1940) with that of "A Bourgeois Revolution?" in *Three British Revolutions: 1641, 1688, 1776,* ed. J. G. A. Pocock (Princeton, 1980), 109–39.

4. See, for example, Hill, ed. *The English Revolution 1640,* 7; Hill and Edmund Dell, eds., *The Good Old Cause: The English Revolution of 1640–60. Its Causes, Courses, and Consequences* (London, 1949), introduction; *Past and Present* 1(Feb. 1952):i–iv. This attitude is also borne out by the regular appearance of Hill's work in periodicals such as *History Today,* the *Listener,* and the *Times Literary Supplement* as well as by his popularity as a reviewer for a wide variety of publications.

5. Hill, *The Century of Revolution 1603–1714* (Edinburgh, 1961; 2d ed., 1980); *Reformation to Industrial Revolution* (Edinburgh, 1967; rev. ed., 1969). Hill's earliest essays on Marvell and Richardson are reprinted in *Puritanism and Revolution* (London, 1958); discussions of Milton appear in most of Hill's works, but the best approach to Hill's view of the poet is his *Milton and the English Revolution* (London, 1977).

6. Except as noted, biographical information relies on Harvey J. Kaye, *The British Marxist Historians* (Cambridge, 1984), 101–3; "Christopher Hill: Some Reminiscences" in Pennington and Thomas, eds., *Puritans and Revolutionaries,* 1–21; Eric Hobsbawm, "The Historians' Group of the Communist Party" in M. Cornforth, ed., *Rebels and Their Causes: Essays in Honour of A. L. Morton* (London, 1978), 21–47.

7. Hill remained on the editorial board of *Past and Present* from its first issue in 1952 until 1968, when he resigned to become vice-president of the Past and Present Society. He has been president of the society since 1970. On the purposes of the journal, see the introductory remarks in the first issue as well as the memoir written by Hill, Hobsbawm and Hilton in the hundredth issue, "Origins and Early Years" (Aug. 1983):3–14.

8. While all of Hill's monographic work on England in the seventeenth century and many of his most influential articles are at least mentioned in this essay, his writings focused outside England, his reviews, his introductions to the work of other people, and many of his essays and occasional pieces have been left out. In any case, a true

assessment of Hill's importance now would be premature; well into formal retirement, he is as productive and as provocative as ever.

9. Hill's publications in what are often considered his unproductive years include "Lenin: Theoretician of Revolution," *Communist Review* (Feb. 1947):59–64; "Marxism and History," *Modern Quarterly,* new ser., 3(1948):52–64; "The Materialist Conception of History," *University History* 1(1951):110–4; "Stalin and the Science of History," *Modern Quarterly,* new ser., 8(1953):198–212; "The Transition from Feudalism to Capitalism, II," *Science and Society* 17(1953):348–51; *Lenin and the Russian Revolution* (London, 1947): "Soviet Interpretations of the English Interregnum," *Economic History Review* 8(1938):159–67; "The Agrarian Legislation of the Interregnum" (based on the work of the Russian scholar S. I. Arkhangelsky), *English Historical Review* 55(1940):222–50; "The English Civil War as Interpreted by Marx and Engels," *Science and Society* 12(1948):130–56; (as K. E. Holme), *Two Commonwealths: The Soviets and Ourselves* (London, 1945); "The University of Moscow, II: The Teaching of History," *Universities Quarterly* 9(1955):332–41. For the importance of these and similar pieces by Hill see R. C. Richardson, *The Debate on the English Revolution* (London, 1977), 98–103.

10. Hill, *The English Revolution, 1640; Good Old Cause;* most of the essays later collected in *Puritanism and Revolution.*

11. "Interview: Christopher Hill," *University History* 1(1951):5.

12. Hill, *Good Old Cause,* 19. Hill's later writings show a greater interest in some of the differences between England and the continent.

13. *The English Revolution, 1640,* 58.

14. Ibid., 61.

15. Ibid., 76.

16. "Interview," 5.

17. *Puritanism and Revolution* also contains essays on agrarian legislation during the Revolution, on revolutionary foreign policy, and some of Hill's best studies using one person or one piece of literature to exemplify a particular social attitude. See particularly, "Society and Andrew Marvell" and "Clarissa Harlowe and Her Times."

18. Alan Simpson, *Journal of Modern History* 29(Sept. 1957):261–62.

19. "Interview," 5–7. On the importance of 1956 for Hill, see also Richardson, *Debate,* 103; Lawrence Stone, "England's Revolution," *New York Review of Books,* 26 Aug. 1965; "Reminiscences," 9–10; Kaye, *Marxist Historians,* 101–3, 106–7.

20. Hobsbawm, "Historians' Group," 38, 44–5.

21. Christopher Hill, *The Economic Problems of the Church: From Archbishop Whitgift to the Long Parliament* (Oxford, 1956; reprinted with corrections, 1961, 1968), xiii.

22. Ibid., xiv.

23. Christopher Hill, "Protestantism and the Rise of Capitalism" originally published in F. J. Fisher, ed. *Essays in the Economic and Social History of Tudor and Stuart England, in Honour of R. H. Tawney,* reprinted in *Change and Continuity in Seventeenth-Century England* (Cambridge, Mass., 1975), 81–102.

24. Christopher Hill, *Society and Puritanism in Pre-Revolutionary England,* 2d ed. (New York, 1967), 511, but see Brian Manning, *English Historical Review* 81(Apr. 1966):358–60.

25. The initial debate was carried on in the pages of *Past and Present;* Charles Webster, ed., *The Intellectual Revolution of the Seventeenth Century* (London, 1974) reprints the important contributions.

26. See "Reminiscences," 10–21.

27. Richard Schlatter, *American Historical Review* 78(Oct., 1973):1054. The "guidebook" was added to in the Barnett Shine Foundation lecture for 1974, "Irreligion in the Puritan Revolution," reprinted in J. F. McGregor and Barry Reay, eds., *Radical Religion in the English Revolution* (Oxford, 1984), 191–211. The earlier essay, "The Many-Headed Monster" is reprinted in *Change and Continuity in Seventeenth-Century England,* 181–204. It appeared originally in *From the Renaissance to the Counter-Reformation: Essays in Honor of Garrett Mattingly,* ed. C. H. Carter (New York, 1965).

28. Christopher Hill, *The World Turned Upside Down: Radical Ideas During the English Revolution* (New York, 1973), 69. The book was first published in England in 1972, and a revised edition appeared in 1975. See also Christopher Hill, "From Lollards to Levellers," in *Rebels and Their Causes,* 49–67; Christopher Hill, "John Reeve and the Origins of Muggletonianism" in Christopher Hill, Barry Reay, and William Lamont, *The World of the Muggletonians* (London, 1983), 64–110.

29. Christopher Hill, *Milton and the English Revolution* (Harmondsworth, 1979), 5.

30. In *God's Englishman: Oliver Cromwell and the English Revolution* (London, 1970; rev. ed., 1972), Hill shows how the same conflict transformed Oliver Cromwell from the hero of the Civil War into the destroyer of the Revolution. See also Hill's *Oliver Cromwell 1658–1958,* Historical Assoc. Pamphlet G38, 1958.

31. Christopher Hill, *Antiquities of Seventeenth-Century England* (London, 1971) was originally delivered as the Riddell memorial lectures at the University of Newcastle upon Tyne, 1969.

32. "The Radical Critics of Oxford and Cambridge in the 1650s" was a lecture delivered at Johns Hopkins University in May, 1970, and printed originally in *Universities in Politics,* ed. J. W. Baldwin and R. Goldthwaite (Baltimore, 1972), 127–48; "The Inns of Court," 149–56, was a review article published in *History of Education Quarterly* 12, no. 4(1972):149–56; "The Medical Profession and Its Radical Critics," 157–80, was the Gideon Delaune Lecture, 1973.

33. Christopher Hill, ed. *Winstanley: The Law of Freedom and Other Writings* (Harmondsworth, 1973); cf. L. Mulligan, J. K. Graham, and J. Richards, "Winstanley: A Case for the Man as He Said He Was," *Journal of Ecclesiastical History* 28(1977):57–75; Mulligan, Graham, and Richards, "The Religion of Gerrard Winstanley," and Hill, "Rejoinder," *Past and Present* 89(Nov. 1980):144–51.

34. The clearest exception to this generalization is Hill's 1980 Neale lecture, a witty dissection of current scholarship on the importance of the English Revolution entitled "Parliament and People in Seventeenth-Century England," published in *Past and Present* 92(Aug. 1981):100–124.

35. Compare Lawrence Stone, "The Bourgeois Revolution of Seventeenth-Century England Revisited," *Past and Present* 109(Nov. 1985):44–54.

36. "Daniel Defoe (1660–1731) and Robinson Crusoe," *History Workshop* 10(Autumn, 1980):6–24, reprinted in *The Collected Essays of Christopher Hill,* vol. 1, 105–30; "Radical Pirates?" in Margaret and J. R. Jacob, eds., *The Origins of Anglo-American Radicalism* (London, 1984), 17–32.

37. "Why Bother About the Muggletonians?" in Hill, Reay, and Lamont, *Muggletonians,* 13.

38. Cf. Kaye, *Marxist Historians,* 102–30 and Stone, "The Bourgeois Revolution Revisited."

39. "Arise Evans: Welshman in London," in Hill's *Change and Continuity,* 48–77;

"The Mad Hatter," *History Today* (Oct. 1957), reprinted in *Puritanism and Revolution*, 303-10.

40. Hill, *The English Revolution, 1640,* 58.

41. Reviews of Hill's work contain the best analysis of Hill's methodology; see particularly the *Times Literary Supplement, New York Review of Books, London Review of Books, English Historical Review,* and *Economic History Review.* Hexter's, "The Burden of Proof" is the most direct discussion of Hill's style of doing history, but other reviews of Hill, and particularly those written by Lawrence Stone, offer a more balanced evaluation. The discussion provoked by Hexter, including a response from Hill, can be found in the *Times Literary Supplement,* 7 Nov. 1975, 1333; 14 Nov. 1975, 1360; 28 Nov. 1975, 1419-20. Hill's occasional pieces and his reviews of the work of other scholars are his only extended comments on methodology, but see also Richardson, *Debate on the English Revolution,* 98-112; Kaye, *Marxist Historians,* 103-30.

42. See, for example, the reviews of *Intellectual Origins of the English Revolution* by Lawrence Stone in the *New York Review of Books,* 26 Aug. 1965; and Gerald Aylmer, *English Historical Review* 81(Oct. 1966):783-89; the reviews of *Milton and the English Revolution* by William Lamont, *English Historical Review* 93(July 1978):621-26; and Quentin Skinner, the *New York Review of Books,* 23 Mar. 1978; and the reviews of *The Experience of Defeat: Milton and Some Contemporaries* (London, 1984) by Conrad Russell, *London Review of Books,* 4 Oct. 1984; and David Underdown, the *New York Review of Books,* 28 Mar. 1985.

43. Hill, *Times Literary Supplement,* 7 Nov. 1975, 1333.

44. Brian Manning, *English Historical Review* 81(Apr. 1966):360. Manning questions the applicability of Hill's materials even for the lives of the middling sort. For similar criticisms, see, for example, the reviews of *The Economic Problems of the Church* by Lawrence Stone, *Economic History Review* 11(1958-1959):518-19, and W. K. Jordan, *American Historical Review* 62(Apr. 1957):613-14; the reviews of *Society and Puritanism* in *Pre-Revolutionary England* by Manning, 358-60; and Hugh Kearney, *American Historical Review* 70(Oct. 1964):118-19; and the review of *Change and Continuity in Seventeenth-Century England* by John Miller, *Times Higher Education Supplement,* 7 Mar. 1975.

45. Norman Sykes, *English Historical Review* (Apr. 1958):294-98. See also the reviews by Jordan and Stone cited in note 44.

46. Lawrence Stone, *New Statesman,* 17 Apr. 1964, 605-6. Hill has often been criticized for the imprecision of his categorization; see especially reviews of *Intellectual Origins of the English Revolution* and *Change and Continuity in Seventeenth-Century England.*

47. Blair Worden, *Times Literary Supplement,* 2 Dec. 1977, 1394-95.

48. Richard Schlatter, *American Historical Review* 78(Oct. 1973):1052-55; and the review of *Milton and the English Revolution* by Lamont cited in note 42.

49. Thoughtful assessments of the books Hill published before 1980 can be found in J. S. Morrill, *Seventeenth-Century Britain 1603-1714* (London, 1980).

50. This has been equally important, but more controversial, as a contribution to Marxist historiography. See Hobsbawm, "Historians' Group," 44-45; Kaye, *Marxist Historians,* 221-49; cf. R. Samuel, "The British Marxist Historians I," *New Left Review* 120(Mar.-Apr. 1980):21-96; Richard Johnson, "Culture and the Historians" in J. Clarke, C. Critcher, and R. Johnson, eds., *Working-Class Culture: Studies in History and Theory* (London, 1979), 41-71.

51. Hill, *Times Literary Supplement,* 7 Nov. 1975, 1333; "Interview," passim.

52. Hill has often used the opportunity of reprinting editions to add emendations to the work and to alert readers to the best critical reviews of his ideas; see, for example, the preface of the second edition of *Society and Puritanism in Pre-Revolutionary England;* n. 1 in the reprint of "William Perkins and the Poor" in *Puritanism and Revolution;* the preface to the second edition of *The Century of Revolution, 1603–1714.* Hill's skill as a teacher is evidenced by the fact that his former pupils include many of the best social historians in England; for a sample of their work, see *Puritans and Revolutionaries.*

53. *English Historical Review* 81(Oct. 1966):789.

Lawrence Stone ⟨⟩
Social Science and History

JOEL BERLATSKY

Since World War II, efforts to enrich historical scholarship with the theories of social science have increased. Among students of English history Lawrence Stone has productively and persistently incorporated the insights of social scientists. As a publishing scholar and as a mentor to graduate students, Stone is a beacon lighting the new pathways. Always in the forefront of new enterprises, in recent years Stone has turned increasing attention to issues of method, evidence, and approach. As J. H. Hexter remarked, Stone, in his attempt to achieve a persuasive picture of past societies, has become a "paradigm of openmindedness" free from "humanistic snobbery" and "scientific priggery." In his pursuit of alternative historiographical paths, Lawrence Stone has expended tremendous energy and for forty years has shown remarkable willingness to examine his own errors and learn from them.[1] Fear of making mistakes has never discouraged Stone from attempting to look at difficult problems on a large scale.

The product of a traditional English education, Lawrence Stone attended one of the best-known public schools, Charterhouse, beginning at age eight. He found Charterhouse little altered from Robert Graves's famous descriptions in *Goodbye to All That,* save for a decline in the use of physical punishment.[2] Already an inveterate collector of stamps, butterflies, and much else, Stone found the antiquated classical curriculum of little use, though it did help to shape a powerful writing style that has resulted in his never having had a manuscript rejected by a journal.[3] Stone turned to a life of learning because of the inspiration he received from a few dedicated teachers at Charterhouse and later at Oxford.

The most influential of these mentors was R. H. Tawney. During World War II, when Stone was in the Royal Navy, he would spend his leaves with Tawney in a ramshackle Bloomsbury flat listening to critiques of modern society intermixed with excursuses into the seventeenth century. In the process Stone was converted from a medievalist to a student of early modern history. Tawney instilled in the young researcher the notion that scholarship could not be divorced from the contemporary world and that there must always be a concern with moral issues.[4]

During his five years in the navy Stone published his first article, an appraisal of English unpreparedness and government bungling at the time of the defeat of the Spanish Armada.[5] The parallel to the writer's own experience in World War II is obvious. Rapid demobilization led Stone back to Oxford, where in June 1946 he was awarded a B.A. degree.

Without the benefit of graduate training, Stone ambitiously started to write a biography of Sir Horatio Palavicino, a Genoese merchant who settled in England and was knighted by Queen Elizabeth I. At the same time Stone submitted to the *Economic History Review* an article that reflected the impact of World War II on his historical concerns. In "State Control in Sixteenth Century England," he concluded that the fear of war and its social consequences were the prime motivators of government economic policy during the reign of Elizabeth I.[6]

Though still a fledgling historian, Stone soon found himself engaged in a tendentious academic battle with H. R. Trevor-Roper. The cause of conflict was Stone's article, "The Anatomy of the Elizabethan Aristocracy," published in 1948 in the *Economic History Review,* in which Stone defended the tenets of his mentor. Tawney's assertion that the "shift in the relative proportions of the national income held by the different classes of society was the basic cause of the upheavals of the mid–seventeenth century" had now been proven beyond reasonable doubt, Stone concluded. The article complemented Tawney's earlier essay, "The Rise of the Gentry," with a portrayal of a declining aristocracy.[7]

As reward for his effort Stone was ravaged by Trevor-Roper who replied in the same journal with "The Elizabethan Aristocracy: An Anatomy Anatomized." A master of the critical cleaver, Trevor-Roper launched a technical attack on Stone's evidence as to the financial state of Elizabethan aristocrats. He accused Stone of multiple errors of detail adding up to a negation of the whole argument. According to Trevor-Roper, Stone had produced not an analysis but a caricature of the Elizabethan magnates. He concluded that the entire subject was an "exaggerated historical problem" for which Tawney and Stone had provided an "unplausible answer."[8]

Such an all-out assault required a reply, especially in an era when the "gentry controversy" had come to be seen as the key that would unlock the secrets of the English Revolution. In his rebuttal, Stone admitted some errors both in statistics and in judgment, but he insisted that the gist of the argument had not been undermined by Trevor-Roper's nit-picking. Stone wisely conceded some technical points, observing at the same time that Trevor-Roper had chosen to ignore qualifications stipulated in the original article.[9] Where the honors of battle lay now seems unimportant, inasmuch as the entire gentry controversy impresses many historians of the 1980s as a relic of a bygone era. Stone's interest in traditional economic history was also waning as he moved toward a more sociological orientation.[10]

Before that shift of emphasis became apparent, Stone ventured into a seemingly unrelated area of inquiry. He contributed *Sculpture in Britain: The Middle Ages* to *The Pelican History of Art* series. Stone's participation was the result of his collecting photographs before the war and an acquaintance with Sir Thomas Kendrick of the British Museum, whose patronage led to the contract. Today, such an unprofessional arrangement would probably be impossible; it was deemed suspect at the time by general editor Nikolaus Pevsner.[11] Spanning the course of English sculpture from Anglo-Saxon times until the Reformation, Stone revealed interests that went well beyond the bounds of econometrics and statistical tables. He was concerned not only with recounting the development of a major art form but also with attempting to place it in the context of historical change. Stone gave particular emphasis to the importance of foreign influences in the shaping of English sculpture. He was appalled by the destruction wrought by the Reformation, in the course of which 90 percent of all medieval sculpture was lost. What survived did so primarily because English landowners "never lost the ability to protect the memorials of their ancestors." Stone sounds positively elitist when he contrasts the "bourgeois quality of mediocrity" in sculptures for the taste of fourteenth-century gentry with those for the more discriminating aristocrats of the previous century. Though interested in the medieval economy, Stone concedes that "there is no correlation between general economic prosperity and the investment of capital in architectural or sculptural undertakings." From the standpoint of art, the Reformation was a disaster, not only for what it destroyed but because a changed religious and political climate ushered in an era of iconoclasm. "Medieval sculpture was strangled by decrees of the state, ruthlessly enforced in the interests of ideological conformity."[12]

The departure into the field of art history was one that confirmed Stone's catholic approach to historical evidence. In several subsequent articles, as in his most recent book, Stone demonstrates how significantly artistic survivals can illuminate other aspects of history.[13]

An Elizabethan: Sir Horatio Palavicino was the concluding work of Stone's earliest, economic history phase. In this book he demonstrates an ability to grasp and to explain such technical matters as the workings of European alum mines and the complexities of Dutch finance. The largest financial rewards, however, came from a close connection with the Crown, and in *Palavicino* Stone illustrates how graft, corruption, jobbery, chicanery, and prevarication permeated the government of Elizabethan England. And yet, Sir Horatio is shown to be more than a mere money-grubber; he also dabbled in espionage and sought to legitimate his position with extensive land purchases. Palavicino tried to run his estates in a businesslike fashion, but he found that his great wealth and foreign origins made him unpopular in a rural society that Stone portrayed as suspicious, faction-ridden, snobbish, tightfisted, and "riddled with prejudice." His heirs squandered Palavicino's huge fortune, and the family descended rapidly into total obscurity.[14]

On the completion of the book on Palavicino, Lawrence Stone headed in a new direction, symbolized by his departure from the pages of the *Economic History Review* and his involvement with a new journal, *Past and Present,* where sociology and the other concerns of the *Annales* school took pride of place. Stone's interest in the elite and in architecture were to recur, but social questions were rapidly replacing his concern with economic matters. His focus shifted to the aristocracy conceived as a group. Thinking more about method and evidence, the developing historian grew less dogmatic as he became more aware of the limits of the available sources. Stone devoted a full decade to a careful analysis of the English aristocracy in the era 1540–1640. The first articles ripened into the prodigious book of 1965, a work that made the early debate with Trevor-Roper on the role of the aristocracy look like child's play.[15] *The Crisis of the Aristocracy, 1558–1640* established Lawrence Stone as a leader in historical scholarship just as—after thirteen years as a fellow at Wadham College, Oxford—he moved permanently to Princeton University in

1963 as Dodge Professor of History and founding director of the Shelby Cullom Davis Center for Historical Studies.[16]

By the time *Crisis of the Aristocracy* was published, various results of the research had appeared as journal articles. Among these was an especially provocative discussion of "The Inflation of Honours, 1558–1641." Stone believed that the government needed the voluntary cooperation of the landed classes, but Elizabeth I was stingy both with real rewards and with substitute honorific titles. As a result, officials and courtiers sought their own rewards through a growth in corruption at a time that many new families moved into the landed class as purchasers of monastic, church, and royal lands. When James I came to the throne, the pressure for honors was great and the King's need for money pressing: thus a flood of new titles was created. Between 1625 and 1628 the number of peers increased from eighty-one to one hundred and twenty-six, many of them connected in some fashion to George Villiers, Duke of Buckingham.[17]

Stone contended that a rapid growth in the peerage had adverse results for the monarchy by reducing respect for nobles and for the very concept of a hierarchical society. Royal finances were strained to endow the new aristocrats, and conspicuous consumption distorted the economy while dividing the society between court and country. The pursuit of honors led to faction at every level, and the lack of useful employment resulted in a divided House of Lords for the first time in one hundred years. Whether James had much choice was doubtful because there had been a genuine growth in the number of wealthy individuals who demanded recognition for their new status but, according to Stone, the inflation of honors destabilized society and ushered in an era of conflict and instability that culminated in Civil War.[18]

The article illustrates the author's concern with social structure, social mobility, and other sociological concepts. The validity of the contention that a rapid expansion of the peerage created instability is difficult to evaluate, but there is little doubt that a proliferation of titles devalues their meaning — however fervent the pride of each new honoree.[19] Thus American campuses proliferate with deans, directors, and professors; to lack such a title is to be prestigeless, paltry, and plebeian. In other articles, Stone explored the changing role of the aristocracy by examining marriage patterns, attitudes toward education, and the importance of office-holding in the creation of aristocratic fortunes.[20]

The Crisis of the Aristocracy involves 753 pages of text and 40 more of appendices. Although Stone concedes that the available statistics could not provide answers for all the questions he had raised, they formed "the bony skeleton of this book" and constituted the best "means of extracting a coherent pattern." The book displays an author willing to bare his methods, acknowledge gaps, concede inadequacies, and admit limitations. The shape of the social structure that his study clarifies is important to Stone, and yet he often seems more fascinated by the attitudes his subjects reveal. Although he has established himself as the major historian of England's top social echelon, paradoxically Stone has admitted his personal dislike for aristocratic society. He is impressed, however, by the collective capacity of the English aristocracy to adapt to changing circumstances, and he remains persuaded that an understanding of its economic, social, and intellectual history is a prerequisite for an adequate explanation of political change.[21]

Fundamental to Stone's theme is his contention that 1580–1640 represented a watershed between medieval and modern England. As the power of the state grew, aristocrats had to adapt. Their failure to find a satisfactory role in relation to the court during the 1630s and early 1640s helped lead to Civil War, but subsequent modifications help account for the stability of the eighteenth century. It is impossible to summarize all the evidence for so provocative a thesis in an essay. Suffice it to say that Stone examined every aspect of the aristocratic way of life: how they managed their estates, how they behaved on the battlefield, how they tipped their hats, and how often they flogged their children. On every subject, the author made clear his sources, his methods, and his assumptions.[22]

Lawrence Stone concludes his monumental enterprise with the view that in the early seventeenth century respect for aristocrats had declined because they possessed relatively little land and wealth, had lost their military functions, had established new relations with tenants, lived beyond their means, were increasingly tied to court, were divided over religion, and were split into factions. Society lacked its old confidence in a graded polity. The temporary abolition of the House of Lords during the Interregnum was the visible evidence of a crisis that marked the climax of a century of changes.[23]

Reviews of Stone's opus ran the gamut from lavish praise to harsh criticism. Most critics conceded that the virtues of the entire mansion much exceeded the imperfections of particular rooms. As David Underdown observed twenty years after publication, "The book's masterly depiction of the aristocratic life-style more than compensates for whichever statistical deficiencies it might contain."[24] One critic who did focus on those statistics was D. C. Coleman. For him the entire controversy over the rise of the gentry was one that, with the exception of Tawney, "no professionally recognizable economic historian has ever taken part in." Coleman attacked Stone for vagueness and for "a certain cavalier quality . . . evident in Stone's general treatment of statistical evidence and economic topics." Although impressed by the comprehensiveness of Stone's project, Coleman was left unpersuaded that the category of titled aristocracy was of significant historical value, inasmuch as the peers were an artificially defined rather than an obvious socioeconomic group. He doubted therefore "whether a statistically-based study of the titular aristocracy as a group in a state of crisis is really the best way to discover a new explanation for the central event of modern English history."[25]

Markedly more favorable was the lengthy review by J. H. Hexter, a historian not noted for undue charity toward participants in what he had once dubbed The Storm Over the Gentry. To focus on the statistical details, Hexter argued, was to miss the merits of Stone's "reconstruction of the patterns of life of a social group [the aristocracy] over a period of almost a hundred years." It was an accomplishment "surely not surpassed in the historical literature of any country in the world." Hexter contended that the author had been exemplary in using statistics and social science concepts. The whole effort was based on a "sound general recipe . . . combining old-fashioned historical methods and newfangled social science notions" while making a fetish of neither. Especially admirable was Stone's willingness to concede past errors. Hexter included in his paean of praise only a few discordant notes; he wondered, for example, why Stone had not treated the corporate role of the aristocracy as displayed in the House of Lords.[26]

It is fair to conclude that more than two decades after first publication *The Crisis of the Aristocracy* remains a historical landmark, a work that placed an entire class in its proper milieu. In persuasive fashion it explains how the most important segment of England's political society temporarily lost its grip, thereby precipitating the slide into revolution and civil war. Subsequent studies and critiques have failed to dislodge Stone's edifice, secured as it is in a bedrock of statistical evidence and in a mastery of the sources. The book elevated Stone to the top rank of modern historians and is an exemplar of the marriage of history with other social sciences.

Stone was not finished with the aristocracy in "Tawney's century." In part responding to critics of the earlier book who asked for case studies, he produced *Family and Fortune: Studies in Aristocratic Fi-*

nance in the Sixteenth and Seventeenth Century, a detailed financial picture of the Cecil family and four other great houses. Stone believed that these portraits illustrated his contention that mere economic considerations could not explain the behavior of people who were "more often concerned with expenditure than with income." In *Crisis of the Aristocracy* Stone had searched for patterns; in *Family and Fortune* his focus was on particulars. He gave most attention to the earls of Salisbury, socially conspicuous and important for the records they left to posterity. Central to the aristocratic ethos of the seventeenth-century Cecils was a building mania that in due course impoverished the family. To finance this life-style, the earls corrupted the government of the day while paying mere pittances in taxes, tithes, and charity. The earls contributed to the aristocratic "crisis" by exceeding contemporary norms of corruption and by ending up as parasitic pensioners of a penurious potentate.[27] The other families discussed offer embellishments to the theme of family fortunes vulnerable to "personal whims and follies, and uncontrolled fertility." They also provide additional evidence of the author's encyclopedic grasp of the life-style of the greatest men of late Tudor and Stuart England.

By the time *Family and Fortune* reached the press, Stone's interests had been drawn to other topics. In an important article appearing in 1966 he discussed his concept of social mobility in an advanced traditional society that had undergone a "seismic upheaval" between 1540 and 1640.[28] Whereas most historians visualized the social structure of traditional societies as a stepped pyramid, Stone preferred to view it as the United Nations building: a low podium with winding ramps (church, law, commerce, and office) leading to a tall, narrow skyscraper. During the period 1500–1700, Stone contended, the English replaced the UN model with a series of vertical towers on a hill. The most important divide in the resulting society was between the 90 percent of the people who worked with their hands and the 10 percent who did no manual labor. Both groups grew as the population expanded, the upper group more rapidly because of the relative increase in the number of lawyers and government officials. Since the number of the very poor also went up, social polarization increased. Stone insisted that in this society upward social mobility was more difficult to achieve than earlier historians had suggested. Education, marriage, and inheritance all might hold the key to such advance in individual cases, but a temporary geographical move—to Ireland or the West Indies or even India—often proved to be a more reliable path.[29]

Opportunities to move upward in society improved temporarily during the later sixteenth century, with the English world destabilized by inflation, by large upper-class families, by a vigorous land market, by expanded educational opportunities, and by Puritanism. In the aftermath of the Civil War of the 1640s, there was a restoration of greater social stability. Family fertility declined; the belief in the efficacy of education was curtailed; and there was a widespread desire in the upper levels to keep a lid on change. In a land again dominated by a hereditary elite, "sponsored" or patronized upward mobility became the norm.[30]

Stone's views on social mobility differed significantly from the conventional historical wisdom. Instead of interpreting the Revolution and Civil War of the 1640s as the consequences of potential changes bottled up too long, Stone has seen the very mobility of the 1540–1640 era as creating discontent and leading to a breakdown in traditional authority. Puritanism was embraced by people moving either up or down as they sought a new source of authority in a changing world. For Stone the Revolution was caused not by specific social changes but by the turmoil of change itself.[31]

The difficulty with Stone's approach is similar to that involving any analysis of social structure during the preindustrial era. The trends and definitions of social groups can be demonstrated only imperfectly and inconclusively. The entire approach can be criticized as a fallacy of composition: a dramatic revolution must have a seismic cause. Yet Stone remains persuaded that important events must have comprehensive if multiple causes.[32]

In order to understand one of those multiple causes more fully, Stone's next research was on education. In "The Educational Revolution in England, 1540–1640" the author conceded that his conclusions were "best guesses rather than hard statistical facts."[33] Using such source materials as did exist, Stone ascertained that all classes of people in early seventeenth-century England had a uniquely high interest in education. The percentage of students in universities was not equalled again until after World War II. The causes of devotion to education were various; they included the end of the clerical monopoly of learning, the acceptance of humanism, and the growth of Puritanism. Stone drew a parallel with the expansion of higher education in Britain and the United States during the 1960s. At both times the spread of knowledge was expected to lead to an improvement in society and an elimination of evils. The university atmosphere of the early seventeenth century was marked by intellectual ferment, enterprising scholarship, and scientific advance. In the course of the century, however, universities came under attack. They were blamed for raising needless questions, for employing teachers with Puritan sympathies, and for radicalizing the young. A ruling class seeking social stability understandably lost interest in university expansion.[34]

In collaboration with his fellow Princetonian, Marius Jansen, Stone attempted to compare the interaction of education and modernization in England with comparable developments in Japan. He emerged from this second look with a less buoyant point of view. Stone now concluded that rather than promoting "intellectual ferment" the universities, by emphasizing the study of Latin, had reinforced "the hierarchical structure of Tudor society." Like the Japanese, the English adopted "as the basis for their elite education a close repetitive study of works written long ago in a foreign language." The purpose was to create an elite "trained to be of service to the state," and appointments were made more on the basis of status than of merit. Advances in knowledge were more likely to take place outside, and even in spite of, the formal educational system.[35]

In a sweeping article in *Past and Present,* Stone argued for the importance of an educational system in preserving a particular form of society.[36] A country's educational structure was, for Stone, a product of its social structure, of available job opportunities, of assumptions of social control, and of demography, as well as of its economic organization. He contended that the stratified nature of modern English society is in part a product of the educational institutions that emerged in the Early Modern Era. In particular he concluded that the "bizarre" development of the public school was no more than "a prolonged male puberty rite" closely related to practices of primitive peoples. Over time the public schools became a means to preserve aristocratic values, institutions, and wealth. Education was meant to keep people in their place. It could provide mobility for a few of the gifted, although it had least impact when high-paying jobs were available for those without degrees or diplomas. Yet the desire for security promoted a quest for certification even in times when few jobs were available. Such observations were, inevitably, influenced by Stone's encounter with an American undergraduate population scrambling from fad to fad, searching for lucrative, risk-free careers. Stone concluded it was not possible fully to explain patterns of literacy over a two hundred and fifty-year period.[37]

Stone's fascination with education as a key to early modern society may also be seen in his contribution to a cooperative effort examining the role of the university in society. He tried to apply statistical techniques to analyze the student body of Oxford, believing, despite the limitations of available sources, that such an effort would "marry intellectual and social history." Stone argued that changes in the size of the student body were "structural pivots around which the history of the university has to be built." Periods of expansion made the university react to "certain of the new developments of the day," while "in periods of numerical depression . . . the university tended to become introverted, and withdrawn from the center of affairs." Primarily, external forces determined the desirability of university education. The supply and nature of jobs for university graduates defined the usefulness of matriculation.[38]

Stone discovered three phases in student population patterns: from 1550 to 1670 there was expansion, followed by a decline that lasted until 1810, thereafter a steady rise in student numbers. In the first epoch, the church and teaching provided employment opportunities, and, since costs were low, plebeians formed 50 percent of the student body. The ruling class felt the university was a preparation for life under strict moral discipline. In the second phase the plebeians gradually disappeared; the church was dominated by aristocrats and the sons of clergy. Grammar schools and universities became more costly and there was a "growing sense of disillusionment about the benefits of higher education." The rich preferred to have their sons obtain social graces on the European Grand Tour. Critics argued that the lax discipline of the universities led youths astray, and the Revolution of the seventeenth century made them appear to be a breeding ground for radical ideas. After 1715, conversely, Whigs suspected that Oxford was a center of Tory subversion. Changes in society during the nineteenth century revived the universities. The growth in population, increased literacy, reform of discipline, and lower costs saw enrollments once again advance. Most of the new students came from the middle class as appropriate jobs opened for those holding degrees.[39]

Little of what Stone found was startling, a fact that may account for the author gradually losing interest in investigating education. Though he integrated his research into later studies, Stone had exhausted what statistics could reveal. In his reviews of works in the field, Stone began to question the importance of the history of education. Intellectual historians of the university were not focusing on important issues; undergraduate education always lacked relevance; and "it is an open question to what extent the things students learn in the university classroom influence their subsequent political and religious beliefs." Activities outside the classroom, Stone concluded, were probably of greater importance. Again it is tempting to wonder if the historian's encounters with the tribal ways of American undergraduates led to a loss of faith in the university as a molder of society.[40]

In accounting for the *Causes of the English Revolution,* Stone looked to social factors not intellectual constructs. Meant as an introduction to a complex subject, this short work was a summation of twenty-five years of thought about the origins of the Civil War.[41] Stone's approach was tersely summed up in his confession "that I still consider constitutional history *in vacuo* as one of the most sterile and meaningless ways of cutting into the tangled thickets of historical change." It was vital to use the insights of social science as "a corrective to the antiquarian fact grubbing to which historians are so prone." But Stone had come a long way from his own earlier views, as he condemned Marxist interpretations as unworkable and the gentry controversy as merely revealing the "shoddy basis of much traditional historical methodology," since it was based on the finding of specific examples in order to demonstrate a sociological proposition. The debate may have helped to establish a more empirical approach, but "in the last resort it is human judgment which determines its reliability."[42]

Describing himself as "an agnostic English liberal," Stone argued that inevitably there is a connection between social order and political structure. Power is the product of many forces interacting; the trick is to discover the precise mix at a given time. The mature scholar was a long way from his early confidence when he stated "so complex is the human personality that materialism and ideals . . . are constantly confused. . . . At bottom it seems to come down to whether he takes an optimistic or pessimistic view of human society: optimists stress ideas, pessimists material interests."[43]

Stone rejected a Marxist picture of seventeenth-century England and saw a political revolution, with abortive social consequences, growing from a multiplicity of causes. The weakness of the state in a changing economy amidst a growing population created instability. In the sixteenth century the church, crown, and aristocracy lost ground while the upper-middle and middle groups made gains that they desired to turn into greater political power. Puritanism gave the opposition an ideology and the sense of righteousness needed to challenge accepted authority. The monarchy could not stave off attacks because it lacked sufficient army, bureaucracy, and leadership. When the traditional order collapsed, religion was left as the best determinant of which side people chose. While few issues were resolved, Stone argued that basic questions were raised and that, despite its failure to change society in a Marxist sense, the English Revolution deserves a fundamental place in Western history.[44]

The Causes of the English Revolution closed a phase in Lawrence Stone's work; revolution, economic determinism, and even Tawney's century were left behind. Under the influence of French historiography, he was moving toward a greater concern with *mentalités* and the *longue durée*. In particular, Stone was looking at the family as the basic unit of society and as a key to understanding change. In a 1976 article on history and the social sciences Stone recapitulated the evolution of the profession of history.[45] His mood was less optimistic than might have been expected from a scholar at the height of his career and reputation, who was about to publish a voluminous study rooted in social science approaches and concerns. The author was disillusioned by what he perceived as the lack of historical awareness by social scientists who got bogged down in senseless jargon, meaningless questions, or elaborate models. Yet traditional history was often myopic, and only in recent decades had the divide between history and social science been partially bridged. In the 1930s the focus for historians had been economics; the 1950s had seen the rise of sociology, replaced by demography in the 1960s and anthropology in the 1970s. Such encounters had caused historians to examine their assumptions and define their terms with more scientific and quantitative exactitude. Yet Stone cautioned against the social sciences leading the unwary into simplistic, monocausal explanations of complex events. The result of the influences from the social sciences was "new history," analytic rather than narrative. The concern was no longer what and how, but why and what are the consequences? Much of the concentration was not on individuals but on groups and institutions. The masses, not just the elite, were of particular concern. Studies developed of mass culture or of family life. Stone conceded the usefulness of computers in such quantitative endeavors, but he warned that they could produce a spurious precision that oversimplified ambiguous situations. One might spend so much time preparing a data base and program that results would be delayed. He expressed a pessimistic fear that the machine might reduce the ability to produce critical thought.[46]

Stone conceded the previous forty years had been tremendously fruitful but "the future looks rather less promising." All pre–twentieth-century statistics are unreliable, yet elaborate edifices are erected on swampy foundations. Evidence that cannot be quantified is too often overlooked, bypassing the wide range of sources that are the best proof of an argument. The writer questioned the tendency to undertake huge statistical enterprises that never reach fruition or are simply useless. He also feared the split developing between quantifiers and traditional historians. No group was as confused as the psychohistorians who "threaten to get out of hand" by developing works "along dogmatically ahistorical lines, based on unproven . . . assumptions about human nature." Such systemized pictures of causation seemed misleading, not "scientific" as claimed. "It may be," Stone wrote, "that the time has come for the historian to reassert the importance of the concrete, the particular and the circumstantial."[47]

The assault on the "new history" was the opening shot of a later bombardment but seemed at the time an aberration, since the author himself was busy with an analysis of family relations in early modern England.[48] A 1975 article on "The Rise of the Nuclear Family" was a preview of another gigantic tome, this time sweeping across centuries to examine *The Family, Sex and Marriage in England, 1500-1800.*[49]

The book's influence has been so great that a decade after publication it is still being subjected to detailed scrutiny.[50] To Stone, the era he studied saw a shift from a society of "deference and patrimony" to one of "affective individualism," a change representing the most important alteration in *mentalité* in the last thousand years.[51]

In the course of more than seven hundred pages Stone sought to explain the movement from an open-lineage family with kinship loyalties to an emphasis on individual autonomy and privacy. Traditionally, marriage was rooted in material values of money and prestige. The family was "open-ended, low-keyed, unemotional, authoritarian," serving "certain essential political, economic, procreative and nurturant purposes." Stone believed the traditional family structure began to erode around 1530 and continued to lose power until 1700. The state, the church, and the nuclear family gained importance at the expense of kin, while patriarchal authority grew. A closer, more domesticated nuclear family came to the forefront based on "affective individualism." The home grew more private and was marked by more intensive affection, individual autonomy, and more personal privacy. While conceding that the pace of these changes varied from class to class, Stone was trying to develop a comprehensive theory of change.[52] Ten years after publication he was ready to concede that his arguments applied best to the upper strata of society, as some critics had suggested from the outset. The product of a short interval of intense examination of literary sources, *Family, Sex and Marriage* became a staple for the study of family history.[53]

Of particular interest was the writer's focus on attitudes rather than forms. Stone believed outward appearances altered less than attitudes, and hence demographically dominated studies had produced misleading results. His harsh picture of sixteenth-century life showed authoritarian parents fostering out their children—who were likely to die young—death everywhere, and medical care a positive menace. Personal relations lacked warmth, tolerance, or care. In one example of hyperbole Stone declared, "The Elizabethan village was a place filled with malice and hatred, its only unifying bond being the occasional episode of mass hysteria . . . in order to persecute the local witch." In the sixteenth and early seventeenth centuries he alleged "a majority of the individuals found it very difficult to establish close emotional ties to any other person."[54]

As the power of the state grew, Stone saw kinship ties weaken and the nuclear family emerge. The Reformation contributed to the development of the ideal of family love, as for many purposes the home replaced the church. True, Puritans prescribed a stern childhood, seeking to break the will of the child with beatings both at home and at school; but paradoxically, according to Stone, such physical punishment was a sign of a new concern for children, who were no longer viewed indifferently. The uncertainty and anxiety produced by the Reformation led to an authoritarian family and state. Only when religious tension declined, after the Civil War, could attitudes be relaxed, and a more sensual nuclear family emerge. Such shifts could, in part, be traced in new laws of inheritance that undermined parental authority.[55]

The eighteenth century emphasized the individual as unique, leading to a concern that marriage be based on affection. Love became an expectation that filtered from upper to lower classes. Relying heavily on literary evidence, Stone inadvertently wandered into the minefield of feminist and women's history. He believed that it was difficult to document the female perception of family life and that eighteenth-century radical feminists had little impact, except to retard change by frightening the few men who were aware of their writings. By linking female education with equality in the family, eighteenth-century feminists had destroyed hope for reform in the family. More education for middle-class women meant increased idleness, a state of affairs acceptable only in marriage. For nineteenth-century spinsters the results were disastrous.[56]

No portion of *Family, Sex and Marriage* attracted more virulent criticism than Stone's discussion of women. Eileen Spring argued that Stone had most of the evidence backwards. For her, the strict marriage settlement—making provision for unborn heirs and entailing estates—indicated an increase rather than a decrease in patriarchal authority. Spring argued that love had little to do with the decline of patriarchy for it "is a normal constituent of the human family." Love is not inconsistent with patriarchy nor with freedom and equality for women. "Patriarchy declines not with the growth of love but with the slow development of democratic and secular thinking." For Spring the radical feminists and their male allies undermined patriarchy. Arguing that love as a basis of attitudinal change was improbable, Eileen Spring lamented that "having at length discovered love, historians may be in some danger of being blinded by it."[57]

Lois Schwoerer attacked Stone's view as elitist and masculine with "his treatment of women in all social categories perfunctory." Women were only discussed as they related to men and "Stone's masculine perspective [distorted] his understanding of early modern family, sex and marriage." Stone was specifically criticized for his failure to note the work women did, and for his dismissal of early feminists. Schwoerer accused him of being blinded toward the poor and women by his elitist pretensions.[58]

Stone now concedes a neglect of the lower classes but is genuinely bemused by the feminist attack. Indeed, a careful reading of the book shows a keen awareness of exceptions that undermine portions of the generalizations. Stone still believes that feminist writers, however much they intended good, simply frightened men into a defensive position for much of the nineteenth century. It may be argued on Stone's behalf that the role of women was not his primary interest. He touched on it solely to illustrate the central theme of changing attitudes about, for example, children, personal hygiene, and sex. Sexual mores interested Stone because of a seventeenth-century pattern of relatively late marriage and emerging ideas of romantic love. A double standard in sexual matters was almost universal, especially in the permissive eighteenth century. Concern for children rose, however, and with it worry about masturbation, homosexuality, and pornography. Here Stone was at special pains to make clear class differences, as the upper classes were the most libertine in the eighteenth century. By 1810 the tide had turned, and the more repressive nineteenth-century mores were taking hold. The evidence for the lower orders was harder to find, but Stone concluded the Puritans in the seventeenth century and the Evangelicals after 1770 provided the main impetus for sexual repression.[59]

Stone contended that the members of the middle class had the greatest incentive to uphold traditional moral standards and were sexually the most inhibited because of their rigidly patriarchal view of society. The discussion of sexual attitudes helped lead Stone toward his conclusion that changes in attitudes were not a direct result of modernization. There were far too many chronological and class discrepancies to make a linear explanation plausible. Most of the changes, in his view, predated industrialization. Indeed, the nineteenth-century fear of a disintegrating society saw an attempt to restore traditional family values. Family life was marked by fluctuations that produced both positive and negative results. From his own observations Stone concluded that the permissive child rearing of the twentieth century "bred a large number of ill-disciplined and poorly socialized children," as had been true in the late eighteenth century. Affective individualism produced "unrealistic fantasy about romantic love . . . [with] exaggerated expectations of sexual and emotional satisfaction" and led to inevitable disappointment. The end result was women who put their jobs "before their duties as wives and mothers," damaging both marriage and children. Conversely, too intense parent-child relationships made it hard for adolescents to cut loose from parental strings.[60]

As if determined to prove his feminist critics correct in principle, if not in detail, Stone pronounced modern day-care little different from the nineteenth-century custom of dumping children into boarding schools, or the seventeenth-century practice of pushing them onto wet nurses. He asserted that the rapid changes of modern life made it increasingly difficult for parents to pass their values on to the next generation. Stone's book, produced in the 1970s, gave a pessimistic interpretation of the modern family without painting a false picture of a past golden age. Although unlikely to meet with feminist approval, Stone did try to emphasize the notion of family patterns constantly being restructured, so that affective individualism is no surer of long-term survival than is any other family model.[61]

The impact of *The Family, Sex and Marriage* can be seen from the articles cited and the wide use of the book in classrooms. Stone's critics were unhappy with some of his sources and the lack of quantifiability. Stone himself had become increasingly doubtful of the importance of statistical evidence and was ready to argue for a new approach. In an extremely controversial article that the author now sees as prophetic, Stone addressed the issue of the use of quantification and the need for a revival of what he called "narrative."[62]

For fifty years the trend of Marxist, *Annales,* and cliometric history had taken historians away from individual people in order to focus on their circumstances. Statistics had replaced the particular and the specific as a more "scientific" approach. In the process, cliometricians, Stone argued, produced methods that were secretive, incomprehensible, and unverifiable. The result was history that divorced intellectual and social developments in a fashion that did not reflect the reality of the past. The big picture got lost in trivial statistics. Sampling by hand, the author contended, was preferable, quicker and "just as reliable as running the whole universe through a machine." Quantification did not solve any major questions, because the evidence was much less sophisticated than the methodology. Economics and sociology with their statistical bias, Stone asserted, were losing their allure for historians who increasingly were looking to anthropology and posing questions about power, authority, leadership, and symbolism. But such an approach, he warned, has pitfalls of its own, for too much attention to a *mentalité* approach may lead to getting bogged down in minutiae, antiquarianism, and trivialization.[63]

Having swung a Luddite ax at most of the machinery of the modern historical profession, it is unsurprising that Stone found his article greeted with cries of outrage.[64] In the light of his own previous efforts, Stone was seen as a traitor to the good old cause of scientific history. However, the author believes that in the last decade his thesis has been proven everywhere except in the pages of the *Economic History Review*. Elsewhere the emphasis has been on the single event, or on political developments, taking into account economic and social factors.[65]

Stone's own essay on the "Results of the English Revolution," reflected the latter approach. Here he tried to take account of all factors in explaining why from 1621 to 1721 the English were "the most politically fickle and volatile people in the Western world." The multiple causes included the "sociopolitical problem of how to accommodate within the existing political system two new economically dynamic, and socially ambitious groups"—the squirearchy and the merchants. But ideas were also important, with the state caught between the dynamic faiths of Puritans and Catholics. The two issues combined after 1660 as merchants became dissenters and squires turned to Catholicism or a strong defense of the established church. Stone concluded that the basic division was best summed up as one between court and country. Country representatives wanted the government to be accountable to Parliament, with low taxes and a small bureaucracy. They also asserted the idea of inalienable individual rights.[66]

For Stone the Revolution succeeded in limiting the King's divine rights, making it impossible to tax without Parliament, and so giving merchants a permanent voice in governing the state. But the Revolution was a complex event with tangled causes that led to unintended consequences. The Irish situation worsened, while the traditional elite consolidated its hold on the English countryside. A fear of reform developed, and suspicion of the military took centuries to dissipate. Cynicism and secularization were the outgrowth of religious enthusiasm turned sour. On balance, Stone now felt compelled to believe that the Great Revolution had mainly negative results, leaving "the preexisting elite . . . more deeply entrenched in property and power." A fear of change leading to revolution was firmly rooted, blocking "reasonable reform to meet new conditions for over a century." The primary consequence of the English Revolution was "an immensely rich legacy of ideas" that reemerged during the American and French revolutions.[67]

If the article on English revolution was a summation of Stone's intellectual evolution since 1972, then his latest work constitutes a return to an earlier project. Even before researching *The Family, Sex and Marriage,* Stone and his wife had begun to study the hypothesis that the English elite was uniquely open to self-made men from the professions and trade. A long-held theory asserted that such openness had led to a willingness to change, leadership in modernization, political stability, and in time even economic decline. The authors' goal was to use computer technology to quantify the elite and see if in fact it had been open and changing. *An Open Elite?* logically fitted into the pattern of Stone's earlier endeavors by focusing on the upper social strata, using art history, and exploiting new technology. The new work was also inspired by the current condition of Britain's ruling class.[68]

To avoid the pitfalls of earlier works, Stone carefully defined the elite as those who had at least one country house and a substantial landed estate. The size of the house was the key denominator, and 1660–1880 was the epoch when the "country elite" had its greatest success. Stone argued that merchants did not rise nearly so consistently as did professionals, who by the eighteenth century had helped create the myth that the hierarchy was open.[69]

To prove or disprove the paradigm of the "aristocratic embrace," the authors examined three counties in three different parts of England. Backed by seventy-eight pages of tables, seven genealogies, photographs, and houseplans, the Stones dissected the changing, or unchanging, elite.[70] They found that established families held onto their property with the greatest tenacity, while new purchasers were more likely to sell. Relatively easy entry to the exalted echelons was available from 1540 to 1640, because of the Reformation, royal largesse, and corruption. Mobility was greatest from office (16th and 17th centuries), legal careers (18th century), overseas trade, brewing, India, banking (after the mid-18th century), and big business (19th century). Wealth alone was not enough, however, because a chasm continued to separate the business and country elites. Professionals were much more acceptable than businessmen, who seldom got to the top before 1880. Only in the Victorian era was there a significant separation of land and money. Prior to the nineteenth century, property was purchased by merchants as a safe investment. The Stones stressed that the downward mobility of younger sons was much more consistent than was any pattern of upward movement. They concluded that traditional perceptions of an easy exchange between land and money "are not borne out by the statistical facts."[71]

As an alternative model of mobility, *An Open Elite?* stressed the close tie between the professions and the land, particularly in the nineteenth century. The unique feature in England was not the degree of mobility "but the ease of cultural assimilation of the children of those relatively few who made the move into a higher social sphere." The Stones felt the rise of a new group to the landed elite was in many ways a myth. The lack of legal barriers had allowed the middling sort to link top and bottom; members of professions emulated their social superiors; and cultural mimicry made the values of the elite a model. The traditional ruling class "psychologically co-opted those below them." Public schools were particularly important in creating "an aristocratic bourgeoisie, not a bourgeois aristocracy." The landed elite, the merchants, and professionals shared a homogeneous outlook, held together by gentility and snobbery.[72]

Critics of the Stones's statistical soufflé emerged as fast as reviews could be printed.[73] One of the basic criticisms was directed at the Stones having concocted a straw man. Both Harold Perkin and the team of Eileen and David Spring stressed that the Stones based much of their argument on having found less mobility than was expected. Had the authors anticipated slower change, they might have reached an opposite conclusion: i.e., that the English elite was open. To declare the whole idea of an open elite dead on the basis of having higher expectations seemed an overstatement. Perkin, in particular, pointed out that virtually the entire sample used by the Stones was new to the elite in an earlier generation. The only legitimate conclusion must be that the pace of social change is largely in the eyes of the beholder.

The Springs' attack went beyond the interpretation of the basic statistical argument. In the second portion of their review article they focused on a much more technical issue, the Stones's interpretation of the "strict settlement" as a means to preserve aristocratic property. Stone was accused of having confused "common law principle and settlement practice, not at all the same thing." The Springs argued that the whole system was patriarchal and reduced female inheritance to as low a rate as possible; "probably nowhere in Europe did daughters and younger children inherit so little." They narrowed in on the strict settlement as an issue that haunted all of Stone's major works, and one that the author had never fully grasped.[74]

In these critiques can be seen the achievement and the problems not only of *An Open Elite?* but also of the corpus of Stone's work. As before, Lawrence Stone had undertaken a gargantuan task, one that even critics admit had not been attempted for any other European society. His labor had been so prodigious that it was impossible to assault the information directly because no one else living had sufficient mastery of the sources and data to undertake the task. Stone had also jumped the normal chronological boundaries of historical inquiry, thereby leaving himself vulnerable to the thrusts of specialists in each period encompassed. Critics, therefore, dispute his interpretation of the data on points where he is vulnerable to specialists because he has painted on so broad a canvas.

An Open Elite? has not fully resolved the issue of what constitutes an open versus a closed elite. Speed of change is such a relative question that the perspective of the observer matters more than statistics.[75] The Stones have put forward a "myth" that few recent historians embrace. However, they do provide an unequaled fund of statistical knowledge based on massive research, a unique use of sources, and an enterprising use of modern technology. Few, if any, other writers are capable of taking such a jumble of data from a multiplicity of sources and turning it into a coherent and readable argument. That such a complex work has stimulated dispute is the greatest compliment to the fertile imagination and hard work of the authors.

While some will argue over Stone's methods and conclusions, others will be puzzled over the author's assessment of the future direction of historical inquiry. Although *An Open Elite?* is based on computer analysis of statistics, Stone questioned the efficacy of computer-based research, as he had done in earlier studies.[76] Yet, even while displaying a growing skepticism about new technology, Stone has not been deterred from undertaking another titanic project—examining the family life of the lower orders—as a response to those who have questioned his exclusive focus on the ruling class. Whether the reader is moved to follow the admonition or the example of the writer will be a matter of individual choice.

For two-score years Lawrence Stone has reflected the changing mood of historical fashion and the evolving society around him. During that time Stone has embraced and then rejected a variety of approaches and conclusions. As shown in *An Open Elite?*, his work has been marked by a fertile imagination, prodigious labor, and powerful prose. By his own admission, he has eschewed the safety of a single narrow field for the more dangerous course of skipping from topic to topic and more recently dancing across centuries. In the process he has made errors that a more narrowly confined vision would have avoided.[77] More cautious academics have seized on these transgressions, multiplied as they have been by Stone's propensity to bring vast projects to rapid fruition.

It is the temerity, however, to leap normal barriers and produce large-scale studies that has made Stone a giant of his profession. The results may have been over-generalized; sweeping schemata provide easy targets for sharpshooters with narrowly focused sights. But willingness to embrace critics, reexamine hypotheses, change his mind, and accept new methods have kept Lawrence Stone at the forefront of Clio's legions. It is with anticipation that we ask: "What will Lawrence Stone be up to next?"

NOTES

I would like to thank Professor Lawrence Stone for providing a typescript of "A Life of Learning," the Charles Homer Haskins lecture presented to the American Council of Learned Societies in the spring of 1985. It was afterward published in the *ACLS Newsletter* (Winter-Spring, 1985):3–22. Professor Stone was also kind enough to provide a complete bibliography and to grant an interview at Princeton during the spring of 1985.

1. J. H. Hexter, "Lawrence Stone and the English Aristocracy," in his *On Historians: Reappraisals of Some of the Makers of Modern History* (Cambridge, Mass., 1979), 162–71. Reprinted from *Journal of British Studies* 8(1968):22–78.

2. Robert Graves, *Goodbye to All That,* pb. ed. (New York, 1957). Lawrence Stone, interview with author, Princeton, spring 1985.

3. Lawrence Stone, "A Life of Learning," *ACLS Newsletter* (1985):4–5; Stone interview.

4. Stone, "Life of Learning," 7–8.

5. Lawrence Stone, "The Armada Campaign of 1588," *History* 29(1944):120–43.

6. Lawrence Stone, "State Control in Sixteenth Century England," *Economic History Review,* o.s., 17(1947):103–20. Reprinted in *Essays in American Colonial History,* ed. Paul Goodman (New York, 1967), 12–32.

7. Lawrence Stone, "The Anatomy of the Elizabethan Aristocracy," *Economic History Review,* o.s., 18(1948):1.

8. Lawrence Stone, "The Elizabethan Aristocracy: An Anatomy Anatomized," *Economic History Review,* 2d ser., 3(1951):279–98.

9. Lawrence Stone, "The Elizabethan Aristocracy—a Restatement," *Economic History Review,* 2d ser., 4(1952):302–21. Stone now sees his encounter with Trevor-Roper as having taught him "that before plunging into a public archive, it is first essential to discover just why and how the records were kept and what they signified to the clerks who made the entries." "Life of Learning," 10.

10. Stone's "An Elizabethan Coalmine," *Economic History Review,* 2d ser., 3(1950):97–106 was an example of traditional economic history.

11. Stone, "Life of Learning," 10; Stone interview.

12. Lawrence Stone, *Sculpture in Britain: The Middle Ages* (Harmondsworth, 1955), 2, 5, 23, 178, 211.

13. See Lawrence Stone, "The Building of Hatfield House," *Archaeological Journal* 112(1955):100–28; "Inigo Jones and the New Exchange," *Archaeological Journal* 114(1957):106–21; "Cole Green Park, Hertfordshire," in *The Country Seat: Studies in the History of the British Country House,* ed. Howard Colvin and John Harris (London, 1970), 75–80; "The Residential Development of the West End of London in the Seventeenth Century" in *After the Reformation: Essays in Honor of J. H. Hexter,* ed. Barbara C. Malament (Philadelphia, 1980), 167–212. See also "Notes on British Painting From Archives," *Burlington Magazine* (1954); "Anglo Saxon Art in Wiltshire" in *Victoria County History of Wiltshire* (1955); "The Verney Tombs of Middle Claydon," *Records of Buckinghamshire* 16(1955):67–82; "An Early Seventeenth Century Wallpaper," *Oxonionsia* (1957); *An Open Elite? England, 1540–1880* (Oxford, 1984), written in collaboration with Jeanne Fawtier Stone.

14. Lawrence Stone, *An Elizabethan: Sir Horatio Palavicino* (Oxford, 1956), 40–45, 182–230, 238, 288, Chap. 3.

15. Lawrence Stone, *The Crisis of the Aristocracy, 1558–1640* (Oxford, 1965).

16. See Mark Silk, "The Hot History Department: Princeton's Influential Faculty," *New York Times Magazine,* 19 Apr. 1987, 42–62.

17. Lawrence Stone, "The Inflation of Honours 1558–1641," *Past and Present* 14(1948):45–70.

18. Ibid., 60–61.

19. Stone called this concept Tawney's Law: "The greater the wealth and the more even its distribution in a given society the emptier become the titles of personal distinction, but the more they multiply and are striven for." *Crisis of the Aristocracy,* 128.

20. Lawrence Stone, "Marriage among the Nobility in the 16th and 17th Centuries," *Comparative Studies in Society and History* 3(1960–1961):182–206; "The Educational Revolution in England, 1540–1640," *Past and Present* 23(1964):41–80; "The Fruits of Office: The Case of Robert Cecil, First Earl of Salisbury, 1596–1612," in *Essays in the Economic and Social History of Tudor and Stuart England in Honour of R. H. Tawney,* ed. F. J. Fisher (Cambridge, 1961), 89–116.

21. Stone, *Crisis of the Aristocracy,* 3–15.

22. Ibid., 15–17, 385–504.

23. Ibid., 747–53.

24. David Underdown, "New Ways and Old in Early Stuart History" in *Recent Views on British History,* ed. Richard Schlatter (New Brunswick, 1984), 108.

25. D. C. Coleman, "The 'Gentry' Controversy and the Aristocracy in Crisis, 1558–1641," *History* 51(1966):169, 174, 175, 178.

26. Hexter, "Stone and the English Aristocracy," 152, 162–64, 167, 171, 187–89, 209–15, 223–24; idem, *Reappraisals in History: New Views on History and Society in*

Early Modern Europe, p.b. ed. (New York, 1963), 117–62; Davis Bitton, *The French Nobility in Crisis, 1560–1640* (Stanford, 1969).

27. Lawrence Stone, *Family and Fortune: Studies in Aristocratic Finance in the Sixteenth and Seventeenth Century* (Oxford, 1973), 18, 32, 41, 57, 58, 119, 160. Some of the materials on the Cecils had appeared in Stone, "Fruits of Office."

28. Lawrence Stone, "Social Mobility in England, 1500–1700," *Past and Present* 33(1966):16–55.

29. Ibid., 16–17, 19–22, 32–37.

30. Ibid., 40–48.

31. Ibid., 48–51.

32. Stone, "Life of Learning," 19.

33. Lawrence Stone, "The Educational Revolution in England, 1540–1640," *Past and Present* 28(1964):41–80.

34. Ibid., 41, 67, 69, 73, 77–80.

35. Lawrence Stone and Marius B. Jansen, "Education and Modernization in Japan and England," *Comparative Studies in Society and History* 9(1966–1967):208–32.

36. Lawrence Stone, "Literacy and Education in England, 1640–1900," *Past and Present* (1969):69–139.

37. Ibid., 71–75, 95, 125.

38. "The Size and Composition of the Oxford Student Body, 1580–1910," in Lawrence Stone ed., *The University in Society,* vol. 1, *Oxford and Cambridge from the 14th to the Early 19th Century* (Princeton, 1974), 3–110.

39. Ibid., 3–5, 9, 16–25, 37–57, 65–69, 75.

40. Lawrence Stone, *The Past and the Present* (London, 1981), 211–21. An expanded edition, *The Past and the Present Revisited,* was published in 1987 with somewhat altered pagination. For a recent exception see Lawrence Stone, "Social Control and Intellectual Excellence: Oxbridge and Edinburgh: 1560–1983," in *University Society and the Future,* ed. N. T. Philipson (Edinburgh, 1983), 3–28.

41. Lawrence Stone, *The Causes of the English Revolution, 1529–1642* (New York, 1972). Earlier versions of the three sections appeared as essays: "Theories of Revolution," in *World Politics* 13(1966):159–76; "The Social Origins" in *Social Change and Revolution in England, 1540–1640* (London, 1965); and "The English Revolution" in *Preconditions of Revolution in Early Modern Europe,* ed. R. Forster and J. P. Greene (Baltimore, 1970), 55–108. For a review and Stone's reply see H. G. Koenigsberger and L. Stone, "Early Modern Revolutions: An Exchange," *Journal of Modern History* 46(1974):99–110.

42. Stone, *Causes,* xii, 32.

43. Ibid., 36, 39–40.

44. Ibid., 57, 66–76, 78–96, 98–100, 116–43, 147. For a recent resurrection of these themes see Lawrence Stone, "The Bourgeois Revolution of Seventeenth-Century England Revisited," *Past and Present* (1985):44–54.

45. Lawrence Stone, "History and the Social Sciences in the Twentieth Century," in *The Future of History,* ed. C. Delzell (Nashville, 1976). Some similar issues had been discussed in "Prosopography," in *Historical Studies Today,* ed. Felix Gilbert and Stephen Graubard (New York, 1971), 107–40. The articles were reprinted in Stone, *Past and Present,* 3–44, 45–73.

46. Stone, "History and Social Sciences," 8, 14–19, 21–26, 28–30.

47. Ibid., 26, 30–38, 40–43. Stone cited the case of one study that revealed the

geographical incidence of hernias in nineteenth century France as the sort of nonsense currently being produced by computerized historians (38).

48. Lawrence Stone, "The Revival of Narrative: Reflections on a New Old History," *Past and Present* 85(1979):3-24. Reprinted in Stone, *Past and Present*, 74-99.

49. Lawrence Stone, "The Rise of the Nuclear Family in Early Modern Europe" in *The Family in History*, ed. Charles E. Rosenberg (Philadelphia, 1975), 13-57; *The Family, Sex and Marriage in England, 1500-1800* (New York, 1977).

50. See, for example, Kathleen Davies, "Continuity and Change in Literary Advice on Marriage," in *Marriage and Society: Studies in the Social History of Marriage*, ed. R. B. Outhwaite (New York, 1981), 55-80; Lois Schwoerer, "Seventeenth-Century English Women: Engraved in Stone?", *Albion* 16(1984):389-403; Eileen Spring, "Law and the Theory of the Affective Family," *Albion* 16(1984):1-20.

51. Stone, *Family, Sex and Marriage*, 4.

52. Ibid., 4-7, 8.

53. Stone, Interview; Schwoerer, "Seventeenth-Century Women."

54. Stone, *Family, Sex and Marriage*, 23-27, 63-98, 99.

55. Ibid., 132-41, 161-74, 217-22, 238-44. For a contrasting view see Spring, "Law and Theory."

56. Stone, *Family, Sex and Marriage*, 253-72, 281-86, 306-58.

57. Spring, "Law and Theory," 12, 13, 19-20. For a detailed discussion of the strict settlement, see Ralph A. Houlbrooke, *The English Family 1450-1700* (London, 1984), Chap. 9.

58. Schwoerer, "Seventeenth-Century Women," 390-91, 400.

59. Stone interview; *Family, Sex and Marriage*, 488-90, 516-33, 545, 623.

60. Stone, *Family, Sex and Marriage*, 637, 648, 658-78, 684, 685.

61. Ibid., 686-87.

62. See Stone, "Revival of Narrative," and "Interpersonal Violence in English Society, 1300-1980," *Past and Present* 101(1983):22-33.

63. Stone, "Revival of Narrative," 3-5, 8-13, 15-23.

64. For two opposing critiques see: Philip Abrams, "History, Sociology, Historical Sociology," *Past and Present* 87(1980):3-16; and E. J. Hobsbawm, "The Revival of Narrative: Some Comments," *Past and Present* 86(1980):3-8.

65. See, for example, Robert Darnton, *The Great Cat Massacre: and Other Episodes in French Cultural History*, p.b. ed. (New York, 1985); Natalie Zemon Davis, *The Return of Martin Guerre* (Cambridge, Mass., 1983); Carlo Ginsburg, *The Cheese and the Worm: The Cosmos of a Sixteenth Century Miller*, p.b. ed. (New York, 1982). To see how Stone's own view shifted see Koenigsberger and Stone, "Early Modern Revolutions," n.58.

66. Lawrence Stone, "The Results of the English Revolutions of the Seventeenth Century," in *The British Revolutions: 1641, 1688, 1776*, ed. J. G. A. Pocock (Princeton, 1980), 23-108. See especially 24, 26-29, 30, 31, 32-37.

67. Ibid., 59-61.

68. Lawrence Stone and Jeanne Fawtier Stone, *An Open Elite? England 1540-1880* (Oxford, 1984); Stone, "Life of Learning," 21.

69. Stones, *Open Elite*, 12-14, 23.

70. The Stones examined 2,296 owners of 362 houses over 340 years. Note that houses had replaced manors as the quantifiable measuring stick.

71. Stones, *Open Elite*, 180, 182-83, 197, 207, 218, 235, 288.

72. Ibid., 249, 292, 407, 411, 423-24.

73. See Harold Perkin, "An Open Elite," *Journal of British Studies* 24(1985):496–500; Eileen Spring and David Spring, "The English Landed Elite, 1540–1879: A Review," *Albion* 17(1985):149–66. In the same issue of *Albion,* Stone replied with "Spring Back," 167–80. Further comments from both sides appeared as "Communications" in *Albion* 17(1985):393–96.

74. Springs, "English Landed Elite," 156–65.

75. Stone, "Spring Back," 167.

76. Stones, *Open Elite,* 458. See also Stone, "History and Social Sciences" and "Revival of Narrative."

77. Stone, "Life of Learning," 20.

J. H. Plumb
and the Whig Tradition

ROBERT C. BRADDOCK

When Professor John Harold Plumb retired from his chair in modern English history at Cambridge University in 1973, friends and colleagues toasted him as the "most famous living English historian."[1] It was a fitting tribute for the occasion, stemming from Plumb's frequent television appearances and his best-selling popular histories that have made him more famous outside academic circles than other historians in this collection. Plumb's reputation rests on more than public recognition, of course. In a series of essays, biographies, texts, and reviews he has made such a mark on the early modern period that the half century of his special interest, 1675–1725, has been labeled "Plumb's territory," confidently placed between "Tawney's century" and "Namier's decades."[2]

J. H. Plumb was born in Leicester in 1911, the third son of a Tory, nonconformist shoe manufacturer, and was educated at Alderman Newton's school. Although he scored highly on the first round of the St. John's Scholarship Examination, he did not get the scholarship that was necessary for him to attend Cambridge, so he attended Leicester University instead. Plumb has since mused that his failure to win a scholarship can be placed to his not being suitably attired for the interview or to his brash preoccupation with theories not in vogue at the rather staid Cambridge of the late 1920s. Perhaps the future student of the Whig oligarchy had not learned to be suitably deferential. At Leicester, he earned the university's first First in history, and this remarkable achievement helped him win the place at Cambridge denied earlier. Except for the war years spent at the Foreign Office, he has remained there. The boy from the obscure grammar school who had not met Cambridge's standards had arrived. From 1946 to his retirement, Plumb moved steadily from lecturer to professor of modern English history (1966–1974) and to master of Christ's College (1978–1982) and a knighthood (1982).[3]

Following his brilliant undergraduate career, Plumb arrived at Cambridge to study under G. M. Trevelyan, who had recently returned to academic life as Regius Professor of Modern History after several decades of writing the biographical and popular histories for which he had become celebrated. When Plumb arrived, Trevelyan was hard at work on his most scholarly work, *England under Queen Anne,* and he encouraged his new—and as it turned out, only—research student to select the parliaments of William III for his Ph.D. thesis subject.[4] It was a conventional enough topic, one which helped shape his later research and eventually led Plumb into conflict with one of Trevelyan's severest critics, Sir Lewis Namier.

Plumb did not set out to attack Namier's interpretation of the eighteenth-century political world straightaway. Indeed Namier's view that the first two Georges had not been mere puppets of the Whig oligarchy coincided with his own view of the Georgian monarchy, but Plumb's view of the electoral process differed greatly from that of Namier and his disciples, and in retrospect it is obvious a clash was inevitable. After completing his degree in 1936, and producing a short history of his father's shoemaking firm,[5] Plumb published an account of some un-Namierlike elections following the Glorious Revolution.[6] Whatever the character of the first election of the reign of George III, Plumb showed that the first election of William III's reign was accompanied by sharp divisions along party lines. Politicians held strong beliefs on the nature of the constitution, even if they did enjoy the spoils of victory as Namier had suggested. Plumb's study had taken him into the constituencies where the battles were fought, away from the drawing rooms of the power brokers familiar to Namier, and thus Plumb described a different political scene.

Having established himself in the profession, Plumb expanded his field of enquiry to the life of Sir Robert Walpole. His statement that "my interest in Sir Robert Walpole was first roused by sitting beneath his picture, which hangs over the High Table at King's, during many silent dinners as a junior fellow" has been disputed by friends who cannot imagine his ever being silent,[7] but it was a logical choice for a student of Trevelyan: it would complement his mentor's study of Queen Anne; it would deal with major political issues; and it would show how personality influenced the course of history.

Plumb's two volumes on Walpole appeared in 1956 and 1960;[8] a third was promised but has not appeared and now can hardly be expected. Times were ripe for a reappraisal of Britain's first prime minister. Namier's works had made it difficult to continue to venerate Walpole as the inventor of the British constitution—as the nineteenth century understood it—and Archdeacon William Coxe's study[9] was not readily available to students. Moreover, Plumb had access to papers denied to Coxe as well as a broader view of his subject. Finally, Coxe and the Victorians had had difficulty understanding and explaining what they took to be corruption run rampant. The best they could do was to praise with faint damns, an attitude no longer satisfying to a generation that had a more skeptical view of human nature.

Plumb erased both the caricature of the Victorians and the uncritical praise of Coxe; instead he depicted a Walpole beset by very real problems. In contrast to Coxe, Plumb demonstrated that Walpole's task was never easy. The Hanoverian kings were never ciphers led by the brilliant politician, an interpretation that had been central to the Whig legend. They expected to be consulted and to make the critical decisions. There was always some faction to be contended with; even the transition from George I to George II was not a foregone conclusion. Plumb came to see that the Jacobites were no idle threat that Walpole could trot out to justify harsh measures, and later research has established that if Walpole at times appeared to be obsessed with Jacobitism, his fears were well grounded.[10]

The question of corruption is another matter. The Victorians had been delighted to be shocked by the bribery that they detected everywhere under the early Hanoverians, and they had resorted to a double standard to defend the man they thought had created the nineteenth-century constitution. Macaulay's conclusion that "Walpole governed by corruption because in his time it was impossible to govern otherwise"[11] served for many who were willing to let the ends justify the means. When pressed, Plumb also excused his hero by observing that "these sharp practices by our standards were legitimate enough by the standards of Walpole's day."[12] The total effect of his study, however, was to show that corruption was not so extensive as the Victorians suspected. When men are deeply committed to causes, they are less likely to be the slaves of their purses.

Perhaps Plumb's most significant reappraisal of his subject concerns Walpole's reputation as a financial wizard. Coxe's Walpole stood out as a paragon of economic wisdom coupled with political virtue during the South Sea Bubble crisis. He alone had the foresight to predict the evils that were soon to come and was appropriately brought to power on a crest of great public acclaim. Coxe's Walpole simply assumed office and got the job done. The Victorians might have challenged Walpole's lack of vindictiveness, but they did not question his financial acumen. Mostly they had not been interested. They preferred to tackle the large constitutional issues presented by the seventeenth century rather than to clear up the financial puzzles provided by the eighteenth.

Plumb was not content with Coxe's explanation, and he had the advantage of having seen the correspondence that passed between Walpole and his financial advisor, Robert Jacombe, during the fateful summer of 1720. These letters reveal several interesting facts. First of all, they show that the famous plan Walpole put forward to solve the crisis was Jacombe's, not his own. But, as Plumb pointed out, it scarcely matters; for as Coxe should have known, the plan was never put into effect. Time, not Walpole's genius, was to be the great healer.

Even more startling was Plumb's revelation that so far from foreseeing the crash, Walpole had had no sense of impending disaster. He had bought South Sea stock no less eagerly than had the rest of the gullible public. Only a pressing need for ready cash led him to be temporarily unencumbered with the tainted stock at the moment the bubble burst. Indeed, Plumb discovered that Walpole had instructed Jacombe to purchase more South Sea stock as soon as possible, but fortunately his letter was delayed in the post; by the time it arrived, Jacombe felt justified in ignoring it. Blind luck, rather than shrewd judgment, carried the day.

Plumb's reassessment of Sir Robert's handling of his personal finances also deflated Walpole's reputation as a financial genius. Although he confessed that it was impossible to determine the sources of Walpole's vast personal wealth, Plumb surmised that some came from manipulation of funds that passed through his hands; some, no doubt, came from what the Victorians would have considered bribes; and much came from careful up-to-date estate management. Probably not much of Walpole's wealth came from his supposed mastery of the stock market. Sir Robert apparently remained a neophyte in such matters. It was land and office that he understood and could exploit best.

Plumb also showed that, once safely in office, Walpole proved to be less of a financial wizard than his legend assumed. The prosperity of the Augustan Age did not rest on his reducing taxes. True, he did ease the land tax, but this reduction was a political gesture to placate supporters and dampen the appeal of the Jacobites, not a measure to stimulate the economy. By switching to indirect taxes, he merely shifted the tax burden to the middling and poorer sort, groups that had been denied the franchise. In fact, a recent study has shown that whatever prosperity early Georgian England enjoyed was not created by lower taxes. Taxes were much higher in Britain than in France.[13]

If Plumb's Walpole was not Coxe's financial genius, neither was he Coxe's popular leader. Walpole was the "skreenmaster general," the most hated man in England. Sympathetic to Namier on this point, Plumb showed how Walpole's unsurpassed knowledge of political reality, careful cultivation of the Crown for support, and sheer good luck had brought him success.

Reviewers pointed out that the second volume of *Walpole* was not as strong as the first. Perhaps the sources were not so rich, perhaps the story was not so dramatic, and perhaps Plumb had already said what he had to say about Walpole's character, and subsequent details would not change the picture very much.[14] Other critics, most notably E. P. Thompson, chided Plumb for being out of sympathy with the common man. If he had studied Walpole's policies from the standpoint of the people, the story might have been one of a "reign of terror" rather than Augustan calm.[15]

Thompson's study of the Waltham Black Act is useful because it reveals another side of the Walpole years. Certainly he was out of sympathy with the people. But if the Black Act protected property rather than the liberties of the unenfranchised, it was because Walpole still thought the Jacobite threat—that Thompson denied—to be a very real possibility. Walpole was, as he confessed: "no saint, no Spartan, no reformer." Plumb's third volume, if it appears, will have to confront the issue of Walpole and the people head-on. In the 1730s the excise crisis and the turnpike and customs riots assumed national dimensions. Plumb's account of Walpole's handling of these events would add another dimension to understanding the man and his times.

In writing his volumes on Walpole, Plumb illuminated many aspects of the early Hanoverian political scene, but his method of doing so was, like Trevelyan's, essentially old-fashioned. Despite glimpses into Walpole's wardrobe, his wine cellar, and—more rarely—his domestic arrangements with his wife and mistress, Plumb wrote a political life, not a personal one. Some historians, like his colleague Sir Geoffrey Elton, would say that that is the way it should be, but modern social historians demand more. Like Thompson, they want to know how Sir Robert's tenants felt about being evicted to improve the view from Houghton and whether the great man ever bothered to ask.

Plumb's study of Walpole was also old-fashioned simply because it was a biography, and modern historiography has tended to focus on problems rather than on the lives of individuals. Plumb was later to lament that academic historians have abandoned biographies to the popular writers.[16] He attributed this shift to their not wishing to run risks, but considering historians' willingness to debate the role of the gentry or the Industrial Revolution, there is obviously more to such reluctance than fear of exposing themselves to attack. The basic issue is: how much does the individual affect the process of historical change, and how does the historian demonstrate that influence? Because he thought that the lives of individuals and details of their hopes and fears remained the stuff of history, Plumb was forced to come to grips with the colossus of eighteenth-century historiography, Sir Lewis Namier.

Namier published *The Structure of Politics at the Accession of George III* in 1929 and *England in the Age of the American Revolution* in 1930, but his views were not embraced for some time by the academic world or the general public. The former did not accept either his method or his conclusions; the latter simply found his work unreadable. But by the time Plumb published his first volume on Walpole this had changed. Namier's views had become orthodox, and his conclusions for the 1760s were being pushed chronologically forward and backward. The result was that all eighteenth-century politicians were perceived as self-serving, petty men, not the appropriate subject of multivolume biographies.[17]

On several occasions, Plumb expressed genuine admiration for Namier's work, but he was also quick to point out its limitations.[18] He declared Namier's study of the Parliament of 1761 to be "exact, patient, tiresome and boring," in short the reverse of what Trevelyan had been accused. More serious was Plumb's claim that Namier's obsession with minutiae could lead him to "get every detail correct, indeed write nothing false, yet by exclusion create a misinterpretation of an age as misleading as the one he was trying to replace." Individual motivation is not everything, Plumb insisted. To say that a particular member voted for a certain measure because he hoped for office does not deny the validity of that measure, nor should it besmirch the motives of others who voted for it.

Namier never took his studies beyond the first decades of the reign of George III and at one time doubted whether the findings would be the same if he had. But by 1952, he had changed his mind and boldly asserted that there probably had been no true political parties during the reign of Queen Anne.[19] A few years later Robert Walcott carried out the research and concluded that Namier's prediction was right. Plumb attacked Walcott's book in the *English Historical Review,* but he did not mount a full-scale assault on the Namier school for a decade. The occasion was his Ford lectures of 1965–1966, "The Growth of Political Stability in England 1675–1725."[20]

Plumb had never had doubts about the existence of parties in the late seventeenth and early eighteenth centuries. In his studies of William III, his life of Walpole, and his survey on the eighteenth century, parties had played a significant part in the story. In "The Growth of the Electorate in England from 1600–1715" Plumb made the point clearer: the larger electorate and the greater number of contested elections indicated the vitality of parties that might not be discernible to a historian using Namier's narrow focus and methods.[21] When he was done, Walcott's position and, by extension, Namier's was no longer tenable, and in the next few years several specialized studies were published overwhelmingly confirming Plumb's conclusion.[22]

The most remarkable aspect of the Ford lectures was not the rediscovery of parties—for Plumb it was hardly a rediscovery—but the general theme of the lectures: stability is no more normal than revolution and therefore cannot be assumed. Stability was a new concept to explain the half-century after the Glorious Revolution.

The predictable hero of the creation of stability was Sir Robert Walpole, and although some of the material Plumb presented was familiar, the way he put it together led to a compelling conclusion. The large electorate and frequency of elections had encouraged party battles in the constituencies, and these, in turn, promoted the chronic instability of Anne's reign. Naturally, Plumb concluded, those who gained the upper hand would try to maintain it. How the victors did so is now familiar: passage of the Septennial Act, use of patronage to subjugate Parliament to the Crown, and the limitation of some of the independence of the country gentlemen. Had the sides been more even after 1715, or had the Whigs been less relentless, the instability might have gone on. Thus what some had seen as the source of corruption was actually a great benefit to the nation.

Plumb took his story further. Stability, he asserted, was also the product of the growth of the executive and of the decline of the cabinet. It had long been known that the size of government grew in the eighteenth century. This growth had usually been seen as a symptom of the increase of corruption—the more places, the more men who could be rewarded. It is now clear that the number of court posts that were truly political sinecures actually declined.[23] What caused the increase in government was not a devious plan of Walpole's but the wars against Louis XIV. These wars required an ever larger army and navy, and larger armed forces required more officials to collect taxes and to procure supplies. No wonder the exciseman became the symbol of a hated government. There were more excisemen than ever, and as their demands kept going up the central government touched the people's lives as never before.[24]

The greater the number of offices, of course, the greater the opportunity for corruption, and Walpole knew better than anyone how to use power. The man who prosecuted editors and closed the theaters to silence his critics was quick to take advantage of the situation, but, Plumb concluded, Walpole had not created the jobs to reward his supporters; he merely exploited a golden opportunity.

Curiously, the issue of corruption had not been a problem for the Namierites. Their theory envisioned a weak central government kept in check by independent landed classes. From this perspective there was little room for corruption to operate. Walpole's use of patronage, which had been such an embarrassment to the great Whig historians, Plumb argued, should be seen as a creative response to a genuine problem. He concluded his lecture by defending corruption as a positive good. By using all the resources at his disposal, Walpole was able to end the struggle for power that had produced the instability. In 1720, for example, rather than rescue the Whigs, he could have led the opposition and toppled the government and possibly the monarchy, but he chose not to. As a reward for saving the Whigs and the Crown, he gained control over patronage, built the "Robinocracy" and became the first prime minister. "Patronage," Plumb concluded, "has been, and is, an essential feature of the British structure of power, no matter how varied the costume it may wear. In the eighteenth century it scarcely bothered to wear a fig-leaf. It was naked and quite unashamed."[25]

Plumb's appreciation of the creation of stability was pragmatic. Patronage kept the constituencies in line, and the Septennial Act put off the periods of potential conflict. What, he asked, would have happened had there been an election in the midst of the South Sea crisis? Nowhere is this theme so clear as in Walpole's handling of the cabinet. For the great nineteenth-century scholars, Walpole had been the father of the constitution, which to them meant government by a cabinet responsible to Parliament. Ironically, Plumb showed that rather than create cabinet government, Sir Robert had done his best to destroy it. The issue was not George I's supposed inability to communicate with his ministers; it was the cabinet's unmanageable size. By George's reign the cabinet had grown large and cumbersome, and as Plumb observed, numbers "bred faction not unity." Walpole accordingly called meetings of the formal cabinet as little as possible, working instead through a very small, informal group of ministers. The new arrangement left no room for opposition; those who disagreed with the great man were ruthlessly weeded out. In this, as in everything he did, Walpole strove to make the world safe for Whigs.

At bottom, Plumb's attack on Walcott and the Namier school was more than an attack on their conclusions about the existence of parties and the importance of ideology in the early eighteenth century. It was also an attack on their method. If they wished to study "English Politics in the Early Eighteenth Century," he pointed out, they had to go beyond the "House of Commons in 1701–1702." And because ideology mattered, it was necessary to examine what was going on in the constituencies as well as to study the activities of the elite. In "Political Man" Plumb made clear what he meant.[26] There were two political nations in the world outside Westminster. The one that voted was vitally concerned with issues of the day. It controlled Parliament. The other was admittedly more amorphous, and, having no vote, it could express itself only sporadically. But the voters and politicians always had to heed the warnings of the disenfranchised. Politics, Plumb concluded, was never a matter merely for the politicians. The trouble with the Namier school was that it had failed to study the world outside Parliament.

At the same time that *Political Stability* dished the Namierites, it provided a stout defense of traditional history. Not only did Plumb stress the role of personality—the stability that had come almost overnight was the work of one man—but also political history, a field coming increasingly under attack. But while Plumb was busy laying the ghost of Namier, a more formidable attack on his interpretation of the eighteenth century was being launched from across the Channel. The *Annales* school of historians did not aim specifically at Plumb, but their long-range historical sweep precluded a study so narrow as Georgian England, let alone Plumb's half-century. They undermined the philosophical base from which Plumb and most of his contemporaries wrote.

For one thing, the *Annales* school rejected the geographic limitations and periodization of traditional history. To them the stuff of history was revealed only over long ranges of time and space. For another, the *Annales* historians tended to reject political history altogether; political events became curious trivia rather than the legitimate focus of historical study. Not surprisingly, the only Walpole to appear in the pages of Fernand Braudel's three volumes covering the early modern period is Horace, not Sir Robert; and the only reference to the South Sea Bubble is to be found not in an analysis of the Whig triumph, but in a discussion of the financial problems of British merchants in India who were left temporarily short of cash.[27]

Reviewers have been quick to point out the errors in detail that Braudel and others who write with such broad scope have made. Undoubtedly Plumb also took delight in pointing out that in one of his books Braudel had got the builder of Houghton wrong.[28] But unlike some of his colleagues, Plumb realized that the new social history had much to offer and urged them not to reject it out of hand. "Social history, in the fullest and deepest sense of the term, is now a field of study of incomparable richness and the one in which the greatest discoveries will be made in this generation."[29]

As befitted a student of Trevelyan, Plumb had never been philosophically opposed to social history. Both of his volumes on Walpole, for example, begin with descriptions of Walpole's world that are excellent introductions to the society of the period. In order to give the reader a broader appreciation for the man, he presented details of Walpole's eating, drinking, and sartorial habits. Plumb did not merely throw in such tidbits to enliven his story; like the great man's fondness for off-color jokes, they were a part of the story. Such details added to the sense of the past that he and Trevelyan both thought essential.[30]

The staggering sums of Sir Robert's wine bill, like the pictures he hung on his wall were, however, aspects of an old-fashioned social history. They were important not in themselves, but for the light they cast on greater political themes. Moreover they represented particular aspects of particular lives. The new social history is concerned with masses of information, the general rather than the particular. It deals with large areas and times ("structures," "conjunctures") rather than specific elections, details of an individual life, or happenings in a reign (*événements*). In short, the new social history has jettisoned the very mortar that held together the edifice constructed by traditional historians like Trevelyan and Plumb, not to mention unashamed defenders of political history like Sir Geoffrey Elton.

Understandably, historians of a small island nation have been reluctant to adopt the broad scope of the new social history, Lawrence Stone's lengthy studies of the aristocracy and intimate life notwithstanding. The one group of English historians that has come closest to duplicating the French approach, Peter Laslett and his colleagues at the Cambridge Center for the History of Population and Social Structure, presented a different eighteenth century from that described by Plumb. At least they have raised different questions, and with the aid of computers, they have produced a massive study of population and a number of smaller studies on topics ranging from bastardy to the impact of cottage industry on early modern towns.

The success of the Cambridge Center led to an understandable reaction. As he had earlier warned against Namier's microscopic approach, Plumb now cautioned against the scholastic gigantism made possible by the use of computers. Will teams of researchers, bringing back masses of data to feed into the machines, produce a better understanding of the age?[31] Even E. P. Thompson, who is usually on the opposite side of Plumb in historical debates, remains unconvinced. He has decried those who seek the "indices of infant mortality" but "cannot be bothered with the cartloads of victims at Tyburn."[32] Although Thompson's *Whigs and Hunters* is a critique of Walpole's government and its historian, he and Plumb have at least agreed that the issue is: should the historian concentrate on the particular or the general; the individual or the group? Plumb thought that new social history might be of value if historians kept their vision narrow and did not reject the study of events. In several articles, he showed how social history on this scale should be done.

One advantage of the new social history is its ability to study groups previously neglected. Philippe Ariès did this when he showed that children were a legitimate focus of historical enquiry.[33] Ariès's pioneering work was attacked by many traditional historians. Some doubted whether the aristocratic portraits that fascinated Ariès proved anything. Others pointed out that he had been rather free with his dates, the mainspring of traditional history. They complained that on the one hand, Ariès picked examples from any century that seemed to support the point he was making at the moment, and that on the other hand, he extended the century in which "childhood" was supposed to have been born for at least three hundred years. Never one to hold back from a good fight, Plumb showed what use could be made of this subject, narrowly defined, in "The New World of Children in Eighteenth-Century England," a detailed confirmation of Ariès' discovery of childhood.[34]

It is somewhat unfair to compare a work of vast interpretation to one with a narrow scope, and yet nothing better reveals the differences between the two approaches to social history. Where Ariès had tried to show the evolution of the concept of childhood, a process that took him across the map of Europe backward and forward over a span of five hundred years and opened him to the charge of oversimplification, Plumb was content to examine what really happened to children in one small country in the critical years following the publication of Locke's *Some Thoughts Concerning Education* (1693).

Significantly, Plumb's findings go further toward proving the point that Ariès wished to make than did those of the French historian himself. For example, Ariès devoted several chapters to changes in educational theory and practice. The proposition that he was trying to establish was that childhood could be said to have arrived when schools had separate curricula for different ages and regular procedures for advancement. Since his evidence was a handful of books on pedagogy and the records of a few elite schools, skeptics rightly asked how pervasive this new attitude really was. Plumb replied for Ariès by showing how newspaper advertisements revealed the large number of schools that actually existed in the eighteenth century. He concluded that most provincial towns had schools and that they charged fees sufficiently low to make education available even to the middling sort. In the absence of modern records, this is probably as good an answer as we are likely to get.

The advertisements reveal another aspect of the advent of childhood: the triumph of the teachings of John Locke. Ariès merely suggested this influence by noting the number of editions of Locke's works on education that had been published and how Locke's ideas had been pirated by others. Plumb's research showed the direct appeal those ideas had to parents. When schools advertised that they followed Locke's theories, it was proof that those theories had triumphed in the public eye.

Plumb's "new world" indicates another measure for the arrival of childhood beyond those indicated by Ariès: the advent of the child as consumer. It was Plumb who pointed out how the multifaceted commercial revolution that was beginning in England included children. In addition to schools, which are a form of juvenile consumerism, the eighteenth century witnessed the birth of the children's book, the toy store complete with "educational toys," and special children's clothing and furniture stores. All of which testified to the social aspirations and fears of middle-class parents. Plumb's few pages thus provided support to the larger work.

Plumb's exploration of the world of eighteenth-century children led to another aspect of social history, "the commercialization of leisure."[35] Here too, by making his focus much narrower than the *longue durée* — at most one hundred years — he was able to show the importance of another change in eighteenth-century life. Plumb again proved himself not merely a political historian but also one who is interested in many facets of the eighteenth century. Newspapers, books on subjects as diverse as gardening and jokes, theaters, and other entertainments prove that the English of the age of George III had more money and time to devote to recreation than ever before. Historians are just beginning to realize the implications of these developments.

The new history can be used to illuminate the old, but the old sources, when used imaginatively, can also yield important information for the new. Plumb showed that old records can reveal new information when asked new questions. It is still up to the historian to impose a historical imagination on the facts, whether they be the price of tickets for boxing matches, the amount of stud fees for racehorses, or the polling results in a parliamentary constituency.

The switch to social history did not require a philosophical shift for Plumb, for he had never taken a single view of history. He wrote political history, but never merely political history. He never claimed, as had Namier, that intellectual history had little value. Nor did he, as the French had done, dismiss political events as ephemeral *événements,* not worthy of the historian's time. Few things better demonstrate Plumb's acceptance of the new social history and his appreciation of the manner in which it complements more traditional approaches than do the research topics chosen by his students. Unlike Trevelyan, Plumb trained a generation of scholars, and they have gone on to dominate the field. Some have continued to write on traditional subjects such as the Jacobites and political parties,[36] others have joined him in applying social history to the particular problem of the Georgian political and social scene.[37]

Plumb realized, perhaps earlier than most of his colleagues, that the historian's real dilemma was not whether to choose between the new history and the old. It was rather: for what audience should the historian write? Fundamentally the issue was the same as the debate between Bury and Trevelyan at the beginning of the century: was history a branch of science or of literature?[38] Plumb's answer was the same as Trevelyan's. The historian must address the public because history does have something to say.

After establishing his place in the academic world and returning to postwar life, Plumb set out to show that academic rigor was compatible with popular history. In 1950 he published *England in the Eighteenth Century* in the *Pelican History of England* series. This was followed by *West African Explorers* (1951); *Chatham* in the *Brief Lives* series (1953); and *The First Four Georges* (1956).[39] Each is an outstanding example of popular history with something to say to the scholar.

England in the Eighteenth Century was, and still is, a remarkable book. A volume in a series designed to bridge the gap between the needs of the student and those of the informed public, it accomplished that rare feat. It became the heart of school and university reading lists but did not fail to appeal to a wider audience. The volume has never been out of print and is available in numerous foreign translations. Its style is considered so noteworthy that it has been selected as a model of English prose by Japanese educators for their students.[40] But its real achievement was that it had something original to say that has stood the passage of time.

In 1950 the gulf between academic or scientific history and popular history was wide. On the one hand there was Namier, whose ideas were finally being accepted by the professionals, but whose style and content had little appeal to the educated public. On the other hand there was Trevelyan, whose *Social History* was enjoying a great popular success in the postwar nostalgia boom while being ridiculed by the academy. While acknowledging the importance of Namier's interpretation of the reign of George III, in *The Eighteenth Century* Plumb introduced themes that he would develop later: political parties, which could best be observed if the focus was removed from the narrow confines of the House of Commons; increasing political stability, which in turn produced social and economic stability; the meaning of corruption. As he was to do later, Plumb chose to emphasize the benefits of stability rather than the abuse of power. Few of his major points would have to be seriously modified today.

Like the *Eighteenth Century, West African Explorers* was part of a series designed to meet the increased demand caused by the postwar education explosion as well as to capitalize on interest in the rapidly vanishing British Empire. Both books looked back to a time of national greatness and self-confidence. With the decline of the once-mighty empire and the prestige and prosperity it had brought, the British were more interested in the acquisition of power under the first Georges than in its surrender under the sixth.

Explorers, although not a major interpretation of its subject, announced that Plumb had the daring to write outside his area of special knowledge, thus exposing himself to the criticism of specialists in addition to the charge of courting popularity rather than pursuing academic rigor. Indeed one reviewer was later to suggest that Plumb had overly dramatized the international conflict of the 1720s and 1730s to enhance the popular appeal of the second volume of Walpole.[41] Characteristically, in a critical tribute to Trevelyan published the same year, Plumb stoutly defended the academic historian's obligation to write for a wider audience.[42] His *Renaissance* demonstrated that he would not let such criticism hold him back. It has proved to be the most popular work on the period since Burckhardt.[43]

Even as an author, Plumb's reputation as the most famous living historian in Britain rests on more than these works of popular synthesis. There are his sparkling introductions to classics of eighteenth-century literature ranging from the *Vicar of Wakefield* to the memoirs of Fanny Hill.[44] But it was his television appearances and subsequent book on Britain's *Royal Heritage* that brought his name to the attention of audiences who might never read his histories.[45]

Plumb was not concerned simply with reaching a wider audience; he thought that history had lessons to teach. But what were those lessons? That was the problem that increasingly confronted historians in the 1960s. The more specialized history became, the less appeal it had to the layperson; and the less it appealed to the layperson, the more specialized it became. Furthermore, some historians were discovering a past that brought little comfort to the present. The great Victorian historians could confidently write the history of progress, but what could a generation that had witnessed two world wars, the Great Depression and the Holocaust find to boast about? Some concluded that if there had been no progress, there was no point in writing history.

Plumb responded to this challenge in characteristic fashion. He had been defending the utility of history all his professional life, and as editor of the *History of Human Society* series he reaffirmed a belief in progress as deep as Macaulay's. It was not the old Whig notion of the triumph of liberty over despotism, of course, but the material progress of the Western world. Here was a theme historians could proudly describe. "The condition of man is now superior to what it was. . . . Two great revolutions—the neolithic and industrial—have enabled men to establish vast societies of exceptional complexity in which the material well-being of generations of mankind has made remarkable advances."[46] This was a remarkable defense of industrial progress. Not only did it answer the critics of past industrialism; it also challenged critics of contemporary industrialism who had warned of the imminent collapse of the industrial West. It was the same optimistic note Plumb had sounded in *Crisis in the Humanities:* mankind *has* made progress, and it is the historian's job to write about it.[47] In his Saposnekow lectures, which he boldly labeled "The Death of the Past," Plumb further defended the utility of history and pointed out the direction he believed the profession should take.[48]

Plumb began by making the distinction between "history" and the "past." The past, according to Plumb, is events that can be used to explain, justify, and even sanctify the present and the future. It may be historical, but it is not history—a term he reserved for the tradition of wishing to see things as they actually happened. He believed that history, with its scientific emphasis on accuracy, was peculiarly Western and that its rise to dominance in the nineteenth century tended to weaken the past. The past, which was more nostalgic than authentic, has been kept alive by its usefulness in teaching the legitimacy of the present. Even as late as the 1940s, the past could conveniently be invoked to justify Britain's struggle against Hitler. But, Plumb sadly concluded, this was a short-lived remission; time was running out for the past. Britain's declining position as a world power and increasingly rapid technological change have combined to render the past obsolete. In a world of constant change, where skills and ideas do not last for a single generation, let alone get passed from one to another, the past does not even explain the present, let alone the future.

Some of Professor Plumb's colleagues have been forced to admit that they think history has no lessons to teach and defend it merely as a useful discipline to train the mind, but ever optimistic, Plumb is not ready to surrender so easily. Specialized, scientific history may have killed the past, but, he argues, the study of history must be continued. Plumb's prescription for the resuscitation of the profession is not simply more or better history. Instead, historians must turn from their specialized studies and write for the general public. Merely summarizing their findings in a readable fashion will no longer do. Since the old past no longer works, historians must create a new one.

The new past, Plumb proclaims, must teach the nature of social change. It "must stress the success as well as point out the failure." Historians must not abandon the rigor of their profession and oversimplify for the popular taste. They must show the complexities of the past. The new past should be "as true, as exact, as we can make it," but it should not abandon its obligation to teach of human successes when people have applied reason to technical and social questions. Moreover, he concludes, historians must not abandon their unique advantage of seeing change over time, an advantage they have over the currently popular social scientists.[49]

In defending the utility of study of history in the conventional sense, Plumb did not merely justify his own career and writings but he also placed himself in the very Whig tradition that he had once criticized—in *Churchill Revised*.[50] Although he had defended the old Whig historians against Namier, he had devoted a lifetime to revising much that they had written, and he could not let Churchill perpetuate their excesses. Yet no less than Churchill and the Whigs, Plumb saw a history of progress and the importance of the lessons of the past, even if that progress tended to be economic and social rather than constitutional. Not surprisingly the three historians he has written about in detail, Macaulay, Trevelyan, and Churchill, each shared his belief in writing for the public, and each was the leading Whig historian of his generation.

Sir John Plumb has enjoyed a long and distinguished career, and he has certainly earned the reputation of being the proprietor of "Plumb's territory." His detailed studies have provided significant information on the events of the period as well as a major reinterpretation of the age. More recently, his studies in social history have not only given new insight into the early modern period, but they have also demonstrated a new method of historical enquiry. In his hands the new history is no longer in opposition to the old, it provides a complement to it.

Throughout his career Plumb has taken an optimistic view of the past. Where some saw corruption, he saw expediency; where others saw repression, he saw stability. Even his interpretation of the discovery of childhood was characteristically optimistic. Where Ariès had to admit that when children gained a childhood they lost their freedom, Plumb saw only the gain. Life in his new world of children was a sort of perpetual Christmas, not Ariès's bittersweet realization that something equally valuable had been lost. This unwavering optimism certainly enhanced Plumb's public reputation and contributed to his being awarded a knighthood.

Plumb's confidence in progress, especially material progress, has led him to defend the study of history with unusual zeal. History, he claimed, is worth knowing because it has lessons for the present. This staunch defense of the utility of history led him to continue to train younger scholars when some argued it was a pointless exercise. It also led him to seek new methods of enquiry to enliven and illuminate his period when others rejected the new approaches. Despite his success in reinterpreting the early eighteenth century, Professor Plumb will not be disappointed if these are his most lasting legacies.

NOTES

A brief version of this paper was read at the annual meeting of the Midwest Conference on British Studies in October 1986. I am grateful for the suggestions given by T. W. Heyck of Northwestern University and Mary Wessling of Stanford University.

1. Neil McKendrick, "J. H. Plumb: A Valedictory Tribute," in *Historical Perspectives: Studies in English Thought and Society in Honour of J. H. Plumb,* ed. Neil McKendrick (London: Europa, 1974), 1.
2. Ibid., 12. McKendrick includes a select bibliography of Plumb's writings, 302-6.
3. McKendrick, "Plumb," passim; *Who's Who.* Plumb's autobiographical essays appeared too late to be consulted. See *The Collected Essays of J. H. Plumb,* vol. 1, *The Making of an Historian;* vol. 2, *The American Experience* (Hemel Hempstead: Harvester Wheatsheaf; Athens: Univ. of Georgia Press, 1989). A third volume is anticipated.
4. McKendrick, "Plumb," passim. See also J. H. Plumb, *G. M. Trevelyan,* rev. ed. (London: Longman, 1971); and John Kenyon, *The History Men: The Historical Profession in England since the Renaissance* (London: Weidenfeld and Nicolson, 1983), 226-35. The conflict between Trevelyan and Namier is described in Plumb, *Making of a Historian.*
5. J. H. Plumb, *Fifty Years of "Equity Shoemaking": A History of the Leicester Co-operative Boot and Shoe Manufacturing Society, Ltd.* (Leicester, 1936).
6. J. H. Plumb, "The Elections to the Convention Parliament of 1689," *Cambridge Historical Journal* 5, no. 3(1937):235-54.
7. McKendrick, "Plumb," 7.
8. J. H. Plumb, *Sir Robert Walpole,* vol. 1, *The Making of a Statesman* (London: Cresset, 1956); vol. 2, *The King's Minister* (London: Cresset, 1960).
9. William Coxe, *Memoirs of the Life and Administration of Sir Robert Walpole, Earl of Orford,* 3 vols. (London, 1798).
10. See Linda Colley, *In Defiance of Oligarchy: The Tory Party, 1714-60* (Cambridge: Cambridge Univ. Press, 1984); and also Quentin Skinner, "The Principles and Practice of Opposition: The Case of Bolingbroke versus Walpole," in *Historical Perspectives,* ed. McKendrick, 93-128.
11. Thomas Babington Macaulay, *Essays,* cited in Kenyon, *History Men,* 251.
12. Plumb, *Sir Robert Walpole* 1:209.
13. Peter Mathias and Patrick O'Brien, "Taxation in Britain and France, 1715-1810, a Comparison of the Social and Economic Incidence of Taxes Collected for Central Government," *Journal of European Economic History* 5, no. 3(1976):603-24.
14. See John B. Owen's reviews in the *English Historical Review* 72(1957):328-31; and 78(1963):557-60.
15. E. P. Thompson, *Whigs and Hunters: The Origins of the Black Act* (New York: Pantheon, 1975), 258.
16. J. H. Plumb, "History and Biography," reprinted in *Men and Centuries* (Boston: Houghton Mifflin, 1963), 217-23.
17. A convenient summary of Namier's impact is "Namier and the Eighteenth Century" in Kenyon, *History Men,* 251-69.
18. J. H. Plumb, "The Atomic Historian," *New Statesman,* 1 Aug. 1969, 141-43.
19. Lewis Namier and John Brooke, *The House of Commons, 1754-1790,* 3 vols. (London: Her Majesty's Stationery Office, 1964), 1:ix; Lewis Namier, *Monarchy and the Party System* (Oxford: Oxford Univ. Press, 1952), 24-30.
20. Robert R. Walcott, *English Politics in the Early Eighteenth Century* (Oxford: Oxford Univ. Press, 1956); J. H. Plumb, *English Historical Review* 72(1957):126-29; idem, *The Growth of Political Stability in England 1675-1725* (London: Macmillan,

1967). The Ford lectures were published in the United States as *The Origins of Political Stability* (Boston: Houghton Mifflin).

21. J. H. Plumb, "The Growth of the Electorate in England from 1600–1715," *Past and Present* 45(Nov. 1969):90–116.

22. See, for example, Geoffrey Holmes, *British Politics in the Age of Queen Anne* (London: Macmillan, 1967); Geoffrey Holmes and W. A. Speck, *The Divided Society: Party Conflict in England, 1694–1716* (London: Arnold, 1967).

23. John M. Beattie, *The English Court in the Reign of George I* (Cambridge: Cambridge Univ. Press, 1967), chap. 7.

24. See John Brewer, "English Radicalism in the Age of George III," in *Three British Revolutions: 1641, 1688, 1776*, ed. J. G. A. Pocock (Princeton: Princeton Univ. Press, 1980), 323–67; and John Brewer, "Commercialization and Politics," in *The Birth of a Consumer Society*, ed. Neil McKendrick et al. (Bloomington: Indiana Univ. Press, 1982), 197–262.

25. Plumb, *Political Stability*, 188.

26. J. H. Plumb, "Political Man," in *Man Versus Society in Eighteenth Century England: Six Points of View*, ed. James L. Clifford (Cambridge: Cambridge Univ. Press, 1969), 1–21.

27. Fernand Braudel, *Civilization and Capitalism, 15th–18th Century*, 3 vols., trans. Sian Reynolds (New York: Harper & Row, 1981–1984), vol. 3, *The Perspective of the World*, 490.

28. J. H. Plumb, review of Braudel's *Capitalism and Material Life* in *New Statesman*, 15 June 1973, 887–89.

29. J. H. Plumb, quoted in McKendrick, "Plumb," 15.

30. See "The Walpoles: Father and Son," in *Studies in Social History: A Tribute to G. M. Trevelyan*, ed. J. H. Plumb (London: Longman, 1955), 179–207; and "Sir Robert Walpole's Wine," and "Sir Robert Walpole's Food," in Plumb, *Men and Centuries*, 147–58.

31. J. H. Plumb, "Bigness in Scholarship," *Horizon* (Winter 1973):46–47.

32. E. P. Thompson, *Whigs and Hunters*, 268.

33. Philippe Ariès, *Centuries of Childhood: A Social History of Family Life*, trans. Robert Baldick (London: Jonathan Cape, 1962).

34. J. H. Plumb, "The New World of Children in Eighteenth-Century England," *Past and Present* 67(1975):64–95.

35. J. H. Plumb, *The Commercialization of Leisure in Eighteenth-Century England* (Reading: Univ. of Reading Press, 1973).

36. See the range of articles in McKendrick, ed., *Historical Perspectives*.

37. See, for example, McKendrick, *Birth of a Consumer Society*.

38. Plumb, *Trevelyan*, 7, 11.

39. J. H. Plumb, *England in the Eighteenth Century* (Harmondsworth: Penguin, 1950); *West African Explorers* (Oxford: Oxford Univ. Press, 1951); *Chatham* (London: Collins, 1953); *The First Four Georges* (London: Batsford, 1956).

40. McKendrick, "Plumb," 13.

41. John B. Owen, *English Historical Review* 78(1963):557–60.

42. Plumb, *Trevelyan*, 13–14, 23–26, 31–33.

43. J. H. Plumb, *The Renaissance* (London: Collins, 1961). See also McKendrick, "Plumb," 13.

44. Several of these are collected in Plumb, *Men and Places*.

45. J. H. Plumb, *Royal Heritage: The Treasure of the British Crown* (New York: Harcourt Brace Jovanovich, 1977).

46. Graham Clark and Stuart Piggott, *Pre-Historical Society* with an Introduction by J. H. Plumb (London: Hutchinson, 1965), 18–19.

47. J. H. Plumb, "The Historian's Dilemma," in *Crisis in the Humanities,* ed. Plumb (Harmondsworth: Penguin, 1964), 24–44.

48. J. H. Plumb, *The Death of the Past* (London: Macmillan, 1969).

49. Ibid., 138–45.

50. J. H. Plumb, *Churchill Revised* (New York: Dial, 1969); J. H. Plumb et al., *Churchill: Four Faces and the Man* (London: Allen Lane, 1969).

E. P. Thompson
Moralist as Marxist Historian

THOMAS WILLIAM HEYCK

Of all the English historians who have come to prominence since 1945, the one most likely to be written about a hundred years from now is E. P. (Edward Palmer) Thompson. More than any other person, he has been responsible for leading the turn to social history and for inspiring the interest in writing history "from the bottom up." Thompson has ranged boldly over the whole of eighteenth- and nineteenth-century English social and cultural history, and he has called attention to a world of popular political and social activity that most historians had either neglected or assumed to be beyond the grasp of empirical research. By viewing the past from a fresh perspective—that of the exploited and nameless population—he has given an enormously fruitful, if often highly controversial, twist to English history. Moreover, by means of new (or newly defined) analytical categories—among them class, class conflict, popular culture, and exploitation—Thompson has compelled historians to consider new issues.

Yet for all his newness, Thompson in many ways is a throwback to an older-style historian. He is deliberately not a "scientific" or "professional" historian. Though he accepts many of the methodological assumptions of modern scholars, Thompson is more like the man-of-letters historian who preceded the professional. Since the early twentieth century, English historians have regarded specialization as a virtue; they have taken other historians as their audience; they have avoided moral judgments; and they have disavowed present-mindedness. While Thompson argues strenuously for rigor in research and inference, he rejects the rest of the professional historian's creed. Like Macaulay or Froude, Thompson is consciously present-minded, polemical, and partisan. He wants to reach a wider audience than just academics; he wants to make a difference in the political behavior of his readers; and he gives priority to moral judgments on the past. This orientation, no less than his tenacious intelligence and his new perspective, have made him a leading intellectual as well as an influential historian. Thus he is best seen not in the line of academic historians ranging from Bury to Namier to Elton, but in the tradition of sages beginning with Blake and Shelley, and extending to Carlyle, Ruskin, Morris, and Leavis. Thompson is the moralist as Marxist historian.

How did such an unusual plant appear in the garden of twentieth-century English historiography? It seems clear that Thompson's family life was all-important. Thompson was born in 1924, into an upper middle class Anglo-Indian intellectual family. Both his mother and father were tough-minded liberals and anti-imperialists.[1] In the 1930s anti-fascism joined anti-imperialism as main articles in the family's creed. As Thompson later recalled, "I must have learned some of my allegiances from my father, himself part academic, part man of letters, who spent so much of himself in the twenties and thirties writing books, pamphlets, letters to the press, and stumping half-empty halls, in the cause of Indian independence."[2] His father had been a Methodist educational missionary in India, but his immersion in Indian culture led him to abandon his faith, a combination of circumstances that helps to explain Thompson's peculiar mixture of moralism and hostility to Methodism. In any case, Thompson's father became a friend of Tagore and Nehru; and young Edward grew up in the 1930s with leaders of Indian nationalism as frequent guests in the home.

Thompson's initial move toward socialism appears to have been a classic case of a youth exceeding the radicalism of his parents. But the most profound influence in Edward's intellectual and emotional commitment to Marxism was his older brother Frank's idealism and heroic death. Here were the roots of Thompson's romantic and libertarian Marxism, which have branched into such passionate history.

Evidence of Frank's influence on his younger brother comes largely from *There Is a Spirit in Europe: A Memoir of Frank Thompson,* written by Edward and his mother.[3] This, Thompson's first book, is a short but moving account of Frank and his service with the Bulgarian partisans during World War II. In Edward's eyes, Frank was an unusually intelligent and idealistic young man. At Oxford he became a socialist and active anti-fascist. In 1939 he joined the Communist party, partly because of conviction and partly because of "frustration at the ineffectiveness of other parties in the face of the approaching war." But there was more to Frank's influence than this. As excerpts from his letters reveal, the two brothers shared a love of literature, especially romantic poetry, and an admiration of the grass roots patriotism of popular front resistance movements in Europe. Frank wrote of his vision of a new Europe, one with "a spirit akin to the Chinese notion of 'human-heartedness' broadening out and complementing the philosophy of dialectical materialism." He believed the cultural and social relations of the Soviet Union to be superior to those of Britain, where the culture of the ruling class, devoted to conspicuous consumption and trivial art, was bankrupt. In Russia, he wrote, there was hope that the "gulf between the poet and the public" could be bridged, and that an authentic, serious popular art could be established.[4]

Frank volunteered for active duty as soon as the war broke out. Having learned Russian and eight other European languages while serving in North Africa and Sicily, he volunteered to serve with the British mission to the partisans of the Balkans. In January 1944 Frank parachuted into the Bulgarian-Yugoslavian border area and for six months fought beside the Bulgarian partisans in their stirring, tragic campaign against the Nazis. He was captured, tortured, and executed in June 1944. E. P. Thompson's account of Frank's mission in Bulgaria remains among the best narratives he has written—clear, taut, and deeply moving.[5] Thompson at this early age—he was not yet twenty-five—showed many of the strengths he would later display as a mature historian: the ability to learn a great deal on the ground from ordinary participants about obscure events in a popular action. He stressed Frank's solidarity with the intrepid partisans and their bravery against terrible odds. Plainly Thompson identified as strongly with the partisans as he did with his brother; these were working people taking their own fight into their own hands. Ever since that first book, a tribute to a beloved brother, Thompson has been a partisan in two senses: as a scholar of commitment to political action, and as a man feeling solidarity with ordinary people, past and present, in their struggle for freedom from oppression.

After the war Frank Thompson was posthumously hailed as a hero in Bulgaria. To the Communists of Bulgaria, the young English officer had made a choice and a difference. To E. P. Thompson, Frank's example of individual "agency" was vivid, personal, and irrefutable. Thompson was learning the same lesson in his academic work. Resuming his university career after military service in North

Africa and Italy, he studied English literature with F. R. Leavis and then finished his degree in history (with first class honors) at Cambridge in 1946.[6] Thompson recalled that at the university he learned most from the works of Christopher Hill, Christopher Caudwell, and, of course, Karl Marx. Hill, who was at the time in his unrevised Marxist phase, impressed Thompson as a man who "restructured whole areas of historical consciousness in England."[7] Caudwell was another Marxist, an erratic, maverick socialist killed in the Spanish Civil War, whose works were all published posthumously. Principally an aesthetic philosopher and literary critic, Caudwell ranged as he pleased over anthropology, neurology, psychoanalysis, psychology, mathematics, and genetics. Thompson found 90 percent of Caudwell's work worthless, but 10 percent brilliant, especially in "the logic of ideological processes."[8] According to Thompson, Caudwell's "way of seeing" was dialectical, emphasizing the interaction of thought and the material world, and the mutual determinations of ideas and culture. Thompson found in Caudwell a theoretical framework for individual agency.[9]

Thompson's learning from Marx is not easy to pin down. He has never been given to textual exegesis. In his early historical work, Thompson often wrote as an orthodox Marxist of the heavy-handed variety, influenced by the later Marx of *Capital* and economic determinism. Yet Thompson recalled in 1976 that what he and others of his generation learned from Marx was not rigid deduction — and the determinism that goes with it — but Marx's historical epistemology: "A lot of what we got from Marx came from the Marx-Engels correspondence, observing them working upon history in the workshop of their correspondence. This gives one a sense of process."[10] Concepts like capitalism and class, then, were not to be derived from "static analysis," but from observations of their patterns over time, and in all their historical varieties. Thompson found Marx enormously suggestive but not scriptural. Not surprisingly, the works of Marx that Thompson has cited most frequently, from the *Theses on Feuerbach* (1845) to the *Communist Manifesto* (1848), are those of the early, "humanistic" Marx. This was a Marx who had much in common with the romantic critics of capitalist society, a tradition much admired by both Frank and E. P. Thompson.

Romanticism and Marxism converged for E. P. Thompson in his first major historical enterprise, a study of William Morris. Thompson's first academic post was in the extramural department of the University of Leeds, where he taught adult classes. He also took an active role in the Communist Party, the Yorkshire Peace Movement, and the Communist Party Historians' Group, thus combining scholarship and activism. He was teaching as much literature as history and had to find ways to make literature significant to his students.[11] That aim led him to study Morris, who provided an example of putting art to the service of social regeneration; and—typically for Thompson—an article grew into an enormous book: *William Morris: Romantic to Revolutionary.*[12]

Thompson wanted to rehabilitate the reputation of Morris as a major intellectual figure, but more specifically to claim Morris as a Marxist and revolutionary, as opposed to a mere exponent of arts and crafts or utopian socialism. Moreover, Thompson set out to show how Morris's initial romanticism extended an anticapitalist and antiindustrial tradition that was to be fulfilled by socialism. Thus Thompson thought it essential to give a full account of Morris's neglected socialist years. Thompson offered Morris as an example for contemporary socialist intellectuals—not least for himself. He succeeded in all these aims. Though his study of Morris is overlong, self-indulgent, and given to intrusive digressions and polemics, there is not a dull passage in it; Thompson's protean intellectual vitality fills every page.

Thompson treats Morris's life as a saga of redemption in which socialism saves romanticism. He begins with a bold and sympathetic, if somewhat reductionist, discussion of romanticism, which he sees as having moved through revolutionary and isolationist phases. His heart is with the revolutionaries—Blake, Wordsworth, and Shelley. What united them was "a search for spontaneity and simplicity as opposed to convention and calculation, a search for the essential moral nature of man."[13] But the romantics were forced into intellectual isolationism by the reality of early capitalist society. Beginning with Keats, the English romantics transmuted their opposition to tyranny into a posing of art against the realities of life. This was the beginning point for Morris: a romanticism in which beauty and art were relegated to an abstract world set against the world of power and fact.[14]

At Oxford, Morris drifted out of the High Church movement, cultivating his opposition to utilitarianism, the cash nexus, and the ugliness and squalor of capitalist industrialism. Carlyle and Ruskin provided vitalizing influences, but the Pre-Raphaelite Brotherhood diverted their potentially revolutionary insights into mere "romance." Here Thompson is quite acute: because the Pre-Raphaelites refused to face the social facts of industrial Britain, romanticism "appears to have lost its last root-holds in the soil of contemporary experience, and to be becoming emaciated, sapless, and drooping."[15] First in his poetry and then in his arts-and-crafts work, Morris continued the struggle against the enemy (now called by Thompson "Victorianism"), while others, like Tennyson, sold out. Thompson has many evocative observations on Morris's work in these "Years of Conflict," but he cannot escape the feeling that they were labors of despair and disillusion, and that Morris's slide into art-for-art's sake was dispiriting, for himself and for subsequent romantics.

But Morris found the Norse sagas, which gave him heart again. He had not known the English working class, who might have saved him; instead, he had to "draw his strength, as it seemed, from the energies and aspirations of a poor people in a barren northern island in the twelfth century."[16] From them he took courage, defiance, and dignity; and started out on the road to salvation. During the Bulgarian agitation, Morris came into contact with working men, and then in the "Anti-Scrape" (antirestoration) movement, he "deepened his insight into the destructive philistinism of capitalist society."[17] Finally, Morris crossed what Thompson calls the "River of Fire" into socialism: he read Henry George, William Cobbett, and A. R. Wallace, and joined the Democratic Federation. This was, according to Thompson, "a true conversion." Now Morris set about completing his critique of modern society by understanding the class struggle. He conversed with other socialists, he entered into socialist activities, he read *Capital,* and illumination was his. And not just his, for, in Thompson's view, Morris was acting on behalf of English intellectual culture: "The long romantic breach between aspiration and action was healed."[18]

In the next section of the book, Thompson examines in great detail Morris's explorations of, and propagandizing for, socialism and communism. He insists, against both left- and right-wing accounts, that Morris was a genuine Marxist. He dismisses as a momentary outburst Morris's well-known remark that he could not understand Marx's theory of value. Morris advocated a "purist," as opposed to an "opportunist" or "palliative" socialism, his policy (and Thompson's no doubt) being "Education towards Revolution." This was, according to Thompson, "a first shadowy English forecast of the 'party of the new type' of Lenin."[19] By 1889 Morris was calling himself a "communist" and placing himself in the tradition of the *Communist Manifesto* and the Paris Commune, as against anarchism and Fabianism. Yet Morris did not forget his romanticism: Thompson says Morris's *Signs of Change* (1889) was one of his finest works, "one of the great achievements of the nineteenth century, the point of confluence of the moral protest of Carlyle and Ruskin, and the historical genius of

Marx, backed by Morris's own lifetime of study and practice in the arts and in society."[20]

In Thompson's view, then, Morris was neither a mere Ruskinian nor a welfare reformer, but a revolutionary Marxist. He admired the cultural coherence of the Middle Ages, but he was no medievalist, for he knew that there was exploitation in feudal society as well as in capitalism. Thus far Thompson was himself a Morrisist; yet he had reservations about Morris's aesthetic theory. He says that Morris's aesthetic philosophy—the idea that art is the expression of the whole person—moved in the right direction but did not go far enough. Morris, Thompson argues, failed to understand "the *ideological* role of art, its active agency in *changing* human beings and society as a whole, its agency in man's class-divided history."[21] On this point, it seems clear, Thompson was working out his own chosen role in life—the intellectual partisan, whose agency would make a difference in healing the cultural and social wounds caused by capitalist industrialism.

Thompson's *Morris* is his forgotten book, although an extremely impressive one. It was written for Britain's embattled left; hence if Thompson was not surprised that academics ignored it, he found the neglect by intellectuals of the left very disappointing. He felt that they had much to learn from Morris's deeply moral, culturally-rooted brand of Marxism. In this view he was right. *Morris* is far from a perfect book; as Thompson later admitted, it is marred by too many lengthy digressions (for example, on positivism, the Socialist League, and the Chicago anarchists) and too many personal intrusions "with moralistic comments and pat political sentiments."[22] He should have added, and from too many immature and simplistic judgments. Two examples suffice: "If Morris had lived to see the love with which Socialist countries to-day defend and preserve their own ancient monuments, he would have known that his confidence was not misplaced."[23] And, "The life of Victorian England was an intolerable life, and ought not to have been borne by human beings. The values of industrial capitalism were vicious and beneath contempt, and made a mockery of the past history of mankind."[24] Thompson edited many such flaws and heavy-handed polemics out of the second edition of the book, published in 1977. But the first version remains an exciting and stimulating book, permeated by Thompson's energy, passion, and overarching thesis. It forces the reader to think of Morris in a new way, if not to accept the argument completely. It displays Thompson's remarkable skill in close reading of texts, in doing a compelling intellectual history, and in writing vividly. If Thompson had written nothing else, his *Morris* would entitle him to the status of a historian—and intellectual—of the first rank.

Thompson was later to say that the central thread of all his historical work was in his book on Morris, "although in a muffled way, because I was then still prisoner of some Stalinist pieties." That thread concerns value systems, about which Marx (and Stalin) had been silent. It concerns "cultural and moral mediations; as to the ways in which the human being is imbricated in particular, determined productive relations; the way these material experiences are handled culturally; the way in which there are certain value systems that are consonant with certain modes of production. . . . "[25] The theme was indeed muffled in *Morris* the book, but implicit in the life of Morris the thinker. And plainly Morrisism simmered in Thompson's mind so as to tenderize his Marxism and to break down his "Stalinist pieties." The new Morris/Marx recipe, with its emphasis on human effectiveness, as against economic determinism, and on historical process, as against static deductive analysis, seemed heretical to orthodox members of the British Communist party. In 1956, their dispute with Thompson heated up with Khrushchev's denunciation of Stalin at the Twentieth Party Congress and exploded upon the Russian invasion of Hungary. Thompson could not accept the violation of an autonomous communist nation. He denounced Stalinism, resigned from the British Communist party, and helped establish the *New Left Review.* Six years later he was evicted from its editorial board by a second generation of the new left.[26]

This was the context in which Thompson wrote *The Making of the English Working Class.* It is important to remember that when writing this epochal work, Thompson was acutely conscious of enemies to his left and right. Indeed, he seems to have had two different audiences in mind: the British left, and a more general public, for whom he was combating the quantifying economic historians, descendants of the nineteenth-century utilitarians and political economists. As he said, he did not write for academics, but for a wider audience of workers, union leaders, and teachers in his adult education courses.[27] In *The Making of the English Working Class,* Thompson sought to refute the determinism of left and right, for both of whom "steam power and the cotton mill = new working class."[28] He wanted to show that the ruling class *chose* to exploit the working population; that working people were no passive mass, but were involved by their own decisions in making themselves into a class; and that in struggling with oppressive forces, the English laboring poor were able to draw on a rich, peculiarly English, traditional culture. *The Making of the English Working Class* is a wonderfully innovative book, but in its underlying sympathies it is moralistic, traditionalist, and even patriotic.[29]

Thompson plots his sweeping drama as a heroic epic, in which the protagonists are the English working people and the antagonists are their oppressors, who sometimes wear the mask of the ruling class, sometimes that of the Industrial Revolution, sometimes that of capitalism. To set the stage, Thompson offers a fresh concept of class, one that has been immensely influential among historians and highly controversial among Marxist intellectuals. He insists that a social class is not a thing, a structure, a category, nor a product of mechanical determinism. Class is a matter of "historical relationship," which happens "when some men, as a result of common experiences (inherited or shared), feel and articulate the identity of their interests as between themselves, and as against other men whose interests are different from (and usually opposed to) theirs." Class, therefore, "owes as much to agency as to conditioning." This definition seems to collapse the difference between class and class consciousness, but Thompson distinguishes between the two by saying that class consciousness is the way people handle their experiences "in cultural terms: embodied in traditions, value systems, ideas, and institutional forms." Thus Thompson successfully avoids the doubtful concept of "false consciousness," asserting that class is a "social and cultural formation," which can only be observed in specific historical processes. In the case of early nineteenth-century England, class happened: "In the years between 1780 and 1832 most English working people came to feel an identity of interests as between themselves, and as against their rulers and employers." By 1832, Thompson argues, the English "labouring poor" had made themselves into "an insurgent working class."[30]

Thompson adopts a three-part structure for his heroic epic. In the first part, he deals not with preindustrial social structure but with certain popular traditions of the eighteenth century that influenced the English Jacobinism of the 1790s and survived in different forms as the popular radicalism of the 1820s and 1830s. The English working people may have stood at the bottom of the social ladder, but in Thompson's view they were neither inert nor without resources. They could draw on ideas of popular democracy going back to the Levellers; on the sense of the rights of the free-born Englishman; on the tradition of Dissent, attenuated though it was after the fading of Puritanism; and on the surprisingly effective instruments of riot and mob action. Finally, Thompson explores English Jacobinism during the years of the French Revolution, when English radicals—mainly artisans—called on these popular traditions to generate a genuine revolutionary movement. "In the 1790s," he says, "something like an 'English Revolution' took place, of profound importance in shaping the consciousness of the post-war working class."[31] That revolution was put down. Consequently, political oppression and the libertarian stance it inspired were crucial formative experiences for the English working class.

In arguing that the English common people of the eighteenth century had a political life, and in emphasizing the role of political repression in the process of class formation, Thompson provided important insights into English political and social history. His implicit linking of the eighteenth-century crowd's sense of a traditional moral economy with the popular ideals of individual rights and liberties leaves a powerful impression that English people were losing ancient and natural protections. Nevertheless, Part One remains only suggestive, because Thompson was not inclined to talk about social structure in a systematic way or to say just how widespread popular political activities were. He gives the impression of frequent mob action and barely suppressed warfare of the common folk against the authorities in eighteenth-century England, even before the 1790s. One may sympathize with Thompson's revulsion against quantification of human experience and yet hunger for hard data. How often did riots occur? How many people were involved? Was the eighteenth century a relatively conflict-ridden or serene period? The same questions remain after his account of English Jacobinism. While Thompson's forays into the ideas of Thelwall, Spence, and Paine are excellent, and his narrative of the London Corresponding Society compelling, his evidence of widespread conspiracy is thin. It is not enough for him to say that one cannot expect more evidence from secret movements. For all his prodigious research, Thompson leaves a skeptical reader in doubt. When it comes to popular movements, Thompson always sees the glass half-full, and never half-empty.

In Part Two, Thompson shifts from narrative to description and analysis and presents the heart of his argument. His main point is that the English working people experienced the Industrial Revolution as a catastrophe. Here Thompson steps forward as a moralist and defiantly takes his stand with the pessimist historians. He overwhelms the statistical arguments of optimists like J. H. Clapham and T. S. Ashton with a flood of qualitative evidence, contending that the quantitative approach loses sight of the context—the human experience as a whole.³² Thompson clearly regards the qualitative approach to history as morally superior to the quantitative. People of the past were living, suffering human beings, and not sociological constructs. Even if aggregate figures indicate an improvement in the standard of living for most people, Thompson argues, "It is quite possible for statistical averages and human experiences to run in opposite directions." Not that he concedes improvement in the standard of living even in quantitative terms: the worker's "share in the 'benefits of economic progress' consisted of more potatoes, a few articles of cotton clothing for his family, soap and candles, some tea and sugar, and a great many articles in the *Economic History Review*."³³

Mainly, Thompson was impatient with the standard-of-living question and wanted to transcend it to show how working people experienced the combined pressure of political repression and industrialization. In a series of exceptionally powerful chapters, handloom weavers, field laborers, and artisans all receive richly detailed, sympathetic, and sensitive treatment. Thompson shows that as capitalism (not necessarily industrialism) penetrated one area after another in the economy, working people lost such control over their own labor as they had once enjoyed, lost the benefits of paternalist social relations, and lost the remnants of independent status. Thompson's discussion of the hopeless struggles of artisans to defend their "honourable" trades against "dishonourable" practices leaves an indelible impression, especially in light of the sensible and workable policies—such as trade unions, apprenticeship regulations, and taxes on certain machinery—that were proposed by various artisanal groups. He reveals political economy as a morally and socially harsh ideology, not the natural law its proponents claimed it to be.

As powerful as Part Two is, it has certain weaknesses. An important flaw is that Thompson largely ignores the population explosion, although much of the social dislocation, decay of artisanal autonomy, and urban misery must be attributed to the sheer staggering growth in the number of people. As Kitson Clark pointed out, the Industrial Revolution seems benevolent in light of the population explosion, since it ultimately provided the means of survival for the swollen numbers of people.³⁴ Moreover, Thompson does not acknowledge that some capitalists, at least, sincerely regarded capitalism as an ideology of human liberation.

A second flaw is Thompson's ambiguity over the term "Industrial Revolution." The Industrial Revolution is the villain of Part Two; yet, as he shows, many of the suffering workers had nothing to do with industrialization—field laborers, for example. Though Thompson has brilliant passages on why the weavers loathed factory work, he provides no separate chapter on factory workers.[35] Thompson sometimes uses Industrial Revolution to denote machine-productive processes, but more often simply to point to the whole period from the 1790s to the 1830s. It is his controlling metaphor rather than a term of precise meaning. As such it allows Thompson to portray the whole process of economic, social, political, and cultural change as moving from the natural to the artificial, and thus to portray that change in moral terms.

Finally, Part Two is flawed by one of its best known and most passionate chapters—"The Transforming Power of the Cross." Here Thompson treats Methodism, which he apparently loathes, as nothing more than "moral machinery." According to him, it was preached by the upper class partly because it provided "ideological self-justification for the master-manufacturers and for their satellites," and partly because it served as a means of disciplining the preindustrial work force. In blackmailing the working people into quiescence, Methodism did grave psychological damage: "The box-like blackening chapels stood in the industrial districts like great traps for the human psyche."[36] Workers accepted it because they were indoctrinated, and because it gave psychic release following the success of counterrevolution. Throughout this argument, Thompson's analytical powers give way to moral outrage and sustained denunciation. There is no question that evangelicalism (not just Methodism) **was** part of the "civilizing process" that helped tame the English people, and that many evangelicals were repressed personalities. But there was more to evangelicalism and Methodism than that. To Wesley and to many of his followers, the worldly benefits of conversion were joy and liberation. To many of the laboring poor, evangelicalism offered a genuine spiritual, as well as social, support when they needed it most. After all, not all religious impulses—not even those of Methodism—can be explained in terms of political and economic instrumentality. But Thompson displays no sense of the autonomy of religious conviction.

The final part of the book is something of an anticlimax after the passions of "The Curse of Adam." In it Thompson resumes his narrative of popular radicalism from the artisan radicals of Westminster to the trades unionists and Luddites and finally to the reform agitators of 1831–1832. The seething array of popular organizations and movements that Thompson uncovers, and the number of artisan intellectuals whose work he explicates, are extremely impressive. Throughout, Thompson balances the illegal and the legal elements in "the working-class presence," never in the sense of posing one wing against another, but in a more subtle sense of workers moving restlessly from one kind of activity to another, depending on political and economic circumstances. His account of the early trade unions and Luddism as two related aspects of the illegal tradition is brilliant, because it gives a sense of the tenacity and resourcefulness of working people in the face of the abrogation of paternalism and the imposition of laissez-faire policies. Always, Thompson portrays the actions of the workers as intelligible and rational and never as blind reaction or self-interest. The Luddites, for instance, were trying to assert "the will and conscience of working people" as a whole against policies and machines that were to them immoral and illegal.[37]

To Thompson, trade unions, Luddites, and all the other political and social activists constituted the genuine "Radical culture" of Cobbett, Hunt, Wooler, Thistlewood, et al. He insists that this was not a minority movement, but "the response of the whole community."[38] His exposition of the works of Cobbett and Owen are marvelous examples of close reading of texts, and his discussions of particular episodes, such as the Pentridge rising and Peterloo, are fascinating. Yet his claims as to the seriousness of the revolutionary threat and the comprehensiveness of radical culture seem strained. Typically, he treats the slim evidence of conspiracies as denoting the tip of a revolutionary iceberg; and he argues by puffing up a seeming blizzard of radical activity that conceals rather than persuades. The shakiness of his claims is revealed in the last chapter, where Thompson admits that radical culture was an affair of the artisan intellectual elite, who "inhabited another world" from that of the unskilled masses, whose attitudes remained demoralized and deferential. Thompson's sense of the Promethean quality of working-class activity in the early nineteenth century is pervasive: "This was, perhaps, the most distinguished popular culture that England has known."[39]

The question is whether Thompson succeeded in showing that the working class had brought itself into being by 1832. Critics have not been satisfied that he demonstrated adequately the extensiveness and unity of attitudes and organizations among working people. Some, for example, say that even after 1832 most workers identified with their particular trades and not with the class as a whole.[40] Others remain unconvinced that early nineteenth-century England was anything like the arena of revolutionary conspiracy that Thompson paints so vividly.[41] Still others dislike Thompson's open partisanship of working people. And there can be no doubt that *The Making of the English Working Class* is partisan, as well as combative, polemical, and imperfectly controlled. But these criticisms, as well as those pertaining to specific points, pale in comparison to Thompson's achievement. Who can doubt that Thompson's evidence—trade unions, cooperative societies, universal suffrage organizations, the movement for humane poor relief, and revolutionary conspiracies—points to the nucleus of the English working class? Or that this working class was and is peculiarly English in its traditions and habitual concerns? Or that Thompson gives a coherent and plausible account of the formation of that peculiar nucleus? Moreover, Thompson has made visible and real the lives of millions of forgotten people. It is true that he neglects the history of women and seems to assume that their experiences were the same as those of working men. Nevertheless, he has challenged all historians—indeed all social scientists—to reconsider their concepts of class and class consciousness. He has made historians of modern Britain rethink an entire historical epoch, and do it with a new sense of the interconnectedness of culture, class, and individual agency.

Scholars have naturally wondered why Thompson did not go on to show the flowering of the working class during the Chartist period. His answer was partly that his wife had long been at work on the Chartists, and partly that "a lot of unfinished problems remained in my mind from the beginning of the book [*English Working Class*.]"[42] During and after his tenure at the University of Warwick (1965–1973) Thompson wanted to work out in depth the nature of popular culture in the eighteenth century. Was the eighteenth century in England a golden age of paternalist community—a "World We have Lost"? Was it a society without class or conflict? Certain aspects of what he had written might lead one to answer yes. This is the logical consequence of casting his story of the working class in the form of a movement from the natural to the artificial, and it is the answer often given by members of the pessimist school with whom Thompson ranged himself. But Thompson answered differently in a remarkable series of essays and one short (for him) book, which together comprise a wonderfully rich study of popular culture before the Industrial Revolution. Throughout these works, Thompson engaged in his usual swordplay with historians to the left and to the right; but he also began to show the influence of cultural anthropology and the *Annales* school of history. Overall, his view is that the eighteenth century in England was a time when two cultures—traditional and modern—were in conflict across a broad front; and that the popular defenders of tradition were not without effect.

The first of these eighteenth-century studies is a carefully crafted and polished piece on the changing concept of time and the way that this change was accelerated by the Industrial Revolution.[43] It is, in effect, a cultural history of time. In preindustrial society, time was task-oriented, depending on the routine tasks of the peasant's day. Time was "passed," but as capitalism spread, time came to be "saved" and "spent." In industrial capitalism, "the employer must *use* the time of his labourer, and see it is not wasted: not the task but the value of time when reduced to money is dominant."[44] With industrialization came "the time-sheet, the time-keeper, the informers and the fines." Further, moralists across the board attacked the whole undisciplined way of life of the laboring population. Factory clocks, bells, and fine-books brought preachings, schoolings, the suppression of old work rhythms, and the forced internalization of new work habits. Gone were the natural variety and autonomy of preindustrial work patterns, which Thompson describes in evocative detail; and gone was the traditional unity of work and of life.[45]

Old habits and work rhythms did not go without a struggle, nor did the traditional sense of legitimate economic activity, which came under severe pressure from the ideas and practices of the market. In "The Moral Economy of the English Crowd in the Eighteenth Century," Thompson argues persuasively that, in what might appear to have been spasmodic outbreaks of violence, English crowds, in fact, expressed a popular consensus about the economic norms, standards, and functions of the various parties in a community.[46] English crowds acted in a disciplined way and with clear objectives, resisting the spread of middlemen (corn dealers, for example), and intimidating millers and bakers into negotiating fair prices. Folk memory recalled the intent of sixteenth- and seventeenth-century laws protecting the consumer. Consequently, the populace expected that in times of dearth food prices would be regulated. The "moral economy" of the crowd derived its "sense of legitimation" from a paternalist model of just economic activity, but Thompson insists that the paternalism admired by many social historians of preindustrial England was badly eroded by the eighteenth century. The laboring poor had to provide their own protection. In Thompson's view they had considerable success until the authorities panicked and jettisoned the vestiges of a paternalistic outlook during the French Revolution, and political economy triumphed.[47]

In examining the moral economy of English crowds, Thompson was less interested in analyzing the frequency and the social composition of crowds than in reconstructing the ideology implicit in crowd behavior—their *"mentalité."* The same can be said for his study of Rough Music, another means by which the English laboring poor expressed their sense of justice.[48] Rough Music took the form of noisy parades, riding a villain (or a surrogate) on a plank, burning effigies, staging ritualized hunts, or combining all of these, and accompanying them always with raucous "music" and obscene gestures. Though the particular form varied from region to region, Rough Music was always ritualized hostility, directed against some individual who was thought to have violated an implicit rule of the community. Sometimes it was a shrewish wife who received the treatment; other times a wife-beater, an adulterer, a sexual deviant, or inappropriate couples (such as a young man and an older woman) who chose to marry. Thompson respectfully rejects Claude Levi-Strauss's interpretation of *le charivari anglais*—namely that it signified a social discontinuity. Thompson, instead, sees Rough Music as the conservative reaction of an oral culture to the decomposition of the patriarchal system of authority.[49] The churches could no longer compel psychological assent; so the people exercised it themselves.

Thompson may underestimate the popular influence of churches in eighteenth-century England, but generally his argument seems plausible. Certainly his emphasis on decoding the theater of Rough Music is a fruitful approach. It is also his technique in attempting to explain a major problem in accepting his view of eighteenth-century culture: given the savage social struggle that seems to have characterized the society, how does one account for the apparent serenity and harmony of the monuments of Augustan high culture? Thompson's answer, in "Patrician Society, Plebian Culture," is cultural hegemony.[50] The upper class, by their rituals of power and their majestic country homes, sought to produce a state of mind among the poor in which exploitation and the structures of authority seemed "to be the very course of nature."[51] The aristocracy and gentry chose very carefully those rare occasions when they met the poor face-to-face: on the judicial bench; as patrons giving favors on formal occasions; in church; at the hunt; or in alms-giving at funerals. All such encounters were carried out with a "studied and elaborate hegemonic style . . . gestures and postures rather than actual responsibilities."[52] But as the upper class and the Church withdrew from their patriarchal duties, the plebeians responded by developing a secularized popular culture of fairs, festivals, songs, sports, Rough Music, rush bearings, and the like. The result was not a class society, but one of sharply divided "patricians and plebs."[53]

In his most unusual book, *Whigs and Hunters: The Origin of the*

Black Act, Thompson deals with a more brutal form of patrician control.⁵⁴ He explores, like a commando parachuting into guerrilla territory, the obscure but intense struggle between the common people and their aristocratic predators in the Windsor Forest area of Berkshire and Hampshire. Thompson uncovers a world in which deer poachers defended customary use-rights of forest land against the Whigs, who appear as the corrupt advocates of the absolute rights of private property. The book is repetitious and long-winded, yet Thompson succeeds brilliantly in describing the intricate forest economy: the ecology of farming, fishing, hunting, and peat-cutting; and the complex interconnection of fields, forest, commons, and wastelands. He shows how the middling sorts of the forest managed to scratch out a living so long as they retained their customary rights to cut peat, take "lops and tops," scavenge waste wood, run pigs on common land, and catch a hare now and then. This traditional use of the land was threatened by the Hanoverians' strict enforcement of the laws protecting deer in the forest.

Thompson reveals that behind the campaign to protect the deer stood a more sinister conspiracy. A forest bureaucracy sought to use deer-stealing by the so-called Blacks as an excuse to advance their own interests. Many of these unscrupulous forest officials were connected to Walpole and his Whig cronies. Hence the second and third decades of the century were years of sporadic conflict between keepers and poachers: arrests, fines, and executions on one side; poaching, threats, extortion, and raids on keepers' houses on the other. Both sides were predators, according to Thompson. Blacks were often declining gentry or yeomen facing newcomers "with greater command of money and of influence, and with greater ruthlessness in the use of both."⁵⁵ Thompson can hardly be said to have emplotted their conflict, yet his analysis takes its usual form—transition from the natural to the artificial, from common custom to individual self-interest.

The Black Act, Thompson concludes, did not work immediately, for "Blacking" continued through midcentury. Nevertheless, the savage act could only have been drawn up by a new kind of exploiter, "by men who had formed habits of mental distance and moral levity to human life," men who saw justice "as no more than the outworks and defences of property and of its attendant status."⁵⁶ It would thus seem perfect evidence for all those Marxists who regard the law as the machinery for oppression by the ruling class. But in an amazing turn, Thompson at the end of *Whigs and Hunters* attacks any Marxist who might think so. The law, he says, may have been an instrument of the ruling class in the eighteenth century, but it was an instrument of an unusual sort. The law functioned as a legitimating ideology for the rulers, and as such its power rested on its impartiality. The law therefore took on—and retains—its own logic of development. Even if it falls short of its own ideal, the law controls the ruling class just as it does the ruled. The English people took it to heart and made it part of the rights of the free-born Englishman. There is a difference, Thompson reminds his Marxist colleagues, between "arbitrary power and the rule of law." The "rule of law is itself an unqualified good."[57]

This Whiggish sentiment is a surprising ending for a book that does so much to demolish the traditional view of the Whigs. Thompson, after all, utterly rejects the view that eighteenth-century English society was one of consensus and deference. He drives that point home in his final (so far) piece on the eighteenth century: "Eighteenth-Century English Society: Class Struggle without Class?"[58] This is his least polished and least satisfactory historical work, for it was, Thompson admits, cobbled together over a six or seven year period. Nevertheless, it offers a stimulating interpretation of preindustrial England. Essentially, Thompson argues that the paternalist explanation will not do. The real features of the society were the importance of money, the exploitation of offices, and a state that stepped back and allowed agrarian and mercantile capitalists to get on with their self-aggrandizement.

Yet there were four restraints on predatory oligarchy: (1) the independent Tory gentry, (2) the press, (3) the law, and (4) the crowd. Thompson is most interested in the last. The plebs could and did unite as consumers, taxpayers, or smugglers on various economic, moral, libertarian, or patriotic issues. They did not form a class, because they lacked the consciousness and modes of class revolt. They were, however, engaged in class struggle. Here Thompson returns to the great theme of *The Making of the English Working Class*. Classes happen in a historical process, as a result of historical experiences. Class struggle *precedes* class: "To put it bluntly: classes do not exist as separate entities, look around, find an enemy class, and then start to struggle."[59] In the process of struggling, people sometimes come to know themselves as a class. Thompson, one may argue, fails to spell out the *type* of circumstances in which class conflict produces class, though in *The Making of the English Working Class* he had detailed the *particular* circumstances in which it happened in England. Even so, his view of the eighteenth century seems credible: the English people were engaged in a *"rebellious* traditional culture" of riots, fairs, Rough Music, and the like.[60] The ruling orders exerted cultural hegemony but could not impose total domination over the plebs, who passed on their traditions to the new working class.

Thompson's eighteenth-century studies brought him full circle, back to the process of class formation, by way of exploring the popular culture that preceded class society. Ever since *The Making of the English Working Class,* Thompson had fought a running battle with the hard-line Marxists to his left, during which he formulated his theory of history. The basis of that theory is Marxism, but a style of Marxism much modified by what Thompson calls "empiricism" — a rigorous dialogue between hypothesis and evidence. Thompson has written about his theory on two levels: (1) grand interpretation, and (2) the logic of historical enquiry. In his view, the former must depend on a proper employment of the latter.

Thompson makes a clear distinction between methodology and theory. Many historians, he says, wrongly think that a method, like quantitative or literary analysis, is theory while, in fact, such methods are the means by which theory (grand interpretation) is broken down and tested. Further, he rightly argues that many economic historians parade cliometric methods as theory, when in truth their methods are only an elaborate disguise for capitalist ideology. Theory on the first level is to Thompson the large-scale interpretations that have to be tested in the practice of writing history. In this sense, all theories are provisional.[61] The best example of his own theorizing on this level appears in his essay, "The Peculiarities of the English."[62] This is a long rebuttal of work by the British Marxists, Perry Anderson and Tom Nairn, who had compared British culture unfavorably with those of certain other European countries.[63] Their view of English history is that England's bourgeois revolution (of the seventeenth century) was premature and incomplete; that it left the landlords in place; that the English bourgeoisie never formulated any significant ideology; that since the bourgeoisie had not done *its* job, workers could not do *theirs;* that the intellectuals were (and are) needed for the critique and evolution of English society; and finally that English intellectuals have failed in their historic role because they were not a coherent group and were too much a part of the dominant culture.

This is a theory that Thompson loves to hate. He argues, with great vigor and wit, that Anderson and Nairn adopted too static and inductive a model of the English past, that they should have been more empirical, and that they had got English history all wrong. In Thompson's view, the seventeenth century *did* leave the landlords in place, but they formed a *capitalist* class, a "true bourgeoisie." Mercantile capitalists grouped themselves around the gentry, and together they constituted an extremely confident and successful capitalist class. True, an aristocratic *style* remained in place, as well as certain archaic aristocratic institutions, but nothing more. After 1832, he contends, the industrial bourgeoisie extended its socioeconomic power, and the new middle class came to dominate certain key institutions such as municipal government, boards of guardians, the police force, and the provincial universities. The middle class broke the aristocratic monopoly on the governing elite, and reduced the aristocracy to the level of "the staff at an elaborate and prestigious hotel, who could in no way influence the comings and goings of the clientele, who or at what time or with whom, but who could arrange the ball and appoint a Master of Ceremonies."[64]

In Thompson's view, Anderson and Nairn had so tightly tied themselves to a model that they could understand neither the achievements of British bourgeois culture nor the importance of British intellectuals. They failed to recognize, for instance, the importance of bourgeois realist fiction, the ideology of political economy, or the discoveries of British natural science. British intellectuals, to be sure, never formed an internally unified and alienated intelligentsia. Nevertheless, they founded multiple centers of intellectual activity, which afforded them opportunity for initiatives and for "the interpenetration of theory and *praxis.*"[65] Further, British intellectuals worked within the tradition of empiricism, which is no emaciated ideology but a powerful and beneficial "idiom." In short, Anderson and Nairn had adopted a model from Marx, but had allowed it to petrify. They had applied their model "to the proliferating growth of actuality," selecting from the past only such evidence as fitted the model.

A non-Marxist historian may well feel that Thompson is as guilty as Anderson and Nairn in building a model derived from Marxian categories. His sense of the eighteenth-century landlords as a capitalist class, for example, seems a crude categorization that captures only part of the qualities of landlordism and gives a distorted view of preindustrial social structure.[66] The distinction that Thompson seems to accept between the mercantile/landlord bourgeoisie and the new middle class of the nineteenth century remains shadowy. His notion of the impotence of the mid-Victorian aristocracy is controversial.[67] Yet Thompson's theory seems more subtle and complex than Anderson and Nairn's, for it is built upon a richer knowledge of nineteenth-century English cultural history. Thompson escapes the false sense that individuals or social groups failed in the historical roles assigned to them by Marx. To him, people are influenced by, and respond to, economic, social, and cultural circumstances, but their thought and behavior are not to be judged by historians' deductions from first principles.

This point leads to the second level of Thompson's historical theory. In his view, the Anderson-Nairn idea of class is static, too dependent on direct economic determinism. They interpret too mechanically Marx's metaphor of base and superstructure, and like Stalin convert a useful metaphor into rigid determinism. They fail to realize that Marx and Engels always kept in mind the mutual interaction of social consciousness and social being.[68] Ironically, Anderson and Nairn, and all such rigid Marxists, are guilty of the same simplistic determinism as the political economists against whom Marx fought. To be sure, Thompson admits, Marx himself was scarred by his struggle with political economy. Marx and Engels thus posed "revolutionary *economic* man . . . as the antithesis to exploited *economic* man." But by bringing romanticism and Marxism together, William Morris had shown that exploitation in capitalist society is "*simultaneously* economic, moral, and cultural."[69] This complex of socioeconomic and cultural factors is properly what history is about.

Thompson makes essentially the same points in his long theoretical and polemical essay, "The Poverty of Theory or an Orrery of Errors," only now the target is Louis Althusser and structuralist Marxists.[70] In this rambling, self-indulgent, inflated, but often telling attack, Thompson accuses Althusser and his allies of putting theory so far first that they neglect historical data; of building rigid models, especially of base and superstructure; of denying human agency; of making a dogma ("theology") of their particular interpretation of Marx and therefore of Stalinism. Indeed, Thompson, by means of rhetoric, jibes, exaggeration, and appeals to common sense, seeks — not entirely successfully — to build an identity between structuralism, determinism, idealism, and Stalinism; and to slay this monster in the name of empiricism.

Thompson never clarifies what he means by "structuralism," and he seems to be unaware of its varieties. But his understanding of its institutional origins and historiographical consequences is acute. He regards structuralism as the result of a highly academic and theoretical epistemology that constructs a self-enclosed system. Like philosophical idealism, it posits a conceptual world "in which it imposes its own ideality upon the phenomena of material and social existence, rather than engaging in continual dialogue with these."[71] The material world that structuralism (or at least Althusser's Marxist variety) assumes is one of economic determinism, an axiom deduced from Marx, but never exposed to historical testing. Althusser, according to Thompson, denies the validity of historical knowledge, while Marx and Engels actually constructed their theory from the study of English history. For Althusser, theory must be liberated from temporality to reach the rigor of mathematics. In Thompson's view, this is rubbish, since any Marxist is trying to understand real people in particular historical circumstances.

Quite apart from what Marx actually said—and Thompson is sure Marx is on his side—Thompson seeks to fight Althusser on the grounds of how historians actually work. Thompson is certain that historical facts *are* out there, and that they are witnesses to historical processes. Of course, facts do not disclose themselves; and all historians know that the evidence must be questioned by sophisticated techniques. But the evidence is there to be interrogated, and the evidence is not "infinitely malleable." A genuine discipline is needed—a dialogue between "thought and objective materials" or a testing of hypotheses by empirical research.[72] Historical knowledge, consequently, is always "provisional and incomplete" but "not therefore untrue."[73] Furthermore, one can safely make moral judgments about the past (a practice ruled out by determinism), provided we hold judgments in reserve until we have decided about facts and causes. If Marxist interpretations are truer than others, it is because they have stood empirical testing better than others, not because of Marx's authority.[74]

Althusser's theory, on the other hand, provides an intellectual rationale for Stalinism. Just as Stalinism crushed individual initiative, heroism, and popular socialism in Eastern Europe, so Althusserianism denies human agency. Stalinism imposes an iron model of society: the economic base determines legal, philosophical, and cultural systems. Yet in Stalinist countries, by a cruel perversion, the base is forced to serve the superstructure—the people serve the Party. Althusser's structuralism interprets Marx's metaphors mechanically, and therefore conceives of individuals as mere "bearers" of structures. Althusser, according to Thompson, denies that people can make their own natures, or that they can use their cultural heritage to deal with their experiences. Unfortunately, Thompson admits, Marx was silent on experience and on choice of values. Hence Stalinism, with some plausibility, has been able to prohibit moral critiques of itself. And in Althusser's work, Stalinism is "reduced to the paradigm of Theory. It is Stalinism at last, theorised as ideology."[75]

As Perry Anderson has shown, Thompson misunderstood Althusser's attitude toward Stalinism; thus the alleged connection between Althusser's ideas and Stalinism is in this sense false. Nevertheless, Thompson's posing of history against "theory" is significant. For the mature Thompson, the historical discipline takes priority even over Marxist categories and interpretations. For him history is the alternative to closed deductive systems, and is therefore the hope for a humane and self-critical Marxism, as well as the basis for a modern critique of industrial capitalism and political economy. Thompson takes his categories, his questions, and his moral judgments from the Marxist tradition (not simply from Marx himself), but he subjects his historical hypotheses to the discipline of historical interrogation. For him, this procedure is crucial, because history has a much more important role than making contributions to the stockpile of academic knowledge. History to Thompson is too important to be left to academic historians.[76] Much as they might have disagreed with him on particular interpretations, Victorian sages like Carlyle and Macaulay would have understood this.

NOTES

1. "E. P. Thompson," interview in *Visions of History*, ed. Henry Abelove et al. (New York: Pantheon Books, 1983), 11.
2. E. P. Thompson, *Writing by Candlelight* (London: Merlin Press, 1980), 37.
3. E. P. Thompson and T. J. Thompson, *There Is a Spirit in Europe: A Memoir of Frank Thompson* (London: Victor Gollancz, 1948).
4. Ibid., 14, 20, 57–58.
5. Ibid., 173–206.
6. Fred Inglis, *Radical Earnestness: English Social Theory, 1880–1980* (Oxford: Martin Robertson, 1982), 194–95.
7. Abelove, ed., "Thompson," 19.
8. E. P. Thompson, "Caudwell," in *The Socialist Register, 1977,* ed. Ralph Miliband and John Saville (London: Merlin Press, 1977), 230; and Abelove, ed., "Thompson," 19.
9. Thompson, "Caudwell," 238–39.
10. Abelove, ed., "Thompson," 20.
11. Ibid., 13; E. P. Thompson, *William Morris: Romantic to Revolutionary,* 2d ed. (New York: Pantheon Books, 1977), 817.
12. E. P. Thompson, *William Morris: Romantic to Revolutionary* (London, Lawrence & Wishart, 1955); all subsequent citations are to this edition, unless otherwise noted.
13. Ibid., 30.
14. Ibid., 43–44.
15. Ibid., 84.
16. Ibid., 215.
17. Ibid., 272.
18. Ibid., 311.

19. Ibid., 477, 498.
20. Ibid., 630.
21. Ibid., 763.
22. Thompson, *Morris,* 2d ed., 817–18.
23. Thompson, *Morris,* 280.
24. Ibid., 16.
25. Abelove, ed., "Thompson," 20.
26. Bryan D. Palmer, *The Making of E. P. Thompson: Marxism, Humanism, and History* (Toronto: New Hogtown Press, 1981), chap. 3; David R. Holden, "The First New Left in Britain" (Ph.D. diss., Univ. of Wisconsin-Madison, 1976), especially chap. 7; Perry Anderson, *Arguments within English Marxism* (London: New Left Books, 1980), chap. 5.
27. Abelove, ed., "Thompson," 6–7.
28. E. P. Thompson, *The Making of the English Working Class* (New York: Vintage Books, 1963), 191.
29. Harold Perkin, *The Structured Crowd* (Brighton: Harvester Press, 1981), 168. Perkin says that Thompson shows the same paternalism for the poor of the past that he "descries in the eighteenth-century squire."
30. Thompson, *English Working Class,* 8–11.
31. Ibid., 111.
32. Ibid., 195.
33. Ibid., 211, 318.
34. George Kitson Clark, *The Making of Victorian England* (New York: Atheneum, 1967), chaps. 3 and 4.
35. For Thompson's account of the weavers, see his *English Working Class,* chap. 9.
36. Ibid., 350, 368.
37. Ibid., 549, 553, and chap. 14.
38. Ibid., 606.
39. Ibid., 814, 831.
40. J. F. C. Harrison, *The Early Victorians, 1832–51* (New York: Praeger, 1971), chap. 2.
41. Norman Gash, *Aristocracy and People: Britain, 1815–1865* (Cambridge, Mass.: Harvard Univ. Press, 1979), Introduction and chaps. 2 and 3; Anderson, *Arguments within Marxism,* 33–39. There is an excellent analysis of *English Working Class* in Harvey J. Kaye, *The British Marxist Historians* (Cambridge: Polity Press, 1984), chap. 6.
42. Abelove, ed., "Thompson," 14.
43. E. P. Thompson, "Time, Work-Discipline, and Industrial Capitalism," *Past and Present* 58(Dec. 1967):56–97.
44. Ibid., 61.
45. Ibid., 82, 93.
46. E. P. Thompson, "The Moral Economy of the English Crowd in the Eighteenth Century," *Past and Present* 51(1971):76–136.
47. Ibid., 129.
48. E. P. Thompson, " 'Rough Music': Le Charivari Anglais," *Annales* no. 2(Mar.–Apr. 1972):285–312.
49. Ibid., 300–304.
50. E. P. Thompson, "Patrician Society, Plebeian Culture," *Journal of Social History* 7(Summer 1974):382–405.

51. Ibid., 387.
52. Ibid., 389–90.
53. Ibid., 395–96.
54. E. P. Thompson, *Whigs and Hunters: The Origin of the Black Act* (New York: Pantheon Books, 1975).
55. Ibid., 108.
56. Ibid., 197.
57. Ibid., 267.
58. E. P. Thompson, "Eighteenth-Century English Society: Class Struggle without Class?" *Social History* 3, no. 2(May 1978):133–65.
59. Ibid., 149.
60. Ibid., 154.
61. Abelove, ed., "Thompson," 15–16.
62. E. P. Thompson, "The Peculiarities of the English," in *The Socialist Register, 1965,* ed. Ralph Miliband and John Saville (London: Merlin Press, 1965), 311–62.
63. See Perry Anderson, "Origins of the Present Crisis," *New Left Review* (Jan.–Feb. 1964):26–54; and "Socialism and Pseudo-Empiricism," *New Left Review* (Jan.–Feb. 1966):2–42; Tom Nairn, "The English Working Class," *New Left Review* (Mar.–Apr. 1964):43–57; Nairn, "The Nature of the Labour Party–I," *New Left Review* (Sept.–Oct. 1964):38–65; and Nairn, "The Nature of the Labour Party–II," *New Left Review* (Nov.–Dec. 1964):32–62. For Anderson's account of the dispute, see his *Arguments within Marxism,* 138–40.
64. Thompson, "Peculiarities of the English," 329.
65. Ibid., 332.
66. For a systematic description of eighteenth-century English social structure, see Harold Perkin, *The Origins of Modern English Society, 1780–1880* (London: Routledge & Kegan Paul, 1969), chap. 2.
67. See Walter Arnstein, "The Survival of the Victorian Aristocracy," in *The Rich, the Well-Born, and the Powerful,* ed. F. C. Jaher (Champaign: Univ. of Illinois Press, 1973).
68. Thompson, "Peculiarities of the English," 351.
69. Ibid., 355, 356.
70. E. P. Thompson, "The Poverty of Theory or an Orrery of Errors," in his *The Poverty of Theory and Other Essays* (New York: Monthly Review Press, 1978), 1–210.
71. Ibid., 13.
72. Ibid., 25–37. For other remarks on historical discipline, see E. P. Thompson, "Anthropology and the Discipline of Historical Context," *Midland History,* no. 1(Spring 1972):41–55.
73. Thompson, "Poverty of Theory," 39.
74. Ibid., 44.
75. Ibid., 182. Anderson's *Arguments within Marxism* is a brilliant reply to Thompson's "Poverty of Theory."
76. Thompson has shown his passionate concern with the present and future most recently in his long novel *The Sykaos Papers* (London: Bloomsbury Press, 1988). In this science-fiction fable, Thompson satirizes current power politics, nuclear arsenals, and environmental destruction, and celebrates agency, human creativity, and rebelliousness.

Norman Gash ᘏᓭ *Peelite*

WALTER L. ARNSTEIN

During an era in which prevalent notions as to the proper content and the appropriate direction of modern British history have been greatly influenced by E. P. Thompson and Eric Hobsbawm, their associates, and their disciples, it is easy to dismiss Norman Gash as a Tory stalwart, the surviving proponent of an older and even outmoded tradition that gave pride of place to political history. That Gash remains persuaded of the centrality of political history, broadly conceived, to our understanding of the past is clear. Yet it would be equally fair to see him as a twentieth-century historical revisionist in his own right.

In his writings Gash has challenged the historical assumptions of the 1920s and 1930s—as popularized by such liberal historians as George Macaulay Trevelyan and by such radical historians as John and Barbara Hammond—on at least five grounds: (1) that it is grossly misleading to describe the 1815–1830 era as one dominated by a powerful and repressive Tory party responsive only to the landed interest; (2) that the significance of the Reform Act of 1832 as a break with Britain's "unreformed" political past has been much exaggerated; (3) that Sir Robert Peel and not the two Pitts, Charles James Fox, Gladstone, or Disraeli was the single most influential British political leader between the 1750s and the onset of the twentieth century;[1] (4) that England's supposedly outmoded and repressive early nineteenth-century governing class was overthrown neither by a middle class revolt at the hustings nor by the agitation of an aroused self-conscious working class. Rather, by a policy of intelligent flexibility and intense involvement in the leading social, religious, and educational movements of the day, the aristocracy and gentry enabled Britain to adapt in an ultimately peaceful and sensible fashion to the challenges posed by rapid population growth, large-scale urbanization, and industrialization; and (5) that historians ought not to leave the writing of political biographies to enthusiastic amateurs but to undertake the task themselves, because biographies remain as important as monographs, essays, and surveys in making the past comprehensible.

Norman Gash was born on January 16, 1912 at Meerut, India, the son of Frederick and Kate Gash. In the course of a twenty-five-year career with the Royal Berkshire regiment, Gash's father rose from the lowly rank of private to that of regimental sergeant-major, serving in India—where three of his five children were born—and also in Canada, the West Indies, and Africa. He fought in the Boer War and World War I—two of his brothers died on the western front—and he was stationed in Ireland during the "Time of Troubles" from 1917 to 1919. Like the youthful G. M. Trevelyan, Norman Gash therefore obtained early personal experience of "the Irish Question" that he was to distill later in his studies of Peel as Irish secretary and as prime minister. Professor Gash's chief recollections of his two years in Dublin remain the school at which he was taught to knit and to unravel and the family departure from the Dublin quayside one wet wintry evening. An Irish street urchin yelled out after them: "I hope the U-boats get you!" By then the war with Germany had been over for a year.[2]

At school in Reading, young Norman found himself initially far more fascinated by languages than by history, an inclination encouraged by the headmaster, a confirmed classicist. When another teacher encouraged Gash during his senior year to turn to modern history instead, the headmaster deplored the decision with "sorrow and anger." Winning in 1930 a scholarship to St. John's College, Oxford, and knowing little of English history before 1400, Gash discovered to his initial regret that Austin Lane Poole, the highly reputed college medievalist, was a poor teacher, whereas the modernist William Conrad Costin, though almost unknown as a scholar, was a first-rate tutor. Although aware that medieval history remained far more prestigious in the Oxbridge world than was the study of later centuries, Gash found himself drawn to the more recent past by a tutor who still referred to "Mr. Gladstone" as a contemporary. Gash's scholarly future was set into motion when Costin asked him to write a paper on the repeal of the Corn Laws and suggested in passing, "Better look at C. S. Parker's *Peel*." Almost immediately it became clear to Gash that when Peel spoke of himself as "Minister of the Crown," he meant something far different from the same phrase when employed by Stanley Baldwin in the 1920s and 1930s. Early–Victorian Britain had as yet scarcely been included in the corpus of modern historical scholarship, so Gash developed his approach to the period "unclouded by the work of other historians."

The notion of becoming a professional historian developed slowly for Gash. For a time he considered a career in the Indian civil service, a choice his parents would have favored. But even in 1933, the days of British imperial administration impressed Gash as numbered, and the home civil service proved less appealing as a prospective career. Having completed his three years at Oxford with first class honors in modern history, Gash was easily persuaded to stay an extra year to write a B.Litt. (now M.Litt.) paper on the agricultural riots of 1830 in Berkshire. The subject interested him because the relevant Home Office documents and local newspapers were accessible and because his own paternal ancestors had worked as agricultural laborers in Berkshire and Oxfordshire. (His great-grandfather had served as village constable at Bix near Henley-on-Thames and his grandfather had become a market gardener for the burgeoning London metropolis.) As he immersed himself in the documents, Gash discovered that—as in the case of Peel and the party system—the conventional historical wisdom seemed to conflict with the evidence. Sentimental social historians, like J. L. and Barbara Hammond in *The Village Labourer, 1760–1832* (1911), had postulated a fundamental conflict between laborers and landlords, whereas the true "villains" of the story were those tenant farmers who took advantage of the Old Poor Law to keep as small a permanent staff of farm workers as they could get away with by hiring extra help for no more than seven or eight months of the rural year. The result of the paper was not only an additional academic degree but Gash's first appearance in a scholarly journal, the *Economic History Review*.[3]

As his tenure at Oxford drew to a close, Gash looked for a teaching post. He needed to earn a living, and, having fallen in love, he required sufficient income to support a wife. Ivy Whitehorn, the daughter of an engineer in Reading, had gone to St. Hugh's College, Oxford, to read French, and it was there that Gash first met her. His first job, as history master at a small school in Dorset run by two brothers, did not last long. By the spring of 1935 the school had gone bankrupt, and when the new proprietor turned out to be a teacher of history Gash was out of work. The wedding was scheduled anyway, and a week before it took place, the University of Edinburgh offered Gash a job as temporary assistant lecturer, primarily to teach a course on nineteenth-century Europe. J. L. Hammond had put in a word on Gash's behalf with Basil Williams, the department head in Edinburgh.

The newly wedded couple sailed to their new home on the London-Leith packet boat and played bridge while the vessel battled a North Sea storm. On the third morning it limped into the Scottish port. Gash met Williams in his office, where he was shocked to learn that he was expected to lecture that very day at 11 A.M. At 10:59, a somewhat rattled young lecturer stepped into the hall to find the redoubtable Professor Williams in the midst of the audience. Gash survived that ordeal, and a year later was able to persuade University College, London, authorities that his knowledge of nineteenth-century British political history sufficed for the post of assistant lecturer in modern history there. He held that post for the next four years, supplementing his income with occasional evening courses taught under the auspices of the Workers' Educational Association (WEA). While in London, Gash began to explore the papers of Sir Robert Peel at the British Museum. They impressed him as a gold mine, an opportunity to explore—as no previous scholar had done—the complexities of post-1832 electoral politics in England.

The first scholarly results of these researches came in the form of two contributions to the *English Historical Review:* in the October 1938 issue a note on "Ashley and the Conservative Party in 1842," and the next year an article on "The Influence of the Crown at Windsor and Brighton in the Elections of 1832, 1835, and 1837." Research came to an abrupt halt in 1940, when—right after Dunkirk—Gash volunteered for army service. The War Office initially insisted that it needed "equipment, not men!" but in November 1940 Gash was accepted as an officer in the Intelligence Corps, promoted to the rank of captain in 1942 and that of major in 1945. He brought to the task of studying and interpreting reports on German army orders of battle and organization the same methodical temperament and sharp analytical mind that he had previously brought to bear on documents in the archives.

As the war ended, Gash was earning a good salary, and he was once again tempted by the income and the security of a peacetime civil service position. His eye was caught, however, by an advertisement for a history position at the University of St. Andrews. The Gashes had already had one happy taste of Scotland, and St. Andrews gave promise of an idyllic refuge from a drab bombed-out London. Before he had formally been offered the post there—as lecturer in modern British and American history—the *Scotsman* of Edinburgh had already announced the appointment. Norman and Ivy Gash moved to

St. Andrews in the summer of 1946. He was briefly diverted to the University of Leeds in 1953, but his wife and two daughters disliked their new environment, and Gash, a southern Englishman by upbringing, also found that he preferred provincial Scotland to industrial Yorkshire. The offer of the post of professor of history drew him back to St. Andrews in 1955, and Gash remained there for the rest of his teaching career. Scottish degrees involved four years of work rather than the three required by English universities; students therefore arrived at a younger age and were exposed to more survey courses and lectures than at Oxford or Cambridge.

During his first years at St. Andrews, Gash lived up to his formal title and taught a survey course in American history on several occasions. After his return in 1955 as professor and department head, his teaching became more specialized. Later he was to serve also in "the nethermost pit of administrator" as vice-principal (1967–1971) and as dean of the Faculty of Arts (1978–1980). Gash thus became one of the few major historians of his generation in Great Britain to combine a steady output of scholarship with academic administration. He ruled the department with a firm paternal hand; there was "none of the democratic nonsense" at St. Andrews in those years. During his regime there was a threefold expansion in faculty and student numbers, but in spite of administrative and family responsibilities, every evening he would be off to his study "messing about with books." During the long vacations he worked steadily on his researches, and except for the spring of 1962, when he taught at the Johns Hopkins University as Hinckley Professor of English History, his philosophy was one of staying on the spot and doing his scholarly work.

Because able undergraduate students at St. Andrews were encouraged to pursue post-graduate study at Oxford or Cambridge, Gash advised relatively few graduate students. Those who did embark on academic careers, however, include Edith Johnston of Macquarie University (Australia) and John Simpson of the University of Edinburgh. Yet others—like John Cookson of the University of Canterbury (New Zealand), David Hampton of Queen's University, Belfast, and F. A. Dreyer of the University of Western Ontario—came to St. Andrews for the specific purpose of doing graduate research with Gash.[4]

The initial results of Gash's own post-1945 researches into early Victorian politics came first in an article in the *English Historical Review*[5] and then as an influential paper, "Peel and the Party System 1830–50," presented to the Royal Historical Society in 1950, the centenary year of Peel's death.[6] In that paper Gash explained the oft-noted historical paradox that Robert Peel had destroyed during the 1840s the very Conservative party that he had created during the 1830s. Gash acknowledged that Peel had contributed enormously to the growth of the party's parliamentary strength during the 1830s but, since "Peel was not good at handling men, and had notoriously little interest in the humdrum and unelevating details of party management,"[7] Gash credited the organization of constituency associations and registration societies to others. Conservatism, "as Peel understood it," Gash insisted, "was not a tactical doctrine designed to draw votes to the Tory party; the Tory party was a tactical device to make Conservatism the basis of government."[8] During the post-1832 era, party had become for Peel a necessary basis for the strong executive that the kingdom required. No wonder that at the time of the 1846 Corn Law crisis Peel had no desire to permit the large but lazy backbench tail to wag the responsible executive head of the party dog. Peel, concluded Gash, was primarily a government rather than a party man.

The magnum opus toward which these studies had been leading had been two-thirds completed by 1940. Gash's postwar research was focused on Part I, the immediate implications of the 1832 Reform Act. Twelve publishers had to be approached, however, before Longman published the work in 1953. *Politics in the Age of Peel* was hailed almost universally as a major contribution to modern understanding of how politics at the constituency level operated in early-Victorian Britain. Part II of the book, "The Working of the System," was prescribed by Asa Briggs as "basic reading for all serious students of the nineteenth century." Chapters like "The Price of Politics," "Electoral Violence," and "Corrupt Boroughs" seemed to demonstrate how many of the abuses that the Reform Bill of 1832 had been designed to correct lived on during the decades that followed. Gash was the first historian to concentrate on "the political practices as opposed to the constitutional theories or legal machinery of the times."[9] He was the first to explain how "legitimate" as opposed to "corrupt" influence was exercised at a time when the franchise (nonsecret) was still interpreted as "a trusteeship" rather than as a right. Landlords influenced tenants, employers influenced contractors, clergymen their parishioners, and customers their shopkeepers. The politics of the day, Gash insists, involved not only the oligarchic (administrative) tradition of government and public opinion as exemplified and manipulated by Chartists and Anti–Corn Law League leaders but also the new registration societies, constituency associations, the central party agents, and the London political clubs (to which the final chapter is devoted). The traditional ability of the government to influence election outcomes in particular constituencies—for example, those in which royal dockyards were located—was, however, rapidly disappearing.

Reviewers like Briggs (then working on his *Age of Improvement, 1783-1867*) gave qualified approval also to Gash's conclusion in Part I of *Politics in the Age of Peel:* that the great Reform Act constituted less a gigantic leap than a modest step along the path of adapting old institutions to an urbanizing and industrializing society. In 1832 Whigs and Tories alike feared revolution, and neither sought to overturn the constitution. For both parties, property, rather than numbers, served as the foundation of good government, and both desired to avoid disorder and bloodshed. "They were in the position of two physicians working according to the same science, differing in their interpretation of a particular case."[10] Briggs disagreed, however, with Gash's contention that on the historic and philosophical plane the Tories of 1832 were better prophets than the Whigs as to the long-range consequences of reform.[11] Doubtless the Tories were right to suggest that the act would not constitute the final constitutional settlement, but those who apocalyptically anticipated the immediate downfall of every ancient institution—the monarchy, the House of Lords, the Church of England—were proved wrong.

Although Part III of *Politics in the Age of Peel,* "Direction from Above," was described by Briggs as "a collection of scraps rather than an analysis," the book established Gash as a major historian of nineteenth-century Britain.[12] In *The History Men,* John P. Kenyon classifies Gash as one of many imitators of Sir Lewis Namier, author of the two-volume *Structure of Politics at the Accession of George III* and related works.[13] This judgment is misleading. It is true that *Politics in the Age of Peel* is concerned with "structure" and that Gash afterwards contributed to a festschrift in Namier's honor, but Gash's book had been largely drafted before he had ever read Namier's *Structure of Politics.* Although Gash and Namier exchanged minor courtesies during the 1950s, Gash remains skeptical "of the collective biography approach" and of Namier's "somewhat teutonic ideas of harnessing gangs of research workers to do the donkey work."[14]

Gash's contribution to the Namier festschrift was a critique of Elie Halévy's thesis that the French Revolution of 1830 influenced the British general election of that year in a pro-reform direction.[15] Drawing in part on a minute appraisal of contemporary newspaper reports, Gash argues persuasively that it did not. He fails to pursue, however, the more significant, though speculative, notion that, had the Revolution of 1830 turned either radical or violent, it might well have undermined the cause of Britain's parliamentary reformers.

The first volume of Gash's monumental biography of Peel was the next of his major works to appear, but it may be appropriate to turn first to a slightly later work. *Reaction and Reconstruction in English Politics, 1832–1852*,[16] the amplified Ford lectures for 1964 at Oxford, constitutes a counterpart to *Politics in the Age of Peel*. Whereas the earlier work had dealt with the substructure of politics, *Reaction and Reconstruction* focuses on the superstructure. The first two chapters assess the monarchy and the House of Lords, the next two the role of religion in contemporary politics, and the final two the Conservative and Liberal parties of the time. Reviewers agreed that Gash had provided a polished brief assessment of the roles played by the monarch and the peers in the years when British politicians came to grips with the implications of 1832. He sets in context the actions of King William IV, that surprising "cauldron of energy,"[17] who dismissed Melbourne as prime minister in 1834. The electorate, in effect, repudiated that action a few months later, but the spell in office was instrumental in reviving Conservative spirits and fortunes and in fixing Peel as the party's leader.

The 1830s and 1840s have been described as an age of industrialism, materialism, and utilitarianism—as well as of Chartists and Corn Law reformers—but, Gash insists, "social legislation was not the primary issue of contemporary politics, and it is only retrospective interest that makes it so."[18] The major controversies of the day all involved religion. It became a Conservative raison d'être to preserve the public role and inner vitality of the Church of England. The Liberal penchant was to sympathize with religious dissent and to chip away at the Church's public role—especially in education. And so the Whig government's moves of 1839 in the direction of secular education were defeated, as also was the Conservative government's attempt in 1843 to entrench the Church in that very arena.

In his final chapters, Gash provides a capsule summary of the meaning of both conservatism and Whiggish liberalism in the minds of each group's parliamentary adherents during the early Victorian era. Gash's friendly rival, Derek Beales, was to criticize the volume's strong Conservative bias and the manner in which its author "treats Peel's remarks with absurd reverence." He acknowledges, however, that the book "provides the most sophisticated analysis available of the Parliamentary politics of the period."[19] He goes on to note how Gash had subtly retreated from the manner in which he had downgraded the significance of party in his 1951 essay, "Peel and the Party System." Gash was now prepared to concede that 1832 had constituted "the point of origin for a new party system"[20] and that, especially between 1835 and 1845, adherents of the two major parliamentary groupings showed a high degree of party loyalty. Peel and his lieutenants, Gash points out, realized more quickly than the Whig grandees or the post-1846 protectionists that "a national party must itself be a diversified party, representing and somehow harmonising diversified interests."[21] Gash followed up *Reaction and Reconstruction* with a 182-page book of documents on the 1828–1851 era, *The Age of Peel*,[22] and he was to return to the subject of the structure, the ethos, and the meaning of the nineteenth-century Conservative party in several subsequent essays and articles.

The keystone of the scholarly arch that Norman Gash has constructed has been his magisterial two-volume biography of Sir Robert Peel.[23] C. S. Parker had completed a three-volume *Sir Robert Peel from His Private Papers* back in 1899, and in 1929 A. A. W. Ramsay had published *Sir Robert Peel,* a biography based in part on manuscript sources; but as Robert McDowell observed in 1961, "a biography of Peel on a scale commensurate with his achievement has long been a desideratum in British historical writing."[24] It has been the all-but-unanimous consensus of Gash's reviewers that this is precisely what Gash has produced, painstakingly, comprehensively, and—in almost 1,400 pages of text—on a grand scale. Inasmuch as Peel had played a central role in the pre-1830 Liverpool and Wellington ministries—first as chief secretary for Ireland, then as home secretary, and after 1828 also as leader of the House of Commons—and since he had subsequently created the post-1832 Conservative party and had twice served as prime minister (1834–1835 and 1841–1846), the surface details of Peel's political career were hardly novel. What Gash added was nuance and context, the result of two decades of immersion in Peel's own surviving correspondence and in that of a score of contemporaries, as well as in the department files (especially those involving Peel's six years as Irish secretary) that no previous biographer had tackled. According to reviewer F. C. Mather, the biography enlarges our understanding of Peel in four main ways: (1) "it enhances the perception of his skill in the conduct of affairs of state"; (2) it "fills out the picture of his private life and personal opinions"; (3) it reveals the importance that Peel "attached to the welfare of the poor"; and (4) it "adds to our knowledge of Peel's constitutional significance."[25]

Several of these observations merit elaboration. Unlike prime ministers Canning, Palmerston, and Gladstone, Peel did not (except on the occasion of his death) become a hero of the masses. Even those parliamentary associates who acknowledged his legislative and administrative talents found it difficult to penetrate Peel's shell of outward reserve; those who did found an unexpected degree of modesty and kindliness beneath. Gash does not seek to explain away this difficulty, conceding that Peel often impressed contemporaries as cold and almost repellent. Especially after the first of his two major voltes-face—the support of Catholic emancipation in 1829—Peel's outward persona hardened.

> The need for self-protection is apt to enlist less amiable qualities, and ingrowing virtues have a trick of developing ingrowing vices. Peel's humour tended to be ironic and sometimes malicious. His integrity could degenerate into self-righteousness. The unnecessary emphasis on the purity of his motives made him on occasion sanctimonious. . . . Only a man of great humility could have held Peel's standards and retained complete humanity, and Peel was not humble. He had the contempt of the professional for the amateur, the impatience of the clever man with the fools, the dislike of the honest man for the rogues.[26]

Gash attributes these characteristics less to the self-consciousness of the social parvenu than to a childhood noted more for discipline than for outward tokens of affection. His father had made with astonishing speed the transition from successful cotton manufacturer to landlord, member of Parliament, baronet, and loyal supporter of William Pitt. His ambitions for his eldest son were boundless. "Bob, you dog," he would tell him, "if you are not prime minister some day, I'll disinherit you."[27]

In both volumes, Gash finds time not only to trace the road to the prime ministership but also to reveal Peel the family man and the connoisseur of works of art. His marriage at the age of thirty-two to the beautiful Julia Floyd (the Indian-born daughter of a British general) was the consequence of a genuine love match. Lady Peel had no desire to become a political hostess like Lady Palmerston, but she did provide Peel with seven children and a proto-Victorian domestic refuge from the battlefields of Westminster. By 1830 Peel had also become one of the great art collectors of his day; his gallery boasted paintings by Rembrandt and Rubens. He was attracted most to "the classical Dutch school with its robust realism and solid landscapes, mirroring nature rather than swathing it in romantic imagination."[28] After 1830, as inheritor of his father's title and two-thirds of his wealth, Peel found it easy and satisfying to play the role of munificent host and generous philanthropist at both his London townhouse and his Tamworth manor house.

His academic success at Harrow and his remarkable double First in classics and mathematics at Oxford (together with the help of the future Duke of Wellington) propelled Peel into the House of Commons at the age of twenty-one and into the cabinet as, in effect, prime minister of Ireland only three years later. Ireland, the prospective political graveyard of innumerable nineteenth-century English politicians, furnished the youthful Peel with a springboard instead. It was in Ireland that he learned the art of public administration:

> the eliciting of specific information by means of detailed questionnaires to the men most likely to have access to the knowledge he needed; the checking of generalities and opinions by reference to the facts; prudent choice of agents; caution in coming to a conclusion and energetic action once a decision had been reached. . . . 'There is nothing like a fact,' he observed when writing to Gregory in June 1814 about his Peace Preservation Bill; and again in April 1816—'facts are ten times more valuable than declamations'. In administration this was an admirable attitude; in politics, where much depends on appearances, it was not always to be so infallible a guide.[29]

It was Peel who "kept the peace" in Ireland during the traumatic transition from wartime boom to postwar depression. It was he who invented there the "police force" that he afterward instituted in metropolitan London. It was he who found ingenious ways of tempering the famine of 1817, the result of a failure of the wheat crop and of a depleted potato harvest. It was Peel finally who, years before Edward Gibbon Wakefield, proposed a state-assisted program of emigration to relieve an overpopulated Ireland.

These efforts did not make Peel the hero of men like Daniel O'Connell, nor did they cause him to support the cause of Catholic emancipation, a subject that perennially divided the Liverpool government. In Peel's judgment, granting Catholics the right to hold public office would do nothing to aid the impoverished Irish peasantry, but it would undermine the ability of the Irish executive to govern effectively. Rather than cementing the Act of Union with Ireland, Catholic emancipation would undermine it. Since Peel was no admirer of the Ulster Presbyterians nor of the stridently anti-Catholic Orange lodges, it was as practical politician rather than as religious ideologue that he increasingly found himself the leader of the "Protestant" cause in Parliament. This very identification was, however, to make the pragmatic turnabout of 1829 so damaging to him.

By then Peel had also established himself as financial expert, the leader of the movement of 1819 to restore the gold standard, and, as home secretary after 1822, the reformer of the English criminal law and prison system. Gash does not contend that Peel pioneered that reform effort. "What the Whig reformers had lacked was tact, influence, and organisation; it was this which Peel made it his business to supply."[30] Even the elderly Jeremy Bentham bestowed a jocular word of praise: "What is this I see? One of His Majesty's Principal Secretaries of State become a Reformist? A Law Reformer in good earnest? . . . Sir, you have passed the Rubicon."[31]

In the second volume of the biography, Gash explains clearly the reasons for the breakup of Wellington's administration and for Peel's subsequent opposition to the Whig Reform Bill. Wellington's government was one of the most economical of the century and "its conduct of affairs as upright and disinterested as the conduct of politics can ever be," but the ministry had an overriding demerit. "It had failed to establish a firm link with either parliament, press, or the public. Publicity and propaganda were almost entirely in the hands of critics and enemies."[32] Although not opposed in principle to some alteration in the franchise rules, Peel decided to resist the specific provisions of what became the Reform Act of 1832. "I was unwilling to open a door which I saw no prospect of being able to close." Peel was convinced, moreover, "that though my opposition will be unavailing, it will not be fruitless, because the opposition now made will oppose a bar to further concessions thereafter."[33] Unlike Wellington, Peel objected in 1832 to the formation of a Tory ministry that might have saved the House of Lords from embarrassment by pushing through a modified Reform Bill of its own. The disagreement of the two party leaders placed additional obstacles in the path of a Conservative recovery that truly began only in late 1834.

Although Gash carefully places the Tamworth Manifesto of 1834 into context,[34] his prime concern in the second volume of the biography is not Peel the party builder but Peel the reforming prime minister. In Gash's judgment, it was Peel's work between 1841 and 1846 in streamlining the tariff system, reforming the banking system, reinstituting the income tax, and repealing the Corn Laws that made possible the relative prosperity and social harmony of the mid-Victorian years. "The age of revolt was giving way to the age of stability; and of that age Peel had been the chief architect."[35] Three-fifths of *Sir Robert Peel* is devoted to those five years, their accomplishments and, for Peel himself, their ultimate frustration. Peel grasped the potential of party as a substitute for the waning powers of Crown patronage and family connection, yet he ultimately sacrificed the short-term interests of his party in favor of what he saw as the long-term interests of his nation. As prime minister, he utilized his cabinet far more than his party. By strength of intellect and by unflagging industry, he dominated that cabinet and coordinated its work, and, when the breakup came in 1846, he succeeded in carrying all but two of his senior colleagues with him.

Gash's ultimate assessment of Peel's role and personality is singularly dispassionate.[36] He acknowledges Peel's occasional failings as party leader (though he molded the modern Conservative party) and as master parliamentarian. Peel's fundamental outlook, Gash insists, remained "executive and governmental. His approach to politics, even in opposition or as a private member, was as a potential minister of the crown."[37] Gash concedes that Peel never altogether resolved the tensions that existed between the several roles that he played, but there is little doubt that Gash finds it easier to sympathize with constructive administrators than with ideologues or rhetoricians.

Even some sympathetic critics found Gash, especially in his first volume, rather too likely to see all events through Peel's own eyes. Thus for David Roberts it remains "hard to make a hero" of a man who for so long had opposed the repeal of the Test and Corporation acts and the enactment of Catholic emancipation and of parliamentary reform. Perhaps, suggests Roberts, Walter Bagehot had been right to attribute to Peel "the powers of a first-rate man and the creed of a second-rate man."[38] Derek Beales, who conducted his own survey of the era, *From Castlereagh to Gladstone, 1815–1885* (1969),[39] acknowledges that Gash's approach to his hero had been less partial in volume II than in volume I. A "Conservative historiography of nineteenth-century politics is now dominant," Beales was to argue in 1974, and Gash had contributed greatly to that tendency.[40] The Chartists and the Anti-Corn Law League, the Benthamites and the Radicals had all declined in status, while the people at the center of government, the ministers and the civil servants, had gained. What Beales objects to most strongly is the manner in which the Conservative reform measures of the 1820s and 1840s have been exalted and the Whig reforms of the 1830s unnecessarily diminished. It was Lord John Russell rather than Peel who proved, in Beales's view, the more effective reformer of the criminal law just as he had been the more effective reformer of Parliament, of education, and of the Anglican church. Beales readily acknowledges—indeed he insists—that Russell's modern biographer, John Prest,⁴¹ does far less justice to his subject than Gash does to Peel.

In a recent article, Ian Newbould similarly upholds the Whig ministries of the 1830s as far less lazy and directionless than often depicted, governing in tacit alliance with Peel in order to weaken the appeal of the Radicals.⁴² In a more recent article, Newbould goes on to challenge Gash's conclusion that the electoral triumph of 1841 was a victory for "the gospel of Peelite Conservatism." In many constituencies, Newbould insists, what counted was a simple pledge to uphold the Corn Laws and to defend the Church of England. In some cases it was opposition to the New Poor Law, in others advocacy of factory regulation, but rarely was it Peel's Tamworthism, those issues "on which Peel had hoped to build a new party." Ultimately, Newbould reminds us, Peel could repeal the Corn Laws only with the aid of the Whigs. Peel "set out to build a party and instead split one, many of the materials of which were not of his making. Might this aspect of his career not be considered a study in failure?"⁴³

Newbould may be right to suggest that Gash underestimates the significance of the Corn Law issue in the 1841 election, but the points in dispute would seem to be primarily a matter of emphasis. Gash has always conceded, after all, that not all of Peel's parliamentary followers during the 1830s shared his hope of "moderate, rational, objective reform as a middle course" between Tory reaction and doctrinaire radicalism. Many of them, as Wellington had lamented, cared for nothing except their own property and the Church. "It was a text," Gash concludes, "for which the years 1841-46 provided an ample sermon."⁴⁴

Boyd Hilton has provided a yet more potent critique in his article, "Peel: A Reappraisal."⁴⁵ He alludes to Gash's work as a "marvellous biography," but contends that, although Peel may have been a pragmatist politically, he tended to be far more doctrinaire in his economic thinking than Gash allows. A consideration of Peel's approach to the resumption of specie payment in 1819, to the Bank Charter Act of 1844, and in due course to "free trade" as a deductive theory all suggest this. There was also a sense of moral urgency in Peel that inspired his disciples far more "than those twin 'altars of honour and duty' which Professor Gash refers to. . . . The lame conclusion must be that Peel was not the founder of the Conservative party but was the progenitor of Gladstonian liberalism."⁴⁶

Obviously no 1,400-page opus will remain exempt from interpretive challenge, but Gash's biography of Peel is likely to remain for the foreseeable future the standard one. The work, concluded the reviewer for the *Times Literary Supplement,* "is fascinating for its style, for the control over the materials, for the insight it gives into the practical workings of politics at the time, in the Cabinet, in Parliament, and at the informal party meetings. Above all, it makes of Peel, however, much he covered up his own springs of feelings, an understandable person."[47] In order to attract the interest of the impatient undergraduate as well as of the painstaking scholar, Gash went on to provide his own 312-page condensation of the two lengthy volumes[48] as well as to record an hour-long cassette tape featuring "Sir Robert Peel: His Early Career and Achievements" on one track and "His Later Career and Achievements" on the other.[49]

In one of his few formal forays into historical theory, Gash understandably mounts a challenge to the point of view put forward by historians as eminent as Sir Lewis Namier and Sir Geoffrey Elton that political biographies are often a debased form of history, that, in Elton's words, a historian "should not suppose that in writing biography he is writing history."[50] In his "Modest Defence of Historical Biography," Gash observes:

> The theory that serious biography is an easy form of writing will hardly survive the experience of attempting one. To know a man's society so that it becomes as familiar as one's own; to discover his true character and convey it convincingly to the reader; to describe the constant interplay of public issues and private motives; to explain with lucidity and authority the different spheres of activity and responsibility that a single career may traverse and yet maintain the constant presence of the man himself . . . to bring to bear on dead evidence a disciplined imagination without which the biography itself remains dead; and to convey all this in readable prose without clogging the narrative, losing direction, or sacrificing depth—that is a task which requires all the skills of which an historian is master.[51]

In that essay, Gash goes on to argue persuasively that—whatever its technical difficulties—the historical biography can be justified as a genre on grounds of philosophical legitimacy, professional value, and human importance. Although he mentions no specific works as exemplars, his own biography of Peel supports his case.

After completing the biography of Peel, Gash found several opportunities to return to the subject of the early nineteenth-century Conservative party. For a volume edited by Donald Southgate, *The Conservative Leadership, 1832–1932,*[52] Gash provided an acute 23-

page distillation, "Wellington and Peel, 1832–1846." Wellington is presented as a party leader by default, a man who lacked tactical skills in politics but who represented enduring conservative qualities such as patriotism, respect for tradition, and a strong sense of public duty. Peel is depicted as the creator of the Conservative party of the 1840s. Though "he had driven his party too far and too fast, the road he had taken had been the right one."[53]

The survey, *The Conservatives: A History from Their Origins to 1965*,[54] provided Gash with an opportunity to take a broader and more original look at the party from its ideological origins in the 1790s to "The Great Disruption of 1846" and its immediate aftermath. The second chapter of the four-chapter, eighty-eight page essay continues the rehabilitation of Lord Liverpool that Gash had begun in his contribution to the collection of essays edited by Herbert van Thal, *The Prime Ministers;* there he had called him "one of the least known and most underrated."[55] It was, in Gash's judgment, Liverpool (not Castlereagh or Canning) who had created the traditions and formulated the principles that underlay the work of Peel's great ministry. Gash places stress on the weakness rather than the strength or repressiveness of Liverpool's government (1812–1827) in the face of a relatively independent House of Commons and an often hostile press. The modified eighteenth-century structure of politics made it difficult for a ministry to utilize either patronage or a sense of party loyalty in order to control Parliament. "It was natural in those circumstances that the emergence of a recognisable conservative policy should historically precede and not result from a recognisable conservative party."[56] In 1977, Gash also brought out a revised edition of his *Politics in the Age of Peel* (1953), with a new introduction and an updated bibliography.[57] A few years later he returned to the subject of "The Organization of the Conservative Party, 1832–1846," both at the parliamentary level—in terms of meetings of M.P.s and the role of whips—and the national level—in terms of provincial organizations, the party's election committee, and the election fund.[58]

The big project of the 1970s, however, was a *New History of England,* for which Gash (together with A. G. Dickens) served as general editor and to which Gash contributed a key volume, *Aristocracy and People: Britain 1815–1865* (1979). Somewhat oddly, the general editors furnished no public explanation as to how the series was to be distinctive, but Gash has made it clear that the volumes (each approximately 350 pages per half-century) are intended to be more than "an ordinary type of textbook." Rather they are meant to convey both the sweep and the continuity of English history since the mid-fifteenth century while at the same time giving emphasis to the major themes of each period. For the volumes published under Gash's immediate supervision, these themes are encapsulated in the titles: W. A. Speck, *Stability and Strife: England, 1714–1760* (1977); Ian R. Christie, *Wars and Revolutions: Britain, 1760–1815* (1982); Gash's own volume; E. J. Feuchtwanger, *Democracy and Empire: Britain 1865–1914* (1985); and Max Beloff, *Wars and Welfare: Britain, 1914–1945* (1985).[59]

Aristocracy and People is organized in a straightforward fashion. Although Gash reminds us in Chapter 2, "Government and Religion," of the significance of local authorities, the seven chronological chapters are focused primarily on the activities of prime ministers, politicians, and parliaments. Only in the first chapter, "Country and People," and in the last, "Peace and Prosperity," does Gash survey the socioeconomic background. The foreign policy of the half century is summed up in Chapter 10, and both the British Empire and those aspects of Irish history that did not directly affect Great Britain are deliberately left out of the story. Subjects not tied to politics receive short shrift, whether "the railway age"—allotted a single paragraph—or the worlds of religious thought and of popular culture. John Stuart Mill is not mentioned in the index, nor are John Keats, Alfred, Lord Tennyson, Augustus Welby Pugin, and J. M. W. Turner. Thinkers are generally neglected in favor of doers. Although "Bentham and the utilitarians helped to colour the thought of their age," Gash notes, "few pure examples of Benthamite reforms ever found their way to the statute book. . . . In practice the expansion of governmental activity in the early nineteenth century was inadequate, unplanned, piecemeal, and spasmodic."[60]

The book obviously owes more to the late George Kitson Clark and W. L. Burn—to whose memory it is dedicated—than it owes, say, to E. P. Thompson and Eric Hobsbawm.[61] To observe that Gash's history does not profess to be "history from the bottom up" is not to suggest that he ignores the subject of working and living conditions or the activities of protest and pressure groups. Like Kitson Clark, Gash concludes that "for all its harshness and crudities, the industrial revolution was the saviour of British society in the conditions which prevailed between 1815 and 1865." Had early nineteenth-century industrialization not coincided with post–Napoleonic War depression as well as with abnormally rapid population growth and urbanization, its supposed "evils" would not have become a platitude of British historiography. Gash agrees with Elie Halévy that at no time was social distress as widespread as in the years 1816–1819, but he is not persuaded that England then, or ever, was divided solely or primarily between the rich and the poor. Society was divided vertically as well as horizontally—city versus country, Anglicans versus Dissenters—and "an immense and complex gradation of classes and incomes stretched between the very rich and the very poor."[62]

Gash is readily prepared to acknowledge that the era under review "is a tempting period for those who turn to history as a kind of storehouse of ideological illustrations. It is rich in evidence that can be extracted from its context to support doctrinaire arguments."[63] What he is not prepared to concede is that some obvious countermodel of modernization existed or that British society was on the verge of being overthrown by a popular revolution. Since there was no active revolutionary group ready to take power, since the traditional governing classes had suffered no loss of nerve, and since soldiers and policemen were, when needed, loyal to the government, it seems reasonable to conclude that "at no time . . . was revolution physically possible in Britain between 1815 and 1848."[64]

For Gash the years 1815–1865 remain, on balance, a great success story: successive ministries adapted old governmental and religious institutions in ad hoc fashion to an industrializing, urbanizing, and increasingly prosperous society. Although he is willing to classify Castlereagh as "the most creative and imaginative of nineteenth-century British foreign secretaries,"[65] it is the underrated Liverpool who is one of Gash's prime heroes on the domestic scene. He was indispensable in holding a divided ministry together and, rather than repressive, "always conscious of the need to distinguish between deliberate political agitation and genuine social grievance."[66] The master statesman and the prime reformer of the age remains, not surprisingly, Sir Robert Peel. "It is probable that Peel's budgets of 1842, 1845, and 1846 did more for the working classes of Britain than all of Shaftesbury's reforms put together."[67] If therefore the aristocracy and gentry remained integral elements of Britain's national life even in the 1860s, this was the consequence of "a process of astute adaptation" that had enabled them to maintain "control so long and with so little resentment on the part of the rest of the community."[68]

The book received generally favorable reviews, especially in the United States, where the *American Historical Review* declared that "this careful study will surely become required reading for students of English history,"[69] and *Choice,* the guide to librarians, recommended it to "all libraries" as "the best available brief history of England 1815–65."[70] English social historians tended to be more critical. Thus Kenneth Fielden commends the work's "great clarity" but views its assessment of early nineteenth-century society as no more than "skin deep. Machinery does not grind, smoke does not billow, city courts do not stink, long hours and mill regulations are not felt on the bone, families hardly exist."[71] Michael Brock sees Gash's underlying theme of aristocratic and gentry adaptability as a nonissue. Unimpressed by the extent of either the civic or the social consciousness of Britain's upper classes, he suggests that their power and influence were so great "that they could have lost their ascendancy only through consistent ineptitude."[72] Eric Hobsbawm posits the opposite complaint: Gash does not take seriously enough the revolutionary nature of the economic and ideological change Britain's people were undergoing. Prepared as ever to condemn "the evils of the industrial revolution," Hobsbawm dismisses Gash's explanations as "unconvincing apologetics." Grudgingly he concedes that "this is a very good conventional history within its limits. But they are narrow limits."[73]

Several of his essays of the 1970s had first demonstrated Gash's interest in the man who had served as prime minister for a longer continuous period (1812–1827) than had any of his successors, the forgotten Lord Liverpool. During the years that followed his formal retirement from St. Andrews in 1980, Gash completed a 265-page biography.[74] Gash does not pretend to have done research on the scale of his masterly *Peel,* but his is the first true life—based on manuscript as well as printed primary sources—since C. D. Yonge's "insipid" mid-Victorian triple-decker.[75] There can be an inverse ratio between length and readability, however, and Gash's *Liverpool* is a small masterpiece, skillfully proportioned and gracefully written. In John Derry's words, it is "a splendid example of distilled learning and mature wisdom."[76] Once again, Boyd Hilton agrees, "Gash's sympathy with a subject enables him to breathe warmth into what might appear to be a rather cold and remote figure."[77]

Indeed he does. Robert Banks Jenkinson, the future peer and prime minister, proves on examination to have had a far from dull background. His ancestry was part (Asian) Indian; his own mother died when he was a baby; at Oxford he was a classmate of the more dynamic and more frivolous George Canning.[78] Young Robert's Grand Tour to the continent provided him with the unexpected opportunity to witness the storming of the Bastille, "a spectacle which gave him a distaste for revolutions."[79] When his father disapproved of his proposed marriage to the daughter of the eccentric Earl of Bristol, he persuaded both the prime minister, William Pitt, and King George III, to plead his case—with ultimate success. Liverpool was a sensitive, serious, determined individual, an experienced parliamentarian who had held the seals of the Foreign Office, the Home Office, and the War Office, and who was in many ways the logical successor in 1812 to the assassinated Spencer Perceval.

Gash presents Liverpool far less as the symbol of "Tory misrule" than as the practical politician who helped win the peace, survived the postwar depression, and contributed greatly to the economic reforms and the relative prosperity of the 1820s. In the process he also inspired the church-building grant of 1818 and the founding of the National Gallery in 1824. Far from being an arrogant or repressive landed aristocrat, Liverpool was a statesman who would have been delighted to keep the wartime income tax and who sought time and again to curb the protectionist impact of the Corn Law of 1815. For him agriculture, commerce, and industry were interdependent, and he often hailed Britain's pioneering industrial engineers. "Liverpool clearly ranks as one of the great though unacknowledged architects of the liberal, free-trade Victorian state, second only to Peel in importance."[80] He may not have been brilliant or heroic, and he was certainly not a great demagogue, but, argues Gash, neither was he the "Arch-Mediocrity" of Disraeli's imagination. Rather was he "a politician's politician . . . that comparatively uncommon and always valuable thing in politics, a man of genuine all-round ability."[81]

Like Peel and Liverpool, Gash has preferred the task of practical historian to that of theoretician, and his retirement years at Langport, Somerset, have seen no letup in his production of book reviews, essays, and books. The most recent book, *Pillars of Government*,[82] includes one of Gash's rare formal forays into the implications of his craft, "Some Reflections on History." In this essay he examines the validity of the historical method and the value for society of historical study. On pragmatic grounds he challenges those skeptical philosophers who have condemned the work of historians as inescapably subjective and as far removed from the people and events they profess to describe. To the contrary, argues Gash, the historian is the spectator "who proverbially sees more of the game" than do the players on the field. Undue preoccupation with conflicts in historical interpretation disguises the degree of consensus to be found among most historians on most matters. Admittedly, "history is a branch of knowledge in which certainty, probability, and speculation all have their part. What may properly be required of an historian is that he distinguishes between certainties and uncertainties. If it is one of his functions to dispel doubt, another is to indicate where doubt must persist."[83]

If the study of history can no longer be justified as a storehouse of moral axioms, it may still be justified as "an extension of our experience of human society." Writers of fiction may have an advantage in illuminating individual psychology, but "history does this certainly as far as collective activities are concerned." Even if historians cannot furnish simple lessons, soldiers, politicians, and diplomats may perform their tasks better if they have learned from the past. It does not follow, concedes the pragmatic Gash, "that a multiplication of professional scholars or research students has in itself any particular social value." History's ultimate worth is a function of its halfway status between the natural sciences and the pure humanities.

> The historian does not set out to construct logical theories. Those who do, like Marx, are only pseudo-historians. Nor does he allow the study of any special cultural activity, whether numismatics or poetry, to become an end in itself though he is happy to make use of the scholarship of those who do. He is a generalist in that he takes any evidence which helps him to understand what he is studying; but his object of study is individual and unique.

Although historians have found large tracts of their intellectual territory invaded by others, it remains Gash's hope that the scholarly autonomy of the discipline will be maintained. "If history is to be of value to others, it must be studied for its own sake by those who have no other purpose."[84]

Among British historians of the post-1945 era, none has done more than Gash to promote or to exemplify that autonomy—as scholar and teacher. In the historical army, he has successfully made his own way from the lowly rank of private to that of regimental sergeant-major. He has pioneered the reexamination of the study of the political structure of early Victorian Britain. He has compelled a new look at the implications of the Reform Bill of 1832. In more recent years, he has persuasively called for a reexamination of that historical cliché, the post-1815 "era of Tory Repression." Since he does not believe that early nineteenth-century Britain underwent a fundamental ideological transformation,[85] he is unwilling to make industrialization the villain it was in the 1920s for the Hammonds and in more recent decades for Thompson and Hobsbawm. To that extent he has resisted the new radical orthodoxy of recent decades. His virtues as a historian have been widely conceded: careful research and examination of evidence; thoughtful synthesis; clarity of exposition; confidence in expression.[86]

What of his limitations? One possible flaw may be an exaggerated opinion of the virtues and significance of Peel. Gash has succeeded in persuading a majority of scholars that Peel truly was the single most influential statesman of the first half of the nineteenth century. Yet, although an occasional statement taken in isolation may suggest otherwise, his own summing up of Peel's strengths and weaknesses remains eminently dispassionate. It may seem inconsistent of Gash to continue to claim for Peel the status of "founding father" of a Conservative party whose rank and file deserted him in the 1840s. Yet, while it is true that subsequent Conservative leaders remained fearful of emulating Peel and breaking up their party, Gash has contended persuasively that, although the party's subsequent myth became Disraelian, "its practice has almost invariably been Peelite."[87] A more legitimate criticism of Gash's work may be that it has been too exclusively political. Such emphasis has provided a useful counterpoise to studies by modern social historians who largely banish politics, especially national politics, from their historical landscape. And it is certainly true that Gash has painted political history with an unusually broad interpretive brush; yet part of that landscape has, in consequence, been left in the shadows.

Eric Hobsbawm has gone on to argue that, although historians like Gash "may survey and summarize a vast and complex field in masterly fashion, and modify accepted interpretations . . . their mission is to rearrange in decent order the furniture of the house of Britain's past that has been disturbed by those who have tried to look under it. This is a pity."[88] If rearranging the furniture is all that Gash has done, then he has done so with elegance and skill, but the issue may be a deeper one. Gash is certainly not oblivious of those scholars who have tried to look under the furniture, nor has he objected to their making the effort. He has remained insistent, however, that historians construct their furniture out of the seasoned timber of evidence rather than out of utopian or counterfactual might-have-beens. Like Peel, he is not an ideologue but a centrist,[89] not a model-builder but a pragmatist. "We are all Peelites now," declared the *Times* in 1852.[90] The generalization may not hold for our day, but as we enter the 1990s, it seems fair to conclude, at least one Peelite remains hard at work among us.

NOTES

I am grateful to Professor Gash for the readiness with which he responded to my questions. I am also grateful to Professor T. William Heyck of Northwestern University and to my wife for reading an earlier draft of this essay and for making a number of helpful suggestions. A shortened version of the paper was presented at the annual meeting of the Midwest Conference on British Studies in October 1986 in Milwaukee.

1. Cf. Derek Beales, "Peel, Russell and Reform," *Historical Journal* 17(1974):873-74.

2. Interview with Norman Gash on June 10, 1985, in Langport, Somerset, and subsequent letters (1985-1989). All biographical information not independently noted draws on that interview and those letters.

3. Norman Gash, "Rural Unemployment, 1815-34," *Economic History Review* 7(Oct. 1935):90-93.

4. Works by these students include Edith Johnston, *Great Britain and Ireland, 1760-1800: A Study in Public Administration* (Edinburgh, 1963); John Cookson, *Lord Liverpool's Administration: The Crucial Years, 1815-1822* (Edinburgh, 1975); David Hampton, *Methodism and Politics in British Society, 1750-1850* (London, 1984); and Frederick Dreyer, "A 'Religious Society Under Heaven': John Wesley and the Identity of Methodism," *Journal of British Studies* (Jan. 1986).

5. Norman Gash, "F. R. Bonham, Conservative 'Political Secretary' 1832-47," *English Historical Review* 63(Oct. 1948):502-22.

6. Reprinted in *Transactions of the Royal Historical Society*, 5th ser., 1(1951):47-69.

7. Ibid., 48.

8. Ibid., 56.

9. Norman Gash, *Politics in the Age of Peel: A Study in the Technique of Parliamentary Representation, 1830-1850* (London: Longman, 1953), ix.

10. Ibid., 4.

11. Ibid., 9. See also *History Today* 3(July 1953):511-12; and *English Historical Review* 69(July 1954):457-60.

12. A. J. P. Taylor in the *New Statesman* 45, 25 Apr. 1953, 490, praised Gash for his distinguished scholarship, "wit and penetration"; the anonymous reviewer in the *Times Literary Supplement*, 3 July 1953, 421 praised Gash's "unflagging skill and zest."

13. John P. Kenyon, *The History Men* (Pittsburgh, 1984), 269.

14. Letter from Norman Gash to author, 20 Aug. 1986.

15. Norman Gash, "English Reform and the French Revolution in the General Election of 1830," in *Essays Presented to Sir Lewis Namier*, ed. Richard Pares and A. J. P. Taylor (London, 1956), 258-88.

16. Norman Gash, *Reaction and Reconstruction in English Politics, 1832-1852* (Oxford: Clarendon Press, 1965).

17. Ibid., 5.

18. Ibid., 129.

19. Review in *Historical Journal* 10(1967):314-15.

20. Gash, *Reaction and Reconstruction*, 122.

21. Ibid., 154.

22. A volume in the *Documents in Modern History* series (London: Edward Arnold; New York: St. Martin's Press, 1968).

23. Norman Gash's first volume was published as *Mr. Secretary Peel: The Life of Sir Robert Peel to 1830* (London: Longman, 1961); the second as *Sir Robert Peel: The Life of Sir Robert Peel after 1830* (London: Longman, 1972). The American distributor was Rowman & Littlefield of Totowa, New Jersey.

24. *Guardian* (London), 12 May 1961, 9.

25. *English Historical Review* 89(1974):128-29.

26. Norman Gash, *Peel* (London and New York: Longman, 1976), 141. "Catholic

emancipation scarred him for the rest of his life, but the effect was not to make him more but less amenable to party claims." Gash, *Sir Robert Peel,* 707.

27. Cited in Gash, *Peel,* 6.
28. Ibid., 59.
29. Ibid., 44–45.
30. Ibid., 69.
31. Cited in ibid., 69.
32. Gash, *Sir Robert Peel,* 3–4.
33. Cited in ibid., 20, 26.
34. Gash also devotes a separate essay to the subject in his *Pillars of Government* (London: Edward Arnold, 1986), 98–107.
35. Gash, *Sir Robert Peel,* 714.
36. Ibid., 705–15. The assessment is followed by a fascinating assemblage of Peel's "Maxims and Reflections," 717–22.
37. Ibid., 707.
38. *American Historical Review* 67(Jan. 1962):392–93.
39. Derek Beales, *From Castlereagh to Gladstone, 1815–1885* (Edinburgh: Thomas Nelson, 1969), in the *History of England* series, ed. Christopher Brooke and Denis Mack Smith.
40. Beales, "Peel, Russell and Reform," 874.
41. John Prest, *Lord John Russell* (London: Macmillan, 1972).
42. Ian Newbould, "Whiggery and the Decline of Reform: Liberals, Radicals and the Melbourne Administration, 1835–39," *Bulletin of the Institute of Historical Research* 53(1980):229–41.
43. Ian Newbould, "Sir Robert Peel and the Conservative Party, 1832–1841: A Study in Failure?" *English Historical Review* 98(July 1983):529–57.
44. Norman Gash, "Wellington and Peel, 1832–1846," in *The Conservative Leadership, 1832–1932,* ed. Donald Southgate (London: Macmillan; New York: St. Martin's Press, 1974), 42, 48. The volume is part of the "Problems in Focus" series.
45. Boyd Hilton, "Peel: A Reappraisal," *Historical Journal* 22(1979):585–614.
46. Ibid., 613–14.
47. *Times Literary Supplement,* 3 Nov. 1972, 1312.
48. Gash, *Peel.* In 1985 Longman also published a new edition of *Mr. Secretary Peel* in which errors are corrected and the bibliography is expanded.
49. Norman Gash, *Sir Robert Peel* (New York: A. L. Educational Sales of Manhasset). Sound cassette.
50. Cited in Gash, "A Modest Defence of Historical Biography" in his *Pillars of Government,* 179.
51. Ibid., 183.
52. See note 44.
53. *Conservative Leadership,* 38–39, 57.
54. The Rt. Hon. Lord Butler [Richard Austen Butler], ed., *The Conservatives: A History from Their Origins to 1965* (London: George Allen & Unwin, 1977).
55. Herbert van Thal, ed., *The Prime Ministers* (New York: Stein & Day, 1974), 283.
56. Butler, ed., *Conservatives,* 38.
57. Norman Gash, *Politics in the Age of Peel,* 2d ed. (London: Longman, 1977).
58. *Parliamentary History* 1(1982):137–59; 2(1983):131–52.
59. All the volumes cited were published in England by Edward Arnold and in the United States by the Harvard University Press, except for the Beloff volume, published

in the United States by Edward Arnold. The authors of the first five volumes, covering the years 1461–1714, are J. R. Lander, Geoffrey Elton, Patrick Collinson, Derek Hurst, and J. R. Jones.

60. Gash, *Aristocracy and People,* 46–47.

61. Ibid., 355. Gash freely acknowledges that Thompson's *Making of the English Working Class,* "despite its bias and exaggeration is eminently readable and provides a quarry of information even for those who do not accept his interpretation."

62. Ibid., 2–3.

63. Ibid., 1.

64. Ibid., 5–7.

65. Ibid., 286.

66. Ibid., 99. Gash provided a preview of Chapter 3, "The Peterloo Years," in a paper read to the Royal Historical Society in 1977, "After Waterloo: British Society and the Legacy of the Napoleonic Wars." It was reprinted in the *Transactions of the Royal Historical Society,* 5th ser., 28(1978):145–57.

67. Ibid., 4.

68. Ibid., 350.

69. *American Historical Review* 85(Dec. 1980):1196. The review was by R. G. Cowherd.

70. *Choice* 18(Sept. 1980):148.

71. *History* 65(Oct. 1980):498.

72. *English Historical Review* 96(Jan. 1981):162.

73. *New York Review of Books* 27, 3 Apr. 1980, 35–37.

74. Norman Gash, *Lord Liverpool* (London: Weidenfeld & Nicolson; Cambridge: Harvard Univ. Press, 1984).

75. The adjective was used by Gash in *Aristocracy and People,* 355. Yonge's work was published in 1867.

76. *History* 70(Oct. 1985):525.

77. *Times Literary Supplement,* 28 Sept. 1984, 1077.

78. The subject is explored by Gash in "The Tortoise and the Hare: Liverpool and Canning," *History Today* 32(Mar. 1982):12–19. Two years earlier he had published "Lord Liverpool: A Private View," *History Today* 30(May 1980):35–40.

79. Gash, *Liverpool,* 16.

80. Ibid., 253.

81. Ibid., 254.

82. Norman Gash, *Pillars of Government: and Other Essays on State and Society, c. 1770–c. 1880* (London: Edward Arnold, 1986). During his retirement years, Gash has also continued to deliver papers (at Oxford, London, Tamworth, and at the annual Prince Albert Society seminar in Coburg, West Germany). In 1988–1989 he was editing for publication by the Manchester University Press a collection entitled *Wellington Essays;* his own contribution is an essay entitled "Wellington as Prime Minister."

83. Ibid., 191–92.

84. Ibid., 194–95.

85. As Gash observed in a review of David Roberts's *Paternalism in Early Victorian England,* "paternalism in one form or another was the traditional social attitude. . . . It provided the common, pervasive background of thought and action. It was the academic doctrines of individualism, utilitarianism, and laissez-faire which were the innovations," but none of these, Gash notes, was ever universally accepted. *English Historical Review* 96(Jan. 1981):168.

86. Cf. Sheldon Rothblatt, "Some Recent Writings in British Political History,

1832–1914," *Journal of Modern History* 55(Sept. 1983):484–85. For a sometime critic, Michael Brock, Gash remains "one of our most distinguished historians." See his review of *Pillars of Government* in the *Times Literary Supplement,* 1 May 1987, 470.

87. Norman Gash, "The Founder of Modern Conservatism," in *Pillars of Government,* 1.

88. *New York Review of Books* 27, 3 Apr. 1980, 37.

89. See Brian Harrison, "The Centrist Theme in Modern British Politics," in his *The Peaceable Kingdom* (Oxford: Clarendon Press, 1982), 309–77.

90. Cited in Lord Butler, ed., *Conservatives,* 106.

F. S. L. Lyons
Historian of Modern Ireland

ALAN O'DAY

Francis Stewart Leland Lyons was born in (London) Derry on November 11, 1923 and after a brief illness died in Dublin on September 21, 1983; he had not reached his sixtieth birthday. During a truncated career, Lyons wrote seven books (six on Irish history), edited or coedited two others, and published numerous articles.[1] He was also much in demand as a lecturer and as a contributor to newspapers; in Ireland Lyons appeared frequently on radio and television. His list of academic appointments and awards is impressive. The most important reason, however, for naming Lyons one of the foremost historians of the British Isles of the post-1945 generation is that he transformed the study of modern Irish history into a respectable field of scholarship—especially within Great Britain. More than anyone else of his era, Lyons came to personify the study of modern Irish history.

In retrospect, Lyons's career reads like a string of successes. After attending preparatory and public schools in England, he entered Trinity College, University of Dublin, in 1941, taking his B.A. with first class honors in modern history and political science four years later. He received a Ph.D. in history from Dublin in 1947. Ireland was neutral in World War II, so Lyons, as an Irish citizen, was one of the comparatively few historians of his generation to miss military service. In 1947 he took up his first post as lecturer in history at University College, Hull (now the University of Hull), where he stayed until 1951 when he returned to Trinity as lecturer in modern history and fellow of the college. While at Hull his first book, based on his Ph.D. thesis, was published under the title, *The Irish Parliamentary Party, 1890–*

1910 (1951). That account, the first of three Trinity College studies on the Irish Nationalist party, established Lyons as an authority on Irish affairs during the late nineteenth and early twentieth centuries—the period to which he was to devote much of his academic life. He remained at Trinity College, progressing slowly through the academic ranks, until 1964, when he accepted a foundation chair at the newly created University of Kent at Canterbury. During his Trinity years, Lyons published several articles and a second major study, *The Fall of Parnell, 1890-91* (1960). In 1960-1961 he served as visiting professor of history at Princeton University. A year later, he was elected a fellow of the Royal Irish Academy, and a book commissioned by the Council of Europe, *Internationalism in Europe, 1815-1914,* was published in 1963.

Lyons had thus established a substantial academic reputation when, at age forty, he took up the challenge of creating an entirely new history faculty and program at the University of Kent. His time there was evidently the most satisfying of his career.[2] He held a number of additional posts, including that of public orator of the university, and between 1969 and 1972 that of master of Eliot College, Canterbury, a quasi-collegiate institution modeled on Oxbridge. In 1966, as a tribute to his writings, he was accorded a Litt.D. degree by his old university, Trinity College. While at Canterbury, Lyons completed two more substantial books, *John Dillon: A Biography* (1968) and *Ireland since the Famine* (1971). It was the latter work that did most to enhance Lyons's reputation, and his account rapidly became the standard survey of modern Irish history. In 1974 he was elected a fellow of the British Academy.

By 1974 Lyons's reputation had been established firmly, and his career could boast more than the customary academic accomplishments. That reputation was to escalate yet further when, in the same year, he was appointed provost (president) of Trinity College, Dublin, and also accepted a commission to become the official biographer of W. B. Yeats. While at Canterbury, Lyons had become immersed in the interdisciplinary approach of the new university, and he found himself increasingly drawn to that academic borderland where the study of history overlaps with that of literature. Canterbury had constituted a critical phase of Lyons's intellectual development. In 1975 he received the first of the five honorary doctorates that were to be awarded to him during his final eight years. Early in 1977 his massive biography, *Charles Stewart Parnell,* was published in London amidst a chorus of acclaim. The book received the esteemed Heinemann Prize for biography.

In 1977-1978 Lyons gave the Ford lectures in English history at the University of Oxford, perhaps the greatest proof of the status he had acquired among British academics. His election constituted a signal personal honor; it also served as a tribute to the advance of modern Irish historiography. Lyons was the first specialist in Irish history to be chosen as Ford lecturer since World War II. The choice was yet more significant because Lyons could claim no previous connection with either Oxford or Cambridge and because Oxford until that time had shown little interest in modern Irish history as a field of study. Lyons's lectures were published by the Oxford University Press in 1979 under the title, *Culture and Anarchy in Ireland, 1890-1939*. During the following year, the book was awarded both the Ewart-Biggs Memorial and the Wolfson prizes. To Lyons must go much of the credit for initiating an interest in modern Irish history in the University of Oxford and its press. In 1978 Lyons's contributions to Yeats studies were recognized by his election as a fellow of the Royal Society of Literature. In 1981 he resigned the Trinity College provostship in order to devote himself to the completion of the Yeats volume. His academic stature had so grown in the previous decade that, but for his early death, he had every reason to expect further marks of recognition.

Yet for all his later eminence, the ascent of F. S. L. Lyons to the highest rank of the historical profession was anything but obvious at the outset. He might easily have assumed the place of a respected minor academic enjoying a satisfying but unspectacular career at Trinity College or at an English provincial university. His Irish Protestant origins were in the prosperous middle class rather than in the former "ascendancy." Lyons's future in Ireland might have been marred by his largely English upbringing and education—and his position in England by the return to Dublin as a student. He was in danger of being part of neither Irish nor English society. Moreover, his class in Ireland occupied an uneasy, indeed, uncertain niche in the new nation. During the 1940s Trinity College was not wholly reconciled to the Irish state and was certainly not revered by state leaders. Nor did Lyons's early historical concern—the Irish Nationalist party—seem likely to attract extensive attention in Ireland or Great Britain. When Lyons went to Hull in 1947, that college ranked as one of the least fashionable—not the sort of place that would elevate a historian's standing. Although Lyons's return to Trinity held many personal advantages, the institution in the 1950s remained on the fringes of both Irish and British university life. His early publications attracted only a small audience, and his articles were published in unglamorous Irish periodicals with small circulations. The first two books, though works of academic merit, enjoyed only modest attention; both were published with the assistance of subventions. Even now, many university libraries do not possess a copy of the first, *The Irish Parliamentary Party, 1890–1910*. Lyons's third book, the study commissioned by the Council of Europe, also remains a rarity. It is not available, for instance, in the Bodleian library of the University of Oxford.

Lyons's appointment at Canterbury was a tribute to his personal and academic attributes, but it gave little hint of Lyons's potential to emerge as a leading historian. Canterbury proved, however, a crucial time in Lyons's development. The spirit of a pioneering university was uplifting, and the interdisciplinary approach brought him into sustained contact with different ideas. During his years as a senior academic at Canterbury, Lyons found himself drawn into the web of English academic life and associations. Increasingly, for instance, he was asked to serve as outside examiner of doctoral theses on Irish subjects presented at British universities. Also, his publications began to appear in more widely circulated journals. It was during this sojourn that Lyons laid the foundation for being the accepted oracle on Ireland for British academics. His time at Canterbury coincided with a developing interest in Britain in Irish affairs.

Lyons's historical studies of Ireland can be examined either chronologically or by type of book. His writings fall into three fairly distinct categories: the scholarly monograph, the biography, and the general interpretative work. Whichever scheme of analysis may be employed, it is clear that his publications throw light on several matters: (1) how and why historians emerge as major forces within their profession and for a broader reading public; (2) how the historian's craft has manifested itself in the British Isles during the past four decades; and (3) how the position and recognition of academics in Britain differ in significant respects from the American pattern.

Lyons's initial book, *The Irish Parliamentary Party, 1890–1910*, is an obvious point to begin considering his rise as a major historian. Though a useful account, it was undoubtedly more decisive in shaping his own career than for its immediate impact on the profession. Lyons later commented self-disparagingly, "that book stinks of the thesis."[3] Yet it was, and remains, a worthy investigation of how the Irish Nationalist party functioned during the years of discouragement after the Parnell divorce scandal split the nationalist movement. In a book of moderate length, Lyons tackled the nature of the party, its structure, its sources of strength, its relationship with the British Liberals, the manner in which certain key personal rivalries impinged upon events, the shifting context within which Home Rulers functioned, and the ultimate shortcomings of the men and the institutions that during those years carried the Irish standard. His study revealed a fascination with the political process, particularly the politics of failure. Lyons's sense of melancholy, his conviction that post-1890 constitutional nationalism contained a tragic flaw that all but doomed it to disaster, pervaded the work. He clearly identified himself with those moderate and liberal nationalists who strove to secure a self-governing Ireland built on principles of mutual respect and toleration between creeds. As a southern Irish Protestant, Lyons regretted the failure of the Irish party and its ultimate replacement by a more virulent sectarian movement. His story, then, is a tale of what might have been had not fate intervened against Ireland once again. The book also demonstrated that Lyons possessed a felicitous pen—an incalculable asset for the future. It merited Emmet Larkin's apt remark, "the quality that distinguished all his published work, and which indeed became his hallmark, was a scrupulous scholarship informed by a lucid and balanced thoughtfulness."[4]

In the Britain and Ireland of the 1940s, *The Irish Parliamentary Party* was an example of a relatively new type of historical writing that sprang from the thesis or Ph.D. dissertation. It was a form of history based on research into a mass of original source materials, which also sought to take a detached and balanced look at historical questions. Until then, modern Irish history had been the preserve of journalists and of participants in the events described. Their intent often amounted to telling, in exciting and heroic manner, the story of the creation of a new nation. By contrast, Lyons's technique was more analytical and relatively bloodless. His contribution to the historiography of the old Irish party in the British House of Commons was to puncture the republican mythology that it had been a thoroughly corrupt and ineffectual organization. Lyons was able to show that, although the leaders of the party may not always have made wise judgments, they had functioned effectively within the severe constraints imposed by the British connection and by Westminster's political alignments. He understood, as the republican tradition did not, that Ireland's destiny then hung on the intentions of British leaders. The task of Irish politicians then was to persuade those leaders to take up and to implement Home Rule.

Where Parnell's successors erred, Lyons concluded, was

> in the last analysis . . . this belief—that Parnell's system could serve later generations as effectively as it had served his own—that was the fallacy lying at the root of the party's disintegration. The leaders did not sufficiently realize that, however much the Irish question might remain the same in essentials, it presented itself in a different form to each generation. In Parnell's time circumstances had conspired to render possible the creation of a highly centralized organization. But such a system was only possible when other means of agitation had for the time being exhausted their resources, when there was a prospect of speedy success for the constitutional approach, and above all when there was an outstanding leader who could compel the admiration and obedience of the country. All these conditions prevailed between 1885 and 1890, but they automatically ceased to do so after the split.[5]

Lyons's account was an early example of an emerging spirit of critical inquiry into his country's recent past. At another level, the book was a stage in the process whereby Trinity College hijacked Irish history during the 1950s and 1960s.

For all its usefulness, Lyons's study had substantial limitations. Some of these, admittedly, were the consequence of the limited resources available in Ireland and Britain. Archives in Britain, notably the British Museum (British Library), had been dislocated during the war, and original research in them was curtailed in the 1940s. Junior lecturers in British universities in postwar Britain were paid modest stipends, and Hull was distant from London. Lyons's own restricted vision accounts for other limitations. His focus was deliberately narrow; for instance, he largely excluded consideration of the Parnellite faction headed by John Redmond in the 1890s. This omission deprives the study of vital texture. His decision to conclude in 1910 instead of 1914 left the Irish party dangling, just at a moment when the patient policy pursued for so many years by John Redmond seemed on the verge of yielding the long-awaited bumper dividend of Home Rule. Nor is Lyons's portrayal of British politics—especially of the role of the Conservative party—perceptive. He paid little attention to the role of the Irish party in wider questions, largely ignoring its involvement in issues of South Africa, women's suffrage, and Liberal social welfare reforms. The book is not so much an account of the Irish party as an analysis of its structure and strategy in pursuit of Home Rule. Lyons's preference for John Dillon is always evident; at times this leads him to underestimate John Redmond's position. Nor does the book compare favorably with the Trinity studies of the Irish party published subsequently. It lacks the flair of Conor Cruise O'Brien's *Parnell and His Party, 1880–90* (Oxford, 1957) or the technical proficiency of David Thornley's *Isaac Butt and Home Rule* (London, 1964). Lyons had the largest subject, but his study was in no sense exhaustive. Despite its defects, however, the book still has no serious rival and remains the standard assessment of the party's later years.

During the 1950s Lyons published a number of journal articles, but his second book, *The Fall of Parnell, 1890–91,* did not appear until 1960, nine years after his first. His account focuses on the reasons why the split in the Irish party took place and why that split defied healing for so long. Lyons anatomized the episode by concentrating almost entirely on the maneuvers of the contesting elements between November 1890 and Parnell's death in October of the next year. Those eleven months, he concluded, sealed the fate of the party for a generation. Lyons's method once more was to dissect the actions of the participants; he paid correspondingly little attention to the formation of a wider public opinion. The book does not attempt a sociological or psychological analysis. Lyons's technique anticipated what has since come to be termed the study of "high politics," but it lacked the strident pretentiousness that has served as the hallmark of that school of historical writing.

Lyons built his study around the issues and personalities of the split, especially the negotiations between William O'Brien and Dillon with Parnell to restore a unified party. He was able to bring fresh intensity to the incident from close examination of important original sources, which had become available during the 1950s. Lyons made particularly effective use of the Dillon, T. P. Gill, William O'Brien, T. C. Harrington, and Redmond papers. His then, was a pioneering use of the source materials of Irish history that is now taken for granted. Lyons's thesis was that attempts to resolve the rending of the party failed because few of the participants actually desired reunion. For Parnell, the negotiations presented an occasion to stall for time and seek to establish a propaganda advantage over his opponents. At the same time, key rivals like T. M. Healy and Michael Davitt were intent on ensuring, as part of any reunification bargain, that Parnell appear to be publicly humiliated. The few men of good intentions — John Dillon and William O'Brien — struggled in the cross fire on behalf of what proved to be a completely forlorn dream. It is a tale filled with pathos, and it reveals once more Lyons's underlying sense of fatalism. Parnell, he concludes, was prepared to bring down his own edifice rather than surrender power. In so doing, he reenacted the role of the flawed titan of a Greek tragedy. In the end, pride destroyed the achievements his political genius had wrought. Lyons clearly identified himself with Dillon, also a pessimist by nature. Most significantly, Lyons undermined the Parnellite myth of the leader being toppled by his rebellious underlings. Parnell is, in reality, shown to be as obstinate as his rivals. If there were any heroes left in the story, they were Dillon and O'Brien.

In many respects *The Fall of Parnell* is a model of its kind, and it may prove to be Lyons's most enduring scholarly work. Emmet Larkin, for instance, has described it as "the most beautifully written of all Lyons' work."[6] It is a tightly argued and elegant book of moderate length. Although it is, in fact, longer than Lyons's first monograph, it succeeds in conveying the atmosphere of the crisis without exhausting the reader with a wealth of unnecessary detail. It may be argued, however, that Lyons placed the party split in too narrow a frame. Although he did not ignore the deeper ideological issues that helped motivate the combatants, he seems to regard these issues as less formative than they may have been. Nor was his understanding of the British side of the story as acute as his interpretation of the Irish dimension. Even on the Irish side, Lyons's touch is less sure when dealing with the position of the Catholic church; his estimate of Parnell's point of view is not always convincing; and the treatment of Healy's role is at times opaque. Yet Lyons succeeds admirably in showing how the contradictions in Parnell's own makeup infused the drama with tension and excitement, and he makes understandable why the deposed leader's reputation was soon to rise much higher than that of his accusers—a matter of profound significance to the unfolding of Irish history. At times the book may seem somewhat bloodless in tone, but it is a fine academic attainment. And if some of Lyons's conclusions have been critically reassessed, the book as a whole still stands as near a definitive account of the episode as seems likely to be published.

In the interval between completion of *The Fall of Parnell* and the appearance of his third book on the Irish party, *John Dillon,* Lyons's work rate was impressive. He did the commissioned study for the Council of Europe, wrote several articles, published a useful pamphlet on Parnell and, of course, had to meet the many problems of establishing a degree in history at Canterbury. The official biography of Dillon opened a new phase in Lyons's career. The book, which he intended as his last on the Irish party, was his first to reach a wider public. It confirmed his sharp literary pen, fully capable of holding the attention of his readers without sacrificing academic integrity. It was Lyons's ability to link thorough research with literary flair that made him so influential a force in Irish historiography. This, his first biography, was the longest by far of Lyons's books to date. His account of Dillon's career occupies nearly as many pages as do his first two books added together. Around this time, Lyons appears to have developed a sense of his future status, for he began to save the drafts of his manuscripts.[7] With the publication of *John Dillon,* there could be little doubt that, in several senses, he had made his mark. Many historians continue to regard the Dillon volume as Lyons's ablest.

Lyons's subject was not at first glance an obvious choice to establish his preeminence among Irish historians. Dillon had been one of the foremost national leaders of his era, but he suffered the misfortune of heading the Irish party during its temporary collapse. Thus, he won no place in its pantheon of heroes for the generation that finally secured the long-desired self-government for most of Ireland. Dillon did not evoke the nobility of Redmond or the deep sense of gratitude that Irish farmers felt for Davitt and O'Brien. He had deserted Parnell and fought against Sinn Fein. Nor was Dillon a naturally lovable character. Moreover, his reputation suffered because he was one of the few leaders of the old Irish party who published no retrospective memoir in his own defense. Dillon, in fact, found himself treated brutally in the accounts of his old comrades, like O'Brien and Healy. Lyons's first two books had gone some distance toward restoring Dillon's standing, but the biography completed his rehabilitation. The volume is something more than a study of a man, for in it Lyons effectively reconsiders, and in many ways revises, the entire history of Irish nationalism and of the parliamentary party during Dillon's career. The book was the first modern scholarly biography of an Irish leader, a book on a par with the very best historical writing being done by British historians.

Lyons's personal sympathy for Dillon had been evident in his earlier books. At the same time he gave full attention to his subject's faults of temper and errors of judgment. The biography is particularly adept at showing how Dillon interpreted the Parnell system of party management and how he sought to reconstruct that system within the framework of post-1891 Irish life. The book's greatest value lies less in its portrait of Dillon, however, than in the manner in which Lyons succeeds in defining the problems faced by liberal nationalism in both their Irish and their British settings. He portrays Dillon as belonging in every respect to the mainstream of nineteenth-century European liberal nationalism at its finest. Dillon sought for Ireland democratic self-rule based on the principles of toleration, compromise, and discussion—even if his attitude toward particular groups, like landlords, was less charitable and inclusive. But, like others who wanted a broadly based national state, Dillon found himself squeezed between cruder and more extreme forms of nationalism in Ireland and in Britain. Dillon's vision, and that of other liberal Nationalists, lost its hold on the people he guided when they encountered the trauma of world war—when so much of the old Europe and its liberalism was laid waste. That Dillon failed impressed Lyons as a misfortune; had Dillon's vision prevailed, the Ireland of the 1920s (in which Lyons was born) might have been a happier place.

The Dillon biography showed Lyons as a man of rich talent and of broad sentiments, but his focus was still largely political. He had not yet attempted "total history" nor was he a historian who deftly borrowed from the social sciences. The book had some blind spots. Lyons's assessment of other major Irish figures, particularly Redmond, O'Brien, and Healy, is unconvincing and unsympathetic. Nor is this book wholly persuasive as an explanation of why Dillon had been able to engage the loyalty of so many colleagues and a significant section of the Irish people until 1916. Lyons is stronger in his appreciation of the subtle interplay between British and Irish politics, even if he is not always an acute guide to the role of Nationalists in Westminster politics. E. R. Norman, who has since won renown as a historian, caught the essence of Lyons's lapse when he noted:

> there is a sense in which Professor Lyons has written an extended history of the party with Dillon as the narrator—which is, of course, something less than biography. The author remarks, for example, that in Parliament Dillon 'played a double role, being virtually the only Irish Member to occupy himself with the major issues of state as well as with specially Irish questions'. But there is no account of this occupation in the book; which is a pity, because he goes on to say that Dillon emerged as one of the 'foremost critics of imperialism, rearmament, and *Machtpolitik* in general'. These, surely, warrant elaboration.[8]

Lyons remained ill at ease with the Conservatives and with the Ulster Unionists in his story. Perhaps though, the outstanding flaw is one inherent in the genre of "official history." Not only did Lyons receive assistance and encouragement from the Dillon family, but also Professor Myles Dillon supervised the final manuscript. In the process, Lyons found Myles Dillon obdurate over references to material in

Elizabeth Matthew's diaries. In arguing his case for inclusion of certain information, Lyons pointed out: "I have a historian's loyalty to my sources and, once having seen this material would find it impossible to behave as if it didn't exist. . . . A public man belongs in the last analysis to history and that the ordinary rules of privacy don't apply—or at least not in the way that they do to private people."[9] He pleaded that inclusion "may lift the book from being an ordinarily competent study to a biography of a different order from any that has yet appeared about an Irish political figure."[10] It is clear that Lyons bowed to Dillon family feeling on several occasions. Furthermore, it is evident from John Dillon's journals, now deposited in Trinity College, that the subject's physical and even more his psychological torment in the early years was suppressed.[11] Finally, Lyons acknowledged that he found the 1890s "distasteful,"[12] an attitude which led to an underestimation of parliamentary nationalism in the post-split decade.

A balance-sheet approach cannot convey why the Dillon biography did so much to enhance Lyons's reputation as a historian. Dillon in the 1960s was not, after all, a well-known historical personality, and capable studies of much better remembered British historical figures were appearing during those years. *John Dillon,* for all its careful workmanship, did not introduce an arresting new methodology or provide a totally novel perspective. An answer may lie in the book's timing. An interlacing of three factors helped ensure the volume's success. First, Anglo-Irish relations were warmer during the 1960s; old feuds appeared to be passing into history. That rapprochement was marked by sending to Ireland the remains of Roger Casement, hanged as a traitor by the British government back in 1916. Until then, successive British governments had denied persistent requests for Casement's remains made by the government of Ireland. During those years, relations between the Irish Republic and the autonomous government of Northern Ireland were placed on a friendly footing. Secondly, the winds of change had largely swept away the British Empire, and many Britons had come to feel almost embarrassed by memories of their imperial past. Thirdly, as a consequence of these shifts of mood, the historical and journalistic establishments in Britain felt the need for an expert on Irish history who could place the relations of earlier decades within a comprehensible framework. Better than anyone else, Leland Lyons filled that bill, and his study of Dillon, a good Irish nationalist who sought only to establish a cooperative working partnership with his British neighbors, suited the times. Both Dillon's and Lyons's liberal nationalism were back in fashion in the 1960s.

Lyons's next and probably most important book, *Ireland since the Famine* (1971) also appeared at a propitious moment. This, his longest work, confirmed a quasi-geometric tendency in Lyons's publications. *Ireland since the Famine* was almost as long as his three earlier books on Irish history combined. His account filled two lacunae. Prior to his survey, no good account of modern Ireland existed that could appeal satisfactorily to a wide audience. The eruption of a new "time of troubles" in Northern Ireland in 1968–1969 had proved difficult for the people of Britain to understand. There was an obvious need for a comprehensive explanation of modern Irish history. Lyons's volume probed deeply the currents, tensions, conflicts, and compromises that animated Irish life and the evolution of Anglo-Irish relations.

Not surprisingly, *Ireland since the Famine* was an instant success. It immediately became the standard history of modern Ireland. Whereas none of Lyons's previous titles had been given paperback editions, this book was issued in soft covers less than two years after its initial publication. The book, subsequently revised by Lyons, has thus far been reprinted ten times. Despite the warm welcome it received in Britain, the book enjoyed less success in the United States, where survey courses in Irish history were proliferating during the 1960s and 1970s.[13] Lyons's erudite yet readable account probably represents the highpoint of his craftsmanship. The book, unlike most general treatments, is not a mere survey or synthesis, but a major example of original historical writing. His chapter on the Irish economy, for instance, was at the time of publication a substantially novel contribution to economic history. Lyons's accomplishment was to weave the political, social, economic, intellectual, cultural, and even the psychological threads of Ireland's story into a single tapestry. Although he never interprets Irish developments in simplistic fashion, Lyons's clarity of exposition saves the reader from feeling a hopeless sense of drift. In this work Lyons moved well beyond the political boundaries that had enclosed his earlier books.

Although old themes reappear in *Ireland since the Famine,* the volume also reveals a transition in Lyons's thinking about Irish nationalism. Yet it is evident that he remained very much a fatalist. Irish history was for him a melancholy tale. He cites the Great Famine of the 1840s as the signal event—a determinant of the country's future, both creative and destructive in its influence. At the beginning of the book he gives color to this perspective when contending that the

Famine, "however much refined and analysed . . . remains an appalling phenomenon, etching itself ineradicably on the hearts and minds not only of those who experienced it, but of all the generations that have lived in Ireland since those terrible years." Lyons goes on to insist, "yet while the immediate effect of the 'great hunger' was to impose an overwhelming burden of suffering upon an impoverished and defenceless people, it may well be that its most profound impact on Irish history lay in its ultimate psychological legacy. Expressed in its simplest terms, this legacy was that the long-standing and deep-rooted hatred of the English connection was given not only a new intensity, but also a new dimension."[14] Subsequent events revolved around how the Irish people contained and unleashed their profound sense of frustration and bitterness. British efforts to remedy the damage and legitimize imperial rule were doomed to failure unless they were accompanied by an intention to release Ireland from the full burden of the Union.

Lyons's earlier liberal nationalism had been supplanted by a harder-edged outlook that verged on the neorepublican. Whereas Trinity historians, including Lyons, had been notable for punching holes in old-style republican mythology, he now placed himself in the vanguard of a subtle and complex neonationalist historiographical revival. Lyons's newly discovered republicanism is displayed in the opening paragraph of *Ireland since the Famine,* where he states:

> The tired old witticism that every time the English came within sight of solving the Irish question the Irish changed the question, contains, like most jokes about Ireland, a small grain of truth submerged in a vast sea of misconception. The Irish did not change the question between the Famine and the war of independence any more than they had changed it between the Union and the Famine. The 'national demand', as it used to be called, remained in essence what Wolfe Tone had declared it to be as long ago as 1791, 'to break the connection with England, the never-failing source of all our political evils'. It is true, of course, that men differed in the nineteenth century, as they have continued to differ in the twentieth about how complete the break should be, or more precisely, perhaps about how far the full separatist ideal was practicable. But whether they took their stand on the rock of the republic, or were prepared to settle for repeal of the Union and some form of Home Rule based upon a reanimated Irish parliament, they were emphatic that the first step towards real independence was to recover for Irishmen the right to control their own affairs.[15]

At first glance it seems ironic that his discovery of Irish republicanism came at a time when Lyons was happily settled at an English university. It is yet more ironic that Lyons's heightened sense of Irish nationalism should strike so responsive a chord in British readers. But, as noted earlier, the climate of opinion often helps determine how particular books and authors are received. The manner in which Lyons linked Irish nationalism to the Famine gave Anglo-Irish misunderstandings a cogency and comprehensibility to his British audience. He made equally intelligible the revival of conflict in Northern Ireland. Lyons's overall appraisal fitted Britain's postcolonial mood. Whereas earlier republican interpretations had been crude, his was sophisticated, and it secured acceptance because of his Irish Protestant and Trinity College pedigree and his reputation for academic objectivity. *Ireland since the Famine* gave Lyons a credence in Britain such as no Irish historian had enjoyed since W. E. H. Lecky.

Americans, in contrast, were trying to cope with the Vietnam experience and the containment of nationalism, and Lyons's theme exerted less attraction, despite a seemingly more fertile soil for Irish national claims. In Ireland, too, reviewers greeted Lyons's achievement with some caveats. One, for example, noted that "two aspects of the Irish community . . . rather escape him — what might be called sentimental Unionism and purely religious Catholicism, which is more than once apparent."[16] The volume has tended to find its warmest reception in Britain, where despite E. R. Norman's belief that it was too long for the general reader, Lord Blake's estimate that it would prove an "essential standby for every student of the subject" has proved correct.[17]

Lyons might have contented himself by basking in the recognition that he had now received, performing his administrative tasks, and periodically revising *Ireland since the Famine*. Instead, during the 1970s he threw himself into all manner of intellectual and organizational activities. He was in continual demand as speaker and writer in different parts of the world. The duties of provost of Trinity proved far more onerous than those of the holder of the chair in history at Canterbury. And he was now a public figure in Ireland, sometimes taken into the councils of state and ever keen to display the Trinity flag to a popular audience. Despite such a heavy schedule, he plowed ahead with his biography of Parnell and took on the huge commission of preparing the official life of Yeats. The latter commitment involved the attempt to acquire the techniques and scholarship of a separate discipline, English literature.

Charles Stewart Parnell, Lyons's second biography, appeared early in 1977. It received immediate and wide acclaim, though a number of reviewers observed that much of the material and outlook had been outlined in Lyons's earlier books. This was the first of his books to be accorded an award, the prestigious Heinemann Prize, and the second to be put out in soft-cover edition, a format intended primarily for the American market. Counting reference notes, the volume was almost seven hundred pages long. *Parnell* was in one sense a book that had to be written, and Lyons was the obvious candidate for the task. The Irish chief's reputation rode as high in the 1970s as it had in his own lifetime, but he had proved an elusive man to capture on paper. R. Barry O'Brien's two-volume study published in the 1890s was a brilliant polemic, but it was conceived as part of the battle for the soul of the post-Parnell Irish party rather than as a work of close scholarship. Yet no subsequent attempt at a biography had matched the power of O'Brien's volumes. Lyons set about providing a definitive study that would place Parnell in context.

To capture the essence of Parnell was a daunting assignment because the Irish leader left a paucity of documents. In his own lifetime Parnell wrote few letters, and he neglected to collect those that were sent to him. He rarely put his thoughts on paper; his views are to be found mainly in speeches and in the reminiscences of his contemporaries. A study of Parnell, therefore, posed a challenge to Lyons quite distinct from that posed by the study of Dillon—not least because the surviving materials for Parnell are often contradictory or replete with ambiguity.

Parnell has now been twice fortunate in his biographers. Both O'Brien and Lyons wielded elegant pens; but in contrast to O'Brien, Lyons clarifies Parnell's failures and errors of judgment as much as he displays his vision and his strength. Once again he portrays the great Irish chief as a man of flawed genius, prepared at the last to place himself above his movement. Thus Lyons dispelled many legends about Parnell without debunking the man. His Parnell emerges as more human and more believable. The most original portion of the book is Lyons's assessment of Parnell's decline between 1886 and 1890 as a combination of indifference, defective judgment, absence of leadership, and poor health that sapped his influence within his party though not among the wider public. In 1890–1891 it was therefore possible for important members of the party to conclude that Parnell's leadership was no longer essential. Lyons gave less attention to the manner in which Parnell's image was sustained in Ireland during these years of semiretirement.

By placing Parnell in a broad context, Lyons sought to demonstrate that, although the leader consistently held aloft a vision of a self-governing nation, his means of gaining that object were not equally farseeing. Parnell emerges less as the flawed giant of *The Fall of Parnell* than as a man whose good fortune before 1886 masked for a time underlying defects of perception. In the end there is no doubt that Lyons has etched a convincing portrait.

If *Parnell* was the book that Lyons *had* to write, it may also be the one he should have foregone. Despite the biography's length—a mark of its author's literary capacity—it contained less fresh material than might have been expected, and most of the interpretative outlook is foreshadowed in earlier books. Perhaps most disappointing, the press of Lyons's many duties made this a less thoroughly researched and thought-out study. Since some of the main sources for Parnell's career are his speeches, Lyons might have exerted himself more to locate all those that have survived. During the autumn of 1877 alone, Parnell made twenty public speeches of which Lyons makes no mention at all. The fullest record of his activities during the 1870s may be found in *Hansard's Parliamentary Debates,* and yet Lyons frequently neglects that source. His observation that Parnell was slow in appreciating the growing land storm in the west of Ireland in 1879 would have been more pertinent had he also noted that the young M.P. was staying up late night after night in the House of Commons in order to participate in debates on non-Irish subjects. Lyons fails to place Parnell's speeches of 1885 into context, and his attempt to analyze Parnell's attitude toward Ulster during the Home Rule episode is not satisfying. Lyons might have been less struck by the novelty of Parnell's radicalism in 1891 had he read more of the leader's speeches in the 1870s.

Paul Bew's short study, *C. S. Parnell* (1980), showed by contrast how a sharp, fresh mind could produce an arresting and original insight that was in vital respects superior to Lyons's.[18] The latter's inability to penetrate Parnell's mind unquestionably resulted from the fact, which Emmet Larkin has noted, that "Lyons was also basically unable to empathize with Parnell because he really did not like him."[19] That attitude had manifested itself in a letter to James Dillon in 1967 when Lyons noted, "writing to Myles the other day I pointed out the contrast between your parents' letters and those between Parnell and Mrs. O'Shea. How shabby and second-rate the latter, how charming and radiantly happy the former."[20]

Although *Parnell* is a lengthy book, it is not genuinely definitive. Yet the volume received more and wider attention than did any of Lyons's previous books, including *Ireland since the Famine.* If

Parnell did not constitute Lyons's best work, the recognition he received for it far outstripped what he had received for any other. This anomaly can be explained by the nature of the historical profession. Lyons had become an established figure, an international academic star, and hence his work automatically received attention.

His final volume, *Culture and Anarchy in Ireland, 1890–1939* maintained Lyons's reputation for graceful presentation. In two respects it marked a departure: he provides a succinct overview, and he focuses special attention on the social and cultural factors in Irish development. The book has had a substantial impact, and soon after initial publication it appeared in a soft-cover edition. It is probably the most widely read of Lyons's books. His theme, that Ireland has been plagued by a clash of four distinct cultures—Gaelic, English, Anglo-Irish, and Ulster Protestant—constitutes a deliberate attempt to shift discussion away from the usual political interpretation of Irish history. In arguing the case, he makes the most of his vast storehouse of erudition. Ultimately, however, the book fails to carry conviction, because Lyons's conception of cultural and social development is unduly restricted. Ireland may well have had more than four cultures or subcultures, and these were not mutually exclusive and antagonistic to the extent that Lyons suggests. The picture was at once more complex and less cloudy.

Culture and Anarchy is a provocative work of interpretation, even if it shows Lyons functioning at a level less effective than earlier. It may also have been intended as a transitional work, taking note of Lyons's increasing absorption in the Yeats project. Perhaps its chief value is for students who are accustomed to placing the Anglo-Irish problem in an exclusively political frame. Although the book proved to be the last of Lyons's major historical works, it was not meant to play that role. He continued to write articles, edited one book, and co-edited another.[21] But for his early death, he would certainly have produced additional works.

It is not easy to situate Lyons in the context of post-1945 British historiography. He achieved a high degree of respect, but his writings did not herald a methodological revolution or give him status as an intellectual guru. He did not inspire a school of history. Yet Lyons's influence has proved pervasive, and his professional reputation may survive longer than that of most of the best-known postwar historians. He has been foremost among those historians who have demonstrated that good political history can be simultaneously interesting and attractively presented. His claim to rank among the post-1945 giants of the historical craft rests ultimately on his success in making Ireland a central problem in British historiography and on the respect and the recognition that he won for Irish studies generally. His influence may resemble that of Norman Gash more than that, say, of Christopher Hill or Edward Thompson—but that remains a truly substantial achievement for one lifetime.

NOTES

I am indebted to Mrs. Jennifer Lyons, Mrs. Doran (librarian of the Royal Irish Academy), and Ms. Daphne Gill (secretary to the provost, Trinity College, Dublin) for biographical information and assistance.

1. A bibliography of Lyons's main academic writings is appended to these notes.
2. R. F. Foster, "Francis Stewart Leland Lyons, 1923–1983," *Proceedings of the British Academy* 70(1985):463–79. Other biographical information is derived from Emmet Larkin, "F. S. L. Lyons: An Appreciation," *Irish Literary Supplement* 3(Spring 1984):6–7.
3. Foster, "F. S. L. Lyons," 466.
4. Larkin, "Lyons Appreciation," 6.
5. F. S. L. Lyons, *The Irish Parliamentary Party, 1890–1910* (London, 1951), 263–64.
6. Larkin, "Lyons Appreciation," 6.
7. The papers are deposited at Trinity College, Dublin, but not all portions are open for inspection.
8. E. R. Norman, *Spectator,* 13 Dec. 1968.
9. Lyons to James Dillon, 13 July 1967. Lyons Papers, Trinity College, Dublin, library.
10. Ibid.
11. Dillon was in a rather bad state in the 1870s. It is more than probable that his problems influenced his outlook on life.
12. Lyons to Myles Dillon, 16 Mar. 1967. Lyons Papers, Trinity College, Dublin, library.
13. See Foster, "F. S. L. Lyons," for some speculations on the reasons.
14. F. S. L. Lyons, *Ireland since the Famine,* rev. ed. (London, 1973), 15–16.
15. Ibid., 3.
16. G. J. Hand, *Irish Independent,* 15 May 1971.
17. E. R. Norman, *Spectator,* 22 May 1971; Blake, *Sunday Times* (London), 9 May 1971.
18. Paul Bew, *C. S. Parnell* (Dublin, 1980).
19. Larkin, "Lyons Appreciation," 6.
20. Lyons to James Dillon, 13 July 1967. Lyons Papers, Trinity College, Dublin, library.
21. He edited *The Bank of Ireland, 1783–1983: Bicentary Essays* (Dublin, 1983) and co-edited *Ireland under the Union* (Oxford, 1980).

BIBLIOGRAPHY

"The Irish Unionist Party and the Devolution Crisis of 1904–1905." *Irish Historical Studies* 6(March 1948).
The Irish Parliamentary Party, 1890–1910. London, 1951.
"The Irish Parliamentary Party and the Liberals in Mid-Ulster, 1894." *Irish Historical Studies* 7(March 1951).
"The Machinery of the Irish Parliamentary Party in the General Election of 1895." *Irish Historical Studies* 8(September 1952).
"Vicissitudes of a Middleman in County Leitrim, 1810–27." *Irish Historical Studies* 9(March 1955).
"The Economic Ideas of Parnell." *Historical Studies* 2(1959).
The Fall of Parnell, 1890–91. London, 1960.
Internationalism in Europe, 1815–1914. Leiden, 1963.
Parnell. Dublin, 1963 (pamphlet).
"George Moore and Edward Martyn." *Hermathena* 98(1964).
"John Dillon and the Plan of Campaign, 1886–90." *Irish Historical Studies* 14(September 1965).
"The Passing of the Irish Parliamentary Party, 1916–18." In *The Irish Struggle, 1916–18,* ed. Desmond Williams. Dublin, 1966.
John Dillon: A Biography. London, 1968.
"The Two Faces of Home Rule." In *The Making of 1916,* ed. K. B. Nowlan. Dublin, 1969.
"James Joyce's Dublin." *Twentieth Century Studies* (November 1970).
Ireland since the Famine. London, 1971; rev. ed., 1973.
"Charles Stewart Parnell"; "The Irish Parliamentary Party"; and "From War to Civil War in Ireland: Three Essays on the Treaty Debate." In *The Irish Parliamentary Tradition,* ed. Brian Farrell. Dublin, 1973.
"The Dilemma of the Irish Contemporary Historian." *Hermathena* 115(1973).
"The Political Ideas of Parnell." *Historical Journal* 16(1973).
"Parnellism and Crime, 1887–90." *Transactions of the Royal Historical Society,* 5th ser., 24(1974).
"Irish Links to American Independence." *Freedom: Then, Now and Tomorrow Symposium* (September 1976).
"The Parnell Theme in Literature." *Irish Literary Studies* 1(1976).
"Sean O'Faolain as Biographer." *Irish University Review* 6(Spring 1976).
"W. B. Years and the Public Life of Ireland." *New Divinity* 7(Summer 1976).
Charles Stewart Parnell. London, 1977.
"The Burden of Our History." W. B. Rankin Memorial Lecture. Belfast: The Queen's University of Belfast, 1979.
Culture and Anarchy in Ireland, 1890–1939. Oxford, 1979.
(ed. with R. A. J. Hawkins). *Ireland under the Union: Varieties of Tension.* Oxford, 1980.
"T. W. M." In *Ireland under the Union,* ed. F. S. L. Lyons and R. A. J. Hawkins. Oxford, 1980.
"Yeats and Victorian Ireland." *Irish Literary Studies* 6(1980).
"Ireland: History's Political Prisoner." *Sooner Magazine* 2(Fall, 1981).
(ed.). *The Bank of Ireland, 1783–1983: Bicentenary Essays.* Dublin, 1983.

Contributors

WALTER L. ARNSTEIN is L.A.S. Jubilee Professor of History at the University of Illinois at Urbana-Champaign, where he has taught since 1968 and also served as department chair from 1974 to 1978. He received his Ph.D. in history at Northwestern University in 1961 under the supervision of Lacey Baldwin Smith, and he has held appointments at Roosevelt University, Northwestern University, and the University of Chicago. In 1982 he was visiting fellow at Clare Hall (Cambridge University) and in 1989 was honorary fellow at the Institute for Advanced Studies in the Humanities (University of Edinburgh). He is a Fellow of the Royal Historical Society and has served as president of the Midwest Victorian Studies Association and of the Midwest Conference on British Studies. His books include *The Bradlaugh Case* (Oxford, 1965; 2d ed., Columbia, Mo., 1984), *Protestant versus Catholic in Mid-Victorian England* (Columbia, Mo., 1982), the winner of the John Gilmary Shea Prize of the American Catholic Historical Association, and *Britain Yesterday and Today: 1830 to the Present,* 5th ed. (Lexington, Mass., 1988).

BARRETT L. BEER is professor of history at Kent State University. He received his undergraduate education at DePauw University and completed his Ph.D. at Northwestern University in 1965 under the supervision of Lacey Baldwin Smith. He has also taught at the University of New Mexico and served as Fulbright Professor of British Studies at the University of Tromsö (Norway) in 1983. His publications include *Northumberland: The Political Career of John Dudley, the Duke of Northumberland* (1973), *The Letters of William, Lord Paget of Beaudesert, 1547–1563* (edited with S. M. Jack, 1974), and *Rebellion and Riot: Popular Disorder in England during the Reign of Edward VI* (1982). His current research includes studies on John Stow and the Edwardian Reformation.

JOEL BERLATSKY is professor of history and chair of the department of history at Wilkes College in Wilkes-Barre, Pennsylvania, where he has taught since 1970. He holds a B.A. from Carleton College, an M.A.T. from Brown University, and a Ph.D. from Northwestern University, completed in 1970 under the supervision of Lacey Baldwin Smith. He is coeditor (with Rosemary O'Day) of the *Letter Book of Thomas Bentham, Bishop of Coventry and Lichfield, 1560–1561* (London, 1979). His articles have appeared in the *Historical Magazine of the Protestant Episcopal Church,* in *Albion,* in the *Journal of Family History,* and in *Eire-Ireland.* He has also contributed to R. Zaller and R. L. Greaves, eds., *A Biographical Dictionary of English Radicals in the Seventeenth Century,* and to Rosemary O'Day and Felicity Heal, eds., *Princes and Paupers in the English Church, 1500–1800.* Currently he is working on a comparison of British colonial attitudes in Ireland and India during the early modern era.

ROBERT C. BRADDOCK has been a member of the history department at Saginaw Valley State University, Michigan, since 1970; from 1976 to 1978 and from 1985 to 1987 he served as department chair. Since 1987 he has been assistant to the vice president for academic affairs. He did his undergraduate work at Middlebury College, Vermont, and completed his Ph.D. in 1971 at Northwestern University under the supervision of Lacey Baldwin Smith. His articles have appeared in *Albion* and the *Journal of British Studies.*

CYNTHIA HERRUP is associate professor of history and law at Duke University. She completed her Ph.D. degree at Northwestern University in 1982 under the supervision of Lacey Baldwin Smith and taught at the University of Michigan at Ann Arbor from 1981 to 1984. Her articles have appeared in *Past and Present,* the *Historical Journal, Comparative Studies in Society and History,* and the *Journal of British Studies.* In 1986 she won the Walter D. Love Prize of the North American Conference on British Studies for the best article in British history published during 1985. In 1987 her book, *The Common Peace: Participation and the Criminal Law in Seventeenth-Century England,* was published by the Cambridge University Press. Her work has been supported by the Fulbright-Hays program, the American Association of University Women, the American Council of Learned Societies, the National Endowment of the Humanities, and the John Simon Guggenheim Memorial Foundation. She is a Fellow of the Royal Historical Society.

THOMAS WILLIAM HEYCK is professor of history at Northwestern University, where he has been a member of the faculty since 1968. He holds the Ph.D. degree from the University of Texas. He has published two books, *The Dimensions of British Radicalism: The Case of Ireland* (Urbana, Ill., 1974) and *The Transformation of Intellectual Life in Victorian England* (New York, 1982; paperback, Chicago, 1989). He has recently completed a volume to be entitled *A History of the British Peoples since 1688* and is currently working on a book concerning intellectual life in twentieth-century Britain.

ALAN O'DAY is senior lecturer in history at the Polytechnic of Northern London where he has taught since 1976. He received his B.A. degree from the

University of Michigan and M.A.s from Roosevelt University and Northwestern University (where he served as an assistant to Lacey Baldwin Smith). He received a Ph.D. from the University of London in 1971. He has taught at German and English universities, including the University of East Anglia. His books include *The English Face of Irish Nationalism* (1977) and *Parnell and the First Home Rule Episode* (1986). He is editor of *The Edwardian Age* (1979), *Reactions to Irish Nationalism, 1865–1914* (1987), and *A Survey of the Irish in England (1872)* (1990) and is coeditor of *Terrorism in Ireland* (1984), *Ireland's Terrorist Dilemma* (1986), *Later Victorian Britain, 1867–1900* (1988), and *Ireland's Terrorist Trauma* (1989).

M. J. TUCKER is associate professor of history at the State University of New York at Buffalo. He received the Ph.D. degree in 1962 from Northwestern University, where he completed his dissertation under the supervision of Lacey Baldwin Smith. He has taught at Colby College and at the Massachusetts Institute of Technology. He is best known for his biography, *The Life of Thomas Howard, Earl of Surrey and Second Duke of Norfolk, 1443–1524* (1964). He contributed a chapter, "The Child as Beginning and End: 15th- and 16th-Century English Childhood" to Lloyd de Mause, ed., *The History of Childhood* (Harper Torch, 1975) and an article, "Life at Henry VII's Court" to *History Today* (May, 1969). His other publications include articles on the Tudor poet, John Skelton, and coauthorship of a meditation manual, *Centering: A Guide to Inner Growth* (Destiny Books, 1983).

Index

Abelove, Henry, 143, 144
Abrams, Philip, 99
Act of Union, Irish, 157, 185, 190, 191
Acton, Lord, 9
Africa: exploration of, 113, 114, 119; North, 123–24; South, 148, 178
Althusser, Louis, 141, 142–43
American: Independence, 191; Revolution, 9, 93, 106
Anarchism, 126, 127
Anderson, Perry, 139, 140, 141, 142, 144, 145
Anglican Church. *See* Church of England
Anglo-Irish: culture, 189; problem, 189; relations, 183, 185
Anglo-Saxon: society, 60; art, 77
Annales school, 3, 10, 78, 91, 109, 113, 134
Anne, Queen, 102, 106, 107, 119
Anthropology, 8, 48, 87, 92, 134
Anti-Corn Law League, 152, 159
Anti-fascism, 122
Ariès, Philippe, 111, 112, 117, 119
Aristocracy, 44, 45, 110; Elizabethan, 76, 96, 97; seventeenth century, 46, 97, 98; eighteenth century, 108, 136; nineteenth century, 140, 147, 166. *See also* Elites; Gentry; Ruling class
Arkhangelsky, S. I., 71
Armada, Spanish, 40, 53, 76, 96
Armytage, Frances, 32; W. H. G., 32, 34
Arnstein, Walter L., 34, 52, 145
Art, 127; history of, 77–78, 93, 97; and Sir Robert Peel, 156; and tyranny, 125

Artisans, 131, 132, 133
Ashley, Cooper, Lord Shaftesbury, 150, 164
Ashton, T. S., 130
Augustan Age, 104, 105, 136
Ausubel, Herman, 11
Aylmer, Gerald, 69, 73

Bacon, Sir Francis, 6, 63
Bagehot, Walter, 159
Baldwin, J. W., 72
Baldwin, Stanley, 149
Bank Charter Act, 160
Banking system, 158
Bank of Ireland, 190, 191
Beales, Derek, 154, 159, 160, 169, 170
Beattie, John M., 119
Beer, Barrett, 7, 11, 52
Bell, H. E., 42
Beloff, Max, 163, 170
Bentham, Jeremy, 9, 158, 159, 163
Berghahn, Marion, 32
Berlatsky, Joel, 8
Bew, Paul, 188, 190
Bindoff, S. T., 25, 43, 47, 53
Biography: autobiography, 48; Gash's defense of, 161; historians' approach to, 6, 28, 48, 106, 148; psycho-biography, 27, 28, 88
Bitton, Davis, 98
Black, J. B., 25
Blake, Lord (Robert), 35, 186, 190
Blake, William, 122, 125
Boards of guardians, 140
Bolingbroke, Viscount, 118
Bonham, F. R., 169

197

Bourgeoisie, 65, 94, 139, 140
Bourgeois revolution, English Civil War as, 58, 66, 70, 72, 98, 139
Braudel, Fernand, 3, 109, 110, 119
Brech, Ronald, 39, 53
Brewer, John, 119
Briggs, Lord (Asa), 9, 152, 153
Bristol, Earl of, 165
Britain, 13, 14, 22, 50; culture and social relations, 123; early Victorian, 125, 149, 167; Empire, 4, 114, 163, 183; history of, 4–5, 9–10; and Ireland, 177, 178, 182, 183, 184, 185; and World War II, 39–40; since World War II, 4, 83, 116. *See also* England
British Broadcasting Corporation, 9, 43
British Museum, 77, 178
Brock, Michael, 165, 172
Bromley, J. S., 50
Brooke, Christopher, 170
Brooke, John, 118
Buckingham, Duke of, 79
Bulgaria, 122, 123; agitation in, 126
Bunyan, John, 69–70
Burckhardt, Jacob, 115
Burn, W. L., 163
Burrow, J. W., 5, 11
Bury, John Bagnell, 113, 122
Bury, J. P. T., 40, 53
Butler, Lord (Richard Austen), 170, 172
Butterfield, Sir Herbert, 10, 30–31, 35; memorial lecture, 30

Cabinet, history of, 107, 108–9, 159, 161
Cambridge Group for Population Studies, 48, 110, 111
Cambridge University: pre-1900, 72, 98; post-1900, 13, 16, 25, 26, 27, 32, 101, 102, 124, 151, 175
Cannadine, David, 4, 11, 35
Canning, George, 155, 162, 165, 171
Capitalism: English Civil War and, 58, 66, 67; religion and the rise of, 13, 62; industrial, 119, 124, 125, 126, 127, 128, 131, 135, 138, 140, 143, 144; transition from feudalism to, 71
Carlyle, Thomas, 3, 4, 122, 125, 126, 143
Carter, C. H., 72

Casement, Roger, 183
Cass, Frank, 53
Castlereagh, Lord, 159, 162, 164, 170
Catholic emancipation, 156, 157, 169–70
Catholicism, Roman, 62, 92, 180, 186
Caudwell, Christopher, 124, 143
Cecil, Robert (Earl of Salisbury), 38, 40, 41, 42, 45, 51, 52, 53, 54, 55, 97
Cecil, William (Lord Burghley), 38, 40, 41, 42, 43, 49
Cecil family, 38, 40, 41, 45, 49, 50, 53, 82, 98
Chadwick, Owen, 16
Chambers, E. K., 24
Charles I, 12, 59
Charles II, 59
Chartism, 134, 152, 154, 159
Childhood, history of, 89–91, 111, 112, 117, 119
Christie, Ian, 9, 12, 163
Churchill, Winston Spencer, 10, 11, 12, 52, 55, 116–17, 120
Church of England: creation of, 19, 20, 22; sixteenth and seventeenth centuries, 60, 61–63, 68, 71, 73, 88, 92; nineteenth century, 125, 153, 154, 159–60, 164, 166. *See also* Religion
Civil Service, British, 50
Clapham, J. H., 130
Clark, George Kitson, 9, 131, 144, 163
Clark, Peter, 53, 54, 55
Clarke, J., 73
Class: social, 124, 127, 128, 134, 138, 141, 144; consciousness, 129, 130, 134; struggle, 121, 126, 138, 144
Clifford, James L., 119
Cliometrics, 4, 10, 91–92, 139. *See also* Computers; Quantitative studies
Coakley, Thomas M., 53, 54
Cobbett, William, 126, 133
Coke, Sir Edward, 60, 63
Coleman, Christopher, 33
Coleman, D. C., 81, 97
Colley, Linda, 118
Collingwood, R. G., 10
Collinson, Patrick, 171
Colwin, Howard, 97
Commercial Revolution, 112
Communism, 10, 123, 126
Communist party of Great Britain, 58,

Index

60, 61, 122–23, 125, 128; Historians' Group of, 58, 61, 70, 73, 125
Computers, and historical research, 27, 87, 92, 93, 95, 98–99, 110–11. *See also* Cliometrics; Quantitative studies
Conservative party, 150, 152, 154, 155, 158, 159, 160, 161–62, 168, 170, 178, 182. *See also* Tory party
Cookson, John, 151, 169
Cornforth, M., 70
Corn Laws, 148, 152, 154, 158, 160, 166
Corruption, governmental: in sixteenth and seventeenth centuries, 41, 44–45, 47, 50, 54, 78, 79, 82, 94; in eighteenth century, 103, 107, 108, 114
Costin, William Conrad, 148
Council of Europe, 174, 176, 180
Counter-Reformation, 72
Court and Country, division between, 92
Court of Augmentations, 19
Court of Wards, 8, 19, 40, 41, 42, 46, 49
Cowherd, R. G., 171
Coxe, Archdeacon William, 103–4, 105, 117
Crab, Roger, 67
Crisis of the Aristocracy, The, 78–82, 97, 98
Critcher, C., 73
Croft, Pauline, 54, 55
Cromwell, Oliver, 6, 63, 72
Cromwell, Thomas, 26, 29, 44; as subject of Elton's career, 6, 13, 15–16, 17; as instigator of the Tudor Revolution, 18, 19, 20, 21–22, 23, 26, 33, 34, 35; Hurstfield's assessment of, 44, 45, 50
Cross, Claire, 32
Crowd, the English, 135, 144
Crown, the: in Elizabethan period, 40–41; in Augustan Age, 105, 107, 108, 120; influence of in early nineteenth century elections, 150
Currin, John, 52
Curti, Merle (lectures), 65

Darnton, Robert, 99
Darwin, Charles, 9
Davies, C. S. L., 23, 33, 35
Davies, Kathleen, 99

Davis, Natalie Zemon, 99
Davitt, Michael, 179, 181
Defoe, Daniel, 65, 72
Delaune, Gideon (memorial lecture), 72
Dell, Edmund, 58, 70
Delzell, C., 98
Democracy, Puritanism and, 61, 63, 66
Demography, 4, 48, 84, 87, 89
Derry, John, 165
Descartes, René, 3
Dickens, A. G., 9, 44, 45, 47, 49, 51, 162
Diggers, 61, 65
Dillon, John, 6, 174, 178, 179, 180, 181–82, 183, 184, 187, 188, 191
Dillon, Myles, 182, 188, 190
Disraeli, Benjamin, 147, 166, 168
Dissenters, 92, 129, 164. *See also* Puritans
Dodd, A. H., 38, 42, 48, 52
Donaldson, Gordon, 9, 11
Dreyer, F. A., 151, 169
Dudley family: Edmund, 26; John (Duke of Northumberland), 22, 26; Robert (Earl of Leicester), 49

Economic determinism, 3, 66
Edinburgh, University of, 149, 150
Education, 25, 27–28, 34; in early modern period, 83–86, 97, 98; in eighteenth century, 111–12; in early nineteenth century, 135, 154, 159; adult, 124, 128; university, 11, 25
Edward VI, 19, 24, 34, 41, 42, 53
Ehrenberg, Geoffrey Rudolph. *See* Elton, Geoffrey
Electorate, 107, 119
Eley, Geoff, 70
Elites, 78, 93–96, 99, 100. *See also* Aristocracy; Gentry; Ruling class
Elizabeth I, 6, 7, 9, 12, 15, 18, 31, 38, 40, 41, 43, 44, 53, 55, 76, 79
Elton, Geoffrey (née Ehrenberg), 4, 6, 7, 10, 11, 33, 34, 35, 37, 44, 45, 50, 52, 53, 55, 105, 110, 122, 161, 171; background and education, 13–16, 32; teaching career, 16–17; research on Thomas Cromwell, 17–26; influence on the historical profession, 27–32
Emmison, F. G., 46, 54

Empiricism, tradition of in British historical studies, 4, 141
Enclosure Act, 21
Engels, Friedrich, 71, 124, 141, 142
England, history of: sixteenth century, 6–7, 12, 13, 15, 17–35, 38–39, 40–45, 48–50, 52, 53, 54, 55, 76–80, 81–86, 88–89, 93–94; seventeenth century, 37–38, 41, 45–46, 50, 57–74, 76–89, 91, 92–94; early modern, 78–80, 83–86, 93–96; eighteenth century, 90, 93, 94, 102–13, 114, 128–34, 135–39; nineteenth century, 90, 91, 93, 94, 125–27, 128–34, 150, 151–61, 162, 163–66; twentieth century, 91. *See also* Britain, history of
English Civil War, 9, 34, 58, 66, 71, 79, 80, 81, 83, 86, 89. *See also* English Revolution
English Commonwealth, The, 53, 54, 55
English Revolution (1640s), 5, 7, 11, 30, 58–61, 63–65, 66, 68, 70, 71, 72, 73, 74, 81, 83, 86–87, 92–93, 98, 99. *See also* English Civil War
Europe: early modern, 13, 59, 99; nineteenth and twentieth century, 123, 174, 182, 191
Evangelicals, 90, 132
Evans, Arise, 67, 72
Exploitation, 121, 128

Factory workers, 132, 135
Family, love and marriage, history of, 88–91, 99
Famine, Irish, 174, 184–85, 186, 188, 190, 191
Farrell, Brian, 191
Feminist history and theory, 4, 10, 89–90, 91
Ferguson, Arthur B., 21
Feuchtwanger, E. J., 163
Feudalism, 59, 71; revival of in Tudor era, 39, 40, 41, 42; fiscal, 8, 40–41, 48, 50, 53
Field laborers, 131, 132
Fielden, Kenneth, 165
Finlayson, Michael, 5, 11
Fisher, F. J., 71, 97
Fletcher, Anthony, 32
Fogel, R. W., 10, 11, 28, 34

Ford, James, lectures, 48, 63, 107, 119, 154, 175
Forster, R. F., 190
Forster, Robert, 10, 98
Fox, Charles James, 147
France, 3, 4, 44, 105, 118
Franchise, parliamentary, 158, 178
Freeman, Edward A., 5, 29
Free trade, 160, 166
French Revolution: of 1789, 9, 93, 130, 135, 165; of 1830, 153, 154
Froude, James Anthony, 5, 29, 121
Fuidge, Nora, 47

Gaelic culture, 189
Gaitskell, Hugh, 37
Galbraith, V. H., 44, 46, 54
Gash, Norman, 6, 7, 10, 144, 190; background and education, 148–50; early research, 149–52; concentration on Sir Robert Peel, 152–61; on Lord Liverpool, 162, 164–66; assessment of, 167–68
Gay, Peter, 10
Gentry, 106, 136, 137, 147; Rise of the Gentry theory, 76–77, 81, 86, 97. *See also* Aristocracy; Elites; Ruling class
George I, 102, 103, 108, 119
George II, 102, 103
George III, 102, 106, 113, 114, 119, 165
Germany, 3, 4, 13, 14, 15, 32, 123, 148
Gibbon, Edward, 3
Gilbert, Felix, 98
Gill, T. P., 179
Ginsburg, Carlo, 99
Gladstone, William E., 147, 148, 155, 159, 170
Gladstonian liberalism, 160. *See also* Liberal party
Glorious Revolution, 102, 107
Goldthwaite, R., 72
Goodman, Paul, 96
Gott, Richard, 32
Graham, J. K., 72
Graubard, Stephen, 98
Graves, Robert, 75, 96
Great Contract, 41
Greece, ancient, 14
Greene, J. P., 98
Greenwich tenures, 42, 53

Index

Guth, D. J., 32
Guy, John, 27

Haigh, Christopher, 27, 35
Hale, J. R., 5
Halévy, Elie, 11, 153, 163
Hammond, Barbara and John L., 147, 149, 150, 167
Hampton, David, 151, 169
Hancock, W. K., 39, 53
Hand, G. J., 190
Handloom weavers, 8, 131, 132
Hanoverian monarchs, 102, 103, 113, 119. *See also* George I; George II; George III; William IV
Harlowe, Clarissa, 71
Harrington, T. C., 179
Harris, John, 97
Harrison, Brian, 172
Harrison, J. F. C., 144
Harriss, G. L., 22, 33
Harrow, public school, 157
Harvey, Gabriel, 22
Haskins, Charles Homer (memorial lecture), 96
Hawkins, R. A. J., 191
Haynes, Alan, 45
Healy, T. M., 179, 180, 181, 182
Hegel, Georg Friedrich, 3
Heinemann Prize, 174, 187
Henry VIII, 9, 12, 15, 17, 18, 19, 20, 22, 24, 26, 29, 30, 33, 44, 45, 50
Herrup, Cynthia, 8
Hexter, J. H., 9, 12, 70, 73, 75, 81, 96, 97
Heyck, T. William, 8, 10, 168
Hibbard, Caroline, 10
Hickes, Sir Michael, 53
Hill, Christopher, 6, 7–8, 10, 70, 71, 72, 73, 74, 124, 190; Marxism of, 7–8, 57–58, 61, 70, 71; background and education, 58; themes in his works, 59–60; on the English Revolution, 59–61, on Puritanism, 61–63; later career and writings, 63–65, criticism and assessment of, 66–69
Hill, Fanny, 115
Hilton, Boyd, 160, 165, 170
Hilton, Rodney, 58, 70
Himmelfarb, Gertrude, 9

Historiography: of the English Civil War, 59, 65, 66; French, 87; and Irish studies, 190; Tudor-Stuart, 48
History: lessons of, 115–16; as a "scientific" discipline, 3, 99; the utility of, 117, 166–67
History, forms of: constitutional, 43, 48; economic, 8, 12, 27, 48, 77, 87, 92, 139; intellectual, 63, 64–65, 127; literary, 48; Marxist, 5, 7–8, 11, 57–58, 58–59, 61, 67, 70, 71, 72, 73, 121, 122, 124, 126–27, 128, 137–38, 139–41, 143; narrative, 7, 8, 28, 91, 99, 100; political, 7, 28, 109, 147, 168, 171, 189; social, 4, 7, 8, 9, 27, 87–88, 109–13, 114, 117, 119, 121, 164, 168; Whig, 27, 31, 60, 101, 103, 108, 115, 116, 117, 138
Hitler, Adolf, 32, 39, 116
Hobsbawm, Eric, 9, 58, 70, 71, 73, 99, 147, 163, 165, 167, 168
Holdsworth, Sir William, 11
Holme, K. E. (pseud. for Christopher Hill), 71
Holmes, Geoffrey, 119
Holocaust, 18, 115
Home Rule (Irish), 177, 178, 179, 185, 188, 191
Hoskins, W. G., 30
Houghton Hall, 105, 110
Houlbrooke, Ralph A., 99
House of Commons: Tudor-Stuart, 24, 37; eighteenth century, 109, 114, 118; nineteenth and early twentieth century, 155, 157, 162, 177, 188. *See also* Parliament
House of Lords: Tudor-Stuart, 24, 79, 80, 81; nineteenth century, 153, 154, 158. *See also* Parliament
Howard, Catherine, 12
Hull, University of, 173, 175, 178
Hungary, Soviet invasion of, 61, 128
Hunt, William, 70
Hunters, 118, 136, 144
Hurst, Derek, 171
Hurstfield, Joel, 6, 8, 10, 30, 52, 53, 54, 55; background and education, 37–39; publications, 39–45; concentration on the Cecil family, 40–41, 45, 49; broadcasting career, 42–46; emphasis

Hurstfield, Joel, (*cont.*)
 on teaching, 46–48; assessment of, 48–52
Hurstfield, Julian, 52, 54

Iggers, Georg, 10
Imperialism, 182; anti-imperialism, 122
India, 82, 94, 110; independence of, 122; Indian civil service, 149
Individualism, 88, 91, 171
Industrial Revolution, 60, 70, 91, 106, 115, 129, 130, 131–32, 134, 135, 148, 153, 154, 163, 165, 167
Inequality: sexual, 89–90; social, 60, 64, 65
Inglis, Fred, 143
Institute of Historical Research, London, 46–47, 50, 54–55
Intellectuals, working class, 139, 140
Interregnum, English, 80; Soviet interpretations of, 71
Ireland, history of, 6, 7, 8; Tudor-Stuart, 82, 93; nineteenth and early twentieth century, 148, 155, 157, 163, 169, 173, 175, 176–78, 180–86, 189, 190, 191
Irish nationalism, 176, 177, 181, 182, 183, 184, 185
Irish Nationalist party, 173–74, 175, 176–82, 190, 191
Irish Unionist party, 191

Jacob, Margaret and J.R., 72
Jacobinism, English, 129, 130
Jacobites, 103, 104, 105, 113
Jacombe, Robert, 104
Jaher, F. C., 145
James VI and I, 41, 53, 79
Jann, Rosemary, 11
Japan, 84, 98, 114
Jensen, Marius, 84, 98
Jews, cultural heritage of, 14
Johns Hopkins University, 72, 151
Johnson, Richard, 73
Johnston, Edith, 151, 169
Jones, Inigo, 97
Jones, J. R., 171
Jones, Maldwyn, 52, 53
Jordan, W. K., 73
Joyce, James, 191

Kaye, Harvey, 5, 11, 70, 71, 72, 73, 144
Kearney, Hugh, 73
Keats, John, 125, 163
Kendrick, Sir Thomas, 77
Kent, University of, 52, 174, 176, 180, 186
Kenyon, J. P., 5, 9, 11, 16, 29, 32, 34, 52, 118, 153, 169
Khrushchev, Nikita, 61, 128
Kiernan, Victor, 58
Koenigsberger, H. G., 98, 99
Kossman, E. H., 50
Kouri, E. I., 32

Labour party, British, 9–10, 12, 38
Lamont, William, 72, 73
Lander, J. R., 171
Landlords, 139, 140, 152; Irish, 182
Larkin, Emmett, 177, 180, 188, 190
Larkin, J. F., 52
Laslett, Peter, 48, 110
Law, 50, 72, 136, 137–38, 158; history of, 28, 48
Lecky, W. E. H., 186
Leeds, University of, 125, 151
Lehmberg, Stanford, 21, 27
Leicester University, 101
Leisure, 112, 113
Leitrim, County (Ireland), 191
Lenin, V. I., 71, 126
Levellers, 60, 72, 129
Levi-Strauss, Claude, 136
Liberal nationalism, 182, 184, 185
Liberal party, 154, 170, 177, 178, 191
Liverpool, Lord, 5, 155, 157, 162, 164, 165, 166, 169, 171
Loades, D. M., 27, 32
Locke, John, 3, 111, 112
Lollards, 64, 72
London police force, 157
London Corresponding Society, 130
London, University of, 13, 14, 15, 27, 31, 37, 38, 39, 43, 47–48, 52, 54, 55, 150. *See also* Institute for Historical Research
Long Parliament, 61, 71
Longue durée, 87, 109, 110, 112
Louis XIV, 107
Lower classes, 8, 87, 89, 90, 95. *See also* Working class

Index

Luddites, 8, 92, 132, 133
Lyons, F. S. L., 6, 7, 8, 10; academic attainments, 173–75, background, 175–77; early works, 176–80; on John Dillon, 180–84; on modern Irish history, 184–86; on C. S. Parnell, 186–89; assessment of, 189–90; bibliography of works, 191

Macaulay, Thomas Babington, 3, 5, 103, 115, 117, 118, 121, 143
MacCaffrey, Wallace, 50
McDowell, Robert, 155
McGrath, Patrick, 44
McGregor, J. F., 72
McIntosh, Marjorie, 53
McKendrick, Neil, 118, 119
McKenna, J. W., 32
Mackie, J. D., 25
Mackrell, John, 32
Maitland, Frederick, 6, 30, 32, 35
Malament, Barbara C., 97
Manning, Brian, 71, 73
Manning, Roger, 32
Marriage, history of, 88–90, 97, 99
Martyn, Edward, 191
Marvell, Andrew, 58, 70, 71
Marx, Karl, 3, 71, 124, 126–27, 128, 140, 141, 142, 167; Marxism, 124, 126, 128, 129, 144, 145; Marxists, 137, 139, 141, 142
Mary I, 19, 26, 41, 52
Materialism, 64, 71, 123, 153, 154
Mather, F. C., 155
Mathias, Peter, 118
Matthew, Elizabeth, 183
Mattingly, Garrett, 40, 53, 72
Medical profession, 72, 89
Melbourne, Lord, 154, 170
Mentalités, histories of, 8, 87, 88, 92, 136
Merchants, 59, 92, 93, 94
Merriman, Roger, 17, 18, 22, 29, 33
Methodism, 122, 124, 132, 169
Meyer, John, 44
Miami University, 54
Middle Ages, 18, 127; medieval art, 77–78
Middle classes, 90, 140, 147. *See also* Bourgeoisie; Merchants

Miliband, Ralph, 143, 145
Mill, John Stuart, 3, 9, 163
Miller, John, 73
Milne, R. S., 40, 53
Milton, John, 6, 58, 63, 64–65, 66, 68, 70, 72, 73
Minnesota, University of, 17
Monarchy, English, 86, 92, 153, 154
Moore, George, 191
"Moral Economy," 135–36, 144
Moral judgements, in historical writing, 76, 121–22
More, Sir Thomas, 24, 34
Morgan, Kenneth O., 33
Morrill, J. S., 73
Morris, William, 6, 122, 124–28, 141, 143, 144
Morrison, John J., 54
Morton, A. L., 70
Moscow, University of, 71
Mulligan, L., 72

Nairn, Tom, 139, 140, 141, 145
Namier, Lewis, 5, 9, 11, 13, 16, 29, 30, 48, 49, 101, 102, 103, 105, 106, 107, 108, 109, 111, 113, 114, 116, 117, 122, 153, 161, 169
Napoleonic Wars, 163, 171
National Gallery, 166
Neale, John Ernest, 13, 15, 23, 24, 31, 35, 37, 38, 40, 42, 43, 47, 49, 51, 55; memorial lecture, 31, 72
Netherlands, 50, 78
Newbould, Ian, 160, 170
Newcastle, University of, 14, 16, 72
New Left Review, 128
New Model Army, 64
Nicholls, C. S., 35
Norman, E. R., 182, 186, 190
"Norman Yoke," 60, 65
Northern Arizona University, 52
Notestein, Wallace, 23, 24, 31
Nowlan, K. B., 191

Oberlin College, 14
O'Brien, Conor Cruise, 179
O'Brien, Patrick, 118
O'Brien, R. Barry, 187
O'Brien, William, 179, 180, 181, 182
O'Connell, Daniel, 157

O'Faolain, Sean, 191
Open University, 65
O'Shea, Katherine, 188
Outhwaite, R. B., 99
Owen, John B., 118, 119
Owen, Robert, 133
Oxford University: pre-1900, 29, 72, 84–85, 98, 125, 157, 165; post-1900, 16, 17, 22, 48, 58, 61, 63, 65, 76, 122, 148, 149, 151, 154, 175, 176

Palavicino, Sir Horatio, 6, 76, 78, 97
Palmer, Bryan D., 144
Palmerston, Lady, 156
Palmerston, Lord, 155
Pares, Richard, 169
Paris Commune, 126
Parker, C. S., 148, 155
Parker, Harold, 3, 10
Parliament: Tudor-Stuart, 15, 20, 21, 23, 24, 31, 33, 34, 35, 38, 44, 47, 50, 51, 59, 66, 67, 72, 92; eighteenth century, 102, 106, 107, 108, 109, 117; nineteenth century, 150, 154, 158, 159, 161, 169. *See also* House of Commons; House of Lords
Parnell, Charles Stuart, 6, 174, 176, 178, 179, 180, 181, 186–89, 191
Parties, political, 106, 107, 108, 114, 118, 149, 150, 151–53, 154, 155, 159, 162, 169. *See also* Conservative party; Liberal party; Tory party; Whig party
Past and Present, 11, 58, 70, 78
Paternalism, 135, 138, 171
Patronage, 108, 162
Peel, Lady Julia (née Floyd), 156
Peel, Robert, Sr., 156
Peel, Sir Robert, 6, 147–52, 154, 155, 156, 157–59, 160, 161, 162, 164, 165, 166, 168, 169, 170
Pelling, Henry, 9
Pennington, Donald, 70
Pentridge rising, 133
Perceval, Spencer, 166
Perkin, Harold, 94, 100, 144, 145
Perkins, William, 74
Peterloo, 133, 171
Pevsner, Nikolaus, 77
Philipson, N. T., 98
Pickthorn, Kenneth, 16
Piggot, Stuart, 120

Pilgrimage of Grace, 20
Pitt, William (Earl of Chatham), 113, 147
Pitt, William (the Younger), 147, 156, 165
Plan of campaign, Irish, 191
Platt, F. J., 52
Plumb, John Harold, 6, 7, 10, 118, 119, 120; background and education, 101; controversy with Namier, 102, 106–7, 109; work on Walpole, 102–6, 107, 108; on social history, 109–13; other works, 113–15; views on progress, 115–17; assessment of, 117
Poachers, 137
Pocock, J. G. A., 70, 99, 119
Police, 140, 157
Political economy, 128, 131, 141, 143
Pollard, A. F., 15, 29, 34, 50
Poole, Austin Lane, 148
Poor Law, 21, 134, 149, 160
Popular culture, 121, 136
Population explosion, in late eighteenth and early nineteenth centuries, 131, 148
Positivism, 127
Pre-Raphaelite Brotherhood, 125
Press, history of the, 108, 112, 158, 162
Prest, John, 160, 170
Prime Minister, office of, 108, 154, 155, 156, 158, 159, 162, 170
Princeton University, 78, 97, 174
Prison system, English, 158
Privy Council, 19, 23
Professional class, 94
Prosopographical techniques, 49, 98
Protectionists, 155
Protestantism, 22, 23, 33, 62, 71; in Ireland, 176, 185. *See also* Puritanism
Psephology, 48
Psychology, 4, 10, 48
Public Record Office, 15, 46, 51
Public schools, 15, 75, 84, 94
Puritanism, 24, 46, 47, 60, 61, 62–63, 68, 70, 71, 72, 73, 83, 84, 86, 89, 90, 92, 129. *See also* Protestantism

Quantitative studies, 8, 87–88, 92, 93, 95, 131. *See also* Cliometrics; Computers

Index

Radicalism, 60, 63–64, 65, 66, 68, 72, 119, 122, 129, 130, 132, 133, 188
Radicals, philosophical, 159, 160, 170
Radio, 43–44
"Railway age," 163
Ramsay, A. A. W., 155
Rankin, W. B. (memorial lecture), 191
Ranum, Orest A., 10
Read, Conyers, 22, 33, 42–43, 49, 52, 55
Reay, Barry, 72
Redmond, John, 178, 179, 181, 182
Reeve, John, 72
Reformation: English, 7, 11, 17, 19, 20, 22, 26, 33, 35, 43, 44, 47, 60, 63, 70, 77, 78, 89, 94, 97; Scottish, 11
Reform Bill (1832), 132, 133, 147, 152, 153, 154, 158, 167
Regius professorships, 16, 29, 32
Reinmuth, Howard, 53
Religion: role of, 13, 60, 61–63, 64, 65, 66, 68, 86, 89; political role after 1832, 154, 163. *See also* Catholicism, Roman; Church of England; Protestantism; Puritanism
Renaissance, 11, 32, 72, 114–15, 119
Restoration (1660), 59, 65
Revolution, threat of in early nineteenth century, 164–65
Richards, J., 72
Richardson, R. C., 71, 73
Richardson, Samuel, 58, 70
Riddell lectures, 72
Riots, 105, 129–30, 138
Roberts, David, 159, 171
Romanticism, 123, 124, 125–26, 141
Rosenberg, Charles E., 99
Rothblatt, Sheldon, 171
Rough Music, 136, 138, 144
Rousseau, Jean-Jacques, 63
Rowse, A. L., 7, 13, 42, 45, 49
Royal Historical Society, 16, 23, 31
Rudé, George, 9
Ruling class, 123, 128, 136, 137. *See also* Aristocracy; Elites; Gentry
Ruskin, John, 122, 125, 126, 127
Russell, Conrad, 23, 33, 34, 73
Russell, Lord John, 159, 160, 169, 170

St. Andrews, University of, 150, 151, 165

Samuel, R., 73
Saposnekow lectures, 115
Saville, John, 143, 145
Scarisbrick, John J., 22, 26, 27, 32, 33
Schlatter, Richard, 5, 11, 55, 72, 73, 97
Schofield, R. S., 11
Schroeder, Paul, 10
Schwartz, Harold, 32
Schwoerer, Lois, 90, 99
Science, Puritanism and, 63, 66
Scotland, 3, 9, 16, 150
Scott, Joan, 10
Scott, Peter, 35
Scott, Tom, 32
Septennial Act, 107, 108
Shaftesbury, Lord, 150, 164
Shakespeare, William, 45, 48, 49, 54
Shelby Cullom Davis Center for Historical Studies, 79
Shelley, Percy B., 122, 125
Silk, Mark, 97
Simpson, Alan, 71
Simpson, John, 151
Sinn Fein, 181
Skinner, Quentin, 73, 118
Slavin, Arthur J., 26, 34
Smith, Alan, 45, 53, 54
Smith, Denis Mack, 170
Smith, Lacey Baldwin, 9, 12, 26, 30
Smugglers, 138
Socage tenure, 42
Social: legislation, 154, 178; mobility, 79, 82, 83, 93–95, 98; sciences, 27, 48, 75, 81, 87, 88, 91–92, 98, 182; structure, 66, 78–80, 81–82, 88–91, 93–95, 110
Socialism, 61, 122; Fabian, 126; utopian, 125. *See also* Marx, Karl
Socialist League, 127
Society for the Protection of Science and Learning (SPSL), 14, 32
Sociology, 8, 48, 99
Southampton, University of, 38, 48, 52
Southgate, Donald, 161
South Sea Bubble, 103–4, 108, 110
Soviet Union, 58, 61, 71, 123
Spain: Civil War in, 124; Empire of, 17
Speck, W. A., 119, 163
Spence, Thomas, 130
Spring, David, 94, 100
Spring, Eileen, 89–90, 94, 99, 100

Squirearchy, 92, 93–94
Stalin, Josef, 61, 71, 128, 141; Stalinism, 128, 141, 142, 143
Standard of living, in late eighteenth and early nineteenth centuries, 131
Starkey, David, 33
State, power of the, 49, 76, 78, 80, 86, 89, 96
Statistics, 91, 95. *See also* Quantitative studies
Statutes: of Uses, 21; of Wills, 21
Stinger, Charles, 55
Stone, Jeanne, 93, 95, 97, 99
Stone, Lawrence, 6, 7, 8, 11, 29, 30, 32, 33, 34, 44, 45, 46, 71, 73, 97, 98, 99, 100, 110; background and education, 75–78; interest in social science techniques, 78, 87–88, 91–92; and *The Crisis of the Aristocracy, 1558–1640,* 78–82; and the "educational revolution," 83–86; on the English Revolution, 86–87, 92–93; on family history, 88–91; on the English social structure, 93–95; assessment of, 96
"Strict settlement," 95, 99
Structuralism, 141
Stuart monarchs, 19, 41. *See also* James VI and I; Charles I; Charles II; William III; Anne, Queen
Stubbs, William, 5
Sutherland, James, 45, 54
Sykes, Norman, 73

Tamworth Manifesto, 157, 158, 160
Tanner, J. R., 25, 34
Tariff system, 158
Tawney, R. H., 11, 13, 24, 29, 30, 35, 48, 49, 62, 71, 76, 81, 87, 97, 101
Taxes, 104–5, 108, 118, 131, 158, 166
Taylor, A. J. P., 8, 13, 32, 169
Television, 44, 115
Tennyson, Alfred, Lord, 126, 163
Test and Corporation Acts, 159
Thatcher, Margaret, 9, 16
Theaters, closure of, 108
Thelwell, John, 130
Thistlewood, Arthur, 133
Thomas, Keith, 70
Thompson, E. P., 6, 7, 8, 10, 11, 105, 111, 118, 119, 144, 145, 147, 165, 167

171, 190; historical approach of, 121–22; background, influences, and education, 122–24; on William Morris, 124–28; on the English working class, 128–34; on the "moral economy" of the English crowd, 135–36; on the Black Act, 136–38; on Marxist theory, 139–43
Thompson, Frank, 122–23, 124, 143
Thompson, T. J., 143
Thomson, M. A., 39
Thornley, David, 179
Tory party: 1714–1760, 118; 1815–1830, 147, 152, 153, 160, 166, 167. *See also* Conservative party
"Total history," 3, 4, 182
Tout, T. F., 30
Toynbee, Arnold, 10
Trade unions, 10, 12, 131, 132, 133, 134
Treason Act, 20
Trevelyan, George Macaulay, 29, 30, 34–35, 102, 105, 106, 110, 113, 114, 117, 118, 119, 147, 148
Trevor-Roper, Hugh, 8, 32, 34, 76–77, 78, 97
Trinity College (University of Dublin), 173, 174, 175, 178, 183, 185, 186, 190
Tudor era: government documents, 17, 20, 25, 34; monarchs, 6, 12, 18, 25, 26, 27, 29, 30, 32, 33, 34, 35, 42, 50, 52. *See also* Henry VIII; Edward VI; Mary I; Elizabeth I
Tudor Revolution, 17–23, 24, 25, 27, 32, 33
Tyacke, Nicholas, 49, 51, 52, 53, 54, 55
Tyburn, 111

Underdown, David, 50, 55, 73, 80, 97
Ulster, 188; Presbyterians, 157; Protestant culture, 189; Unionists, 182
United States, 4, 14, 17, 22, 27–28, 38, 48, 52, 83, 184
Universities, in early modern era, 83–84, 84–85, 98
Urbanization, 148, 153
Utilitarianism, 125, 128, 154, 163, 171

Van Thal, Herbert, 163, 170
Victoria County History, 45, 50
Victorian era, 3, 103, 104, 127;

Index

aristocracy, 140; historians, 11, 29, 115; history, 9; ideas, 9; social mobility, 94; wine industry, 9; "Victorianism," 126

Wakefield, Edward Gibbon, 157
Walcott, Robert, 106–7, 109, 118
Wallace, A. R., 126
Walpole, Horace, 109, 119
Walpole, Sir Robert, 6, 102–5, 106, 107, 108–9, 110, 111, 117, 119, 137
Walsingham, Sir Francis, 49
Walters, Elizabeth Valmai, 39
Waltham Black Act, 105, 118, 137, 144
War Cabinet, Office of, 38
Wardship, 40–43, 50, 53
Warfare, eighteenth century, 107, 114
Warwick, University of, 134
Waterloo, Battle of, 171
Webster, Charles, 71
Wedgwood, Cecily Veronica, 9, 12, 44
Wellington, Duke of, 155, 157, 158, 160, 162, 170, 171
Werham, R. B., 43
Wesley, John, 132, 169
West Indies, 82
Whig party: eighteenth century, 85, 102, 107, 108, 109, 110 117, 118, 136–37, 145; nineteenth century, 153, 154, 155, 158, 159, 160, 170
Whitgift, John, Archbishop of Canterbury, 61, 71
William III, 102, 107
William IV, 154
Williams, Basil, 150
Williams, Desmond, 191
Williams, Penry, 22, 23, 30, 33, 55
Willson, David Harris, 53
Windsor Forest, 137
Winstanley, Gerard, 60, 63, 65, 66, 72
Wisconsin, University of, 65
Witchcraft, 89
Wolfe Tone, Theobald, 185
Wolsey, Thomas, Cardinal, 18, 50
Women: history of, 89, 134; role in society of, 89–90, 95; suffrage for, 178
Wooler, Thomas J., 133
Worden, Blair, 73
Workers Educational Association (WEA), 150
Working class, 7, 126, 128–33, 134, 138, 144, 147, 164, 171. See also Lower classes
World War I, 4, 148, 182
World War II, 4, 10, 15, 38–39, 51, 60, 75, 76, 122, 123, 150, 173, 178
Wrigley, Edward A., 11

Yearley, Clifton, 53
Yeats, William Butler, 174, 175, 186, 189, 191
Yonge, C. D., 165, 171
York, 14, 58
Yorkshire Peace Movement, 125
Yugoslavia, 123

Zeewald, W. Gordon, 21